Build a repertoire of go-to recipes
that you can easily and deliciously adapt
for every season throughout the year.

Panzanella

SUMMER
baguette, tomato, nectarine,
corn, jalapeño, cilantro, basil

FALL
sourdough, clementine, kale, squash,
sage, pomegranate

WINTER
rye, orange, roasted sweet potato,
Castelvetrano olives, feta, red onion

SPRING
everything bagels, fava,
baby arugula, dill, chives

Pasta with Meatballs

SUMMER
spaghetti, syrupy roasted tomato
sauce, arugula, basil

FALL
penne, pesto, sweet potato,
crushed red pepper

WINTER
fusilli, tomato sauce,
kale, dried herbs

SPRING
orecchiette, garlic herb brown
butter, carrot, snap pea, asparagus

Fish Tacos

SUMMER
peach cucumber salsa,
coriander seed and leaf

FALL
cumin-lime pumpkin,
pepitas, pomegranate

WINTER
Southern-style greens, corn

SPRING
radish, spicy coleslaw

Fruit Tarts

SUMMER
graham cracker crust, almond
custard, mixed berries, apricot glaze,
sliced almonds

FALL
cookies and cream, chocolate
ganache, passion fruit curd

WINTER
biscoff, cheesecake,
fennel grapefruit curd,

D1379037

A DISH *for* ALL SEASONS

A DISH *for* ALL SEASONS

125+ Recipe Variations for Delicious Meals All Year Round

Kathryn Pauline

CHRONICLE BOOKS
SAN FRANCISCO

Library of Congress Cataloging-in-Publication Data available.

ISBN 978-1-7972-0771-1

Manufactured in China.

Design by Lizzie Vaughan.
Typesetting by Frank Brayton.
Typeset in Fouriner and Neurial Grotesk.

Din Tai Fung is a registered trademark of Din Tai Fung USA. Jell-O is a registered trademark of Kraft Foods Group Brands LLC. Jolly Ranchers and Milk Duds are registered trademarks of Huhtamaki Finance B.V. LLC. Laughing Planet Cafe is a registered trademark of Laughing Planet Industries LLC. Moosewood is a registered trademark of Moosewood, Inc. Monterey Bay Aquarium is a registered trademark of Monterey Bay Aquarium Foundation. Oreo is a registered trademark of Nabisco Brands Company. Pop-Tarts is a registered trademark of Kellogg North America Company. Vidalia is a registered trademark of Georgia Department of Agriculture. Wonder Bread is a registered trademark of Flowers Foods, Inc.

10 9 8 7 6 5 4 3 2 1

Chronicle books and gifts are available at special quantity discounts to corporations, professional associations, literacy programs, and other organizations. For details and discount information, please contact our premiums department at corporatesales@chroniclebooks.com or at 1-800-759-0190.

Chronicle Books LLC
680 Second Street
San Francisco, California 94107
www.chroniclebooks.com

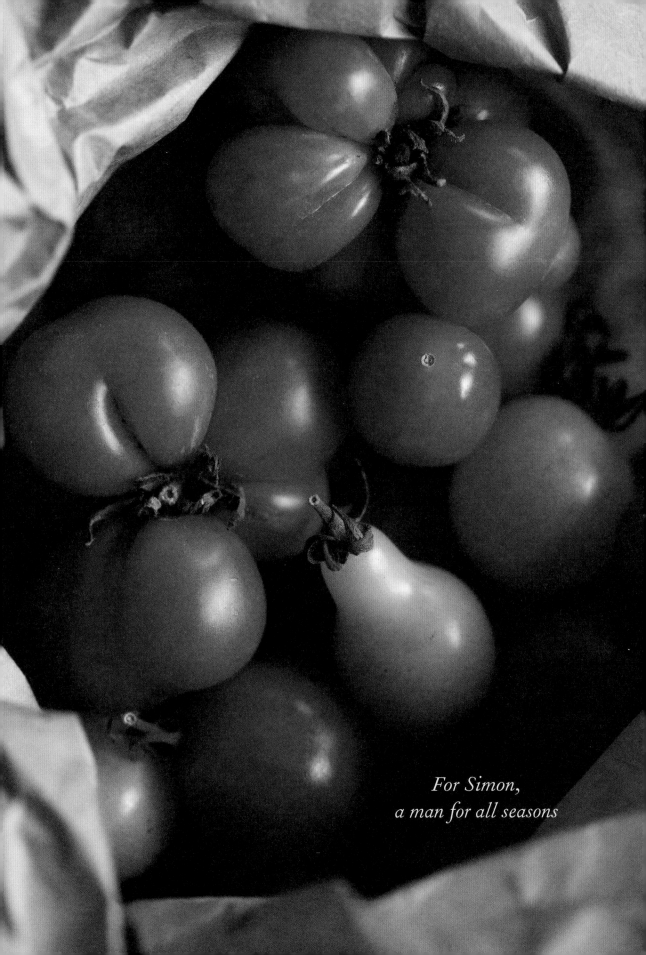

For Simon,
a man for all seasons

TABLE OF CONTENTS

HERBS
$3 BUNCH.

INTRODUCTION

When I first started cooking, I aspired to shop for seasonal
produce and cook with the intuitive confidence of a professional
chef, but this was easier said than done. If you've ever seen an
interview with a famous chef, you probably know just what I'm
talking about: "So, how do you think of ideas for all your fabulous
recipes?" "Oh, I just go to the market and see what looks good."

I was twenty the first time I heard someone say this. At the time, I had a little one-bedroom apartment to myself, and I'd spend many twee Saturdays walking to the farmers' market to "see what looked good" for myself. I'd come home with a bunch of tomatoes, zucchini, mushrooms, and Swiss chard, and I would cook them the only way I knew how: coat them in olive oil, sprinkle them with salt and pepper, and roast them. They were delicious, and I basked in my small triumph.

After a while, I got a little bored of my whole inspired-chef schtick. I mean, surely Ina isn't just roasting every single thing she brings home from the farmers' market, right? So I decided to switch over to actual recipes for a while to build my repertoire.

In the years following those one-bedroom farmers' market days, my then boyfriend (now husband) and I moved in together, got married, and eventually started hosting Thanksgiving at our place for our grad school friends. For our first Thanksgiving, I planned a French- and Italian-inspired menu and decided to make some sweet potatoes coated in homemade basil pesto.

I went from store to store, searching for enough reasonably priced fresh basil to feed the whole gang, and realized that if I were to buy the amount called for, I would have to spend a small fortune on a dozen tiny bunches of hydroponic basil. I had gotten used to the $3 pageant-sized bouquets I bought at the farmers' market all summer (and the bunches gardening friends would occasionally leave at our doorstep), and I assumed I would find the same in November.

If you've done any gardening at all, my mistake is probably pretty obvious: When you live in a temperate climate, fresh basil is not a Thanksgiving-friendly ingredient. I learned an important lesson that day: Being a good cook is all about knowing how to

adapt your plan to make use of what's in season, because in-season produce tends to be the best quality, the least expensive, and the easiest to find.

I've cooked many more meals in the years since—I've made two international moves, worked in a commercial kitchen, written hundreds of recipes mostly from a twenty-eight-square-foot room with no dishwasher, won a *Saveur* award for my blog *Cardamom and Tea*, traveled a bunch, and written this cookbook.

Because of this, I can now truly "go to the market and see what looks good," then go home and make a delicious gratin, galette, or whatever strikes my fancy. This is partly because I've learned what to expect at farmers' markets and grocery stores at different times of the year; but I've also learned the real secret to on-the-fly seasonal shopping: Build a repertoire of easily adaptable recipes to use with whatever produce you find.

This cookbook celebrates this type of seasonal improvisation. With twenty-five adaptable base recipes, one hundred variations, and lots of bonus content, you'll learn to think on your feet, use what you have, and find inspiration in the present moment.

Each base recipe comes with instructions for changing things up to suit the season and your own personal tastes. Plus, each base recipe is followed by four seasonal variations, so you can always find something delicious to make, whether you feel like doing your own thing or following a composed step-by-step recipe.

Once you have the tools to adapt any recipe to suit the time of year, seasonal cooking becomes second nature, and you'll no longer spend long winters pining for those well-loved tomato-stained pages. Make what you want when you want it with what you have.

HOW TO USE THIS BOOK

This book does things differently from most seasonal cookbooks. Rather than dividing recipes into four or five seasonal chapters, it's organized like a conventional cookbook, with everything divided into dishes and meals, so you can flip through and see what strikes your fancy. You'll find the seasonal varieties distributed throughout the entire book. Above all, remember that no page is ever off-limits, no matter the time of year. Whether you plan to use the base recipes or the seasonal variations (or both), you can put this book into practice in a number of ways.

How It's Organized

○ There are twenty-five base recipes so you can learn how to make some of your favorite dishes with whatever seasonal ingredients you'd like.

○ Each of these twenty-five guides comes with four seasonal variations (plus a few bonus recipes and many grid variations), for more than one hundred and twenty-five total recipes.

○ Most of these seasonal variations include additional tips for changing things up for different seasons and tastes, and there are many opportunities to borrow components of one recipe to use in another.

Ways You Can Use This Book

There is more than one right way to use this cookbook. There are those who appreciate the structure and promise of a conventional recipe. On the other hand, there are those who have fun only when they're improvising. Whether you're meticulous, free-spirited, experienced, or still finding your footing, you'll find something here for you.

Let's say you want to make an upside-down cake and it's the middle of summer. Here are a few ways you might go about doing so:

Follow a seasonal variation. You flip to the Summer Upside-Down Cake (page 269), which happens to be apricot and raspberry with a chocolate chip almond cake. You pick up the ingredients, follow the summer recipe, and enjoy.

Learn how to make a few simple changes to a seasonal variation. You thought you were going to make the apricot raspberry cake, but when you get to the market you find out that apricots aren't in season for another week, so you pick up another stone fruit instead. When you get home, you skim over the upside-down cake base recipe to learn how to adapt the summer variation.

Create something unique. You choose the semolina cake batter from page 270, blackberries, and rose water. You use the upside-down cake base recipe to figure out how to bring it all together.

Use the ingredients you already have at home. Your weekly produce box gave you more peaches than you know what to do with, so you use the upside-down cake base recipe to turn some of them into a cake.

Adapt one of the out-of-season variations to make it suit your current season. You notice that the winter pineapple gingerbread upside-down cake has instructions to adapt it for summer. You substitute the classic buttermilk batter on page 267 instead of the gingerbread batter, and you use fresh pitted cherries instead of jarred maraschinos.

Do your own thing. Use these recipes as mere suggestions, take inspiration to make something else, and have fun. Scribble in the margins, add new things to the produce lists, and make this book your own.

Go to the market and see what inspires you! Besides all the produce, many of these recipes feature mostly staples you probably already have at home, so you can go to a farmers' market, see what inspires you, come home, and find something delicious to make.

Finding Flavor Inspiration

Each of this book's base recipes will steer you in the right direction when it comes to its technical aspects. For instance, if you follow my guide to Panzanella (page 69), yours will be just the right chewy-soft consistency. But the *fun* part is choosing which ingredients to put together for their combination of flavors. Here are a few ways to find inspiration in case you're ever feeling a little stuck:

Look through other seasonal variations in this book for inspiration: Maybe the nectarine, basil, corn, and tomatoes in my Summer Panzanella (page 69) seem like they would also work wonderfully on a crostini or in a garden salad. (Hint: They do!)

Look to some of your favorite dishes for inspiration: If you love elote preparado, make a romaine salad with grilled corn kernels, cotija crumbles, cilantro, a little sprinkling of cayenne pepper, and a creamy mayo-based dressing (e.g., page 62). Go with what you already know works together, and apply it elsewhere.

Imagine one of those lush Instagrammable cheeseboards: What would you go for? Pecans, Manchego, and dried cranberries? Raw apple, basil, and aged Cheddar? This is especially helpful for brainstorming sweet and savory combinations.

Use this book alongside a book that focuses on flavor: A couple of my favorites are *The Flavor Bible* (Dornenburg and Page) and *The Flavor Equation* (Sharma).

Think about flavors that show up together time and time again:

Classic Flavor Pairings

- Apple cinnamon
- Tomato basil
- Strawberry banana
- Honey fig
- Pistachio rose water
- Chocolate raspberry
- Coconut lime
- Carrot dill
- Watermelon feta
- Strawberry rhubarb
- Lemon poppyseed

- Lime, chipotle, cilantro
- Fennel, apple, honey mustard
- Sweet potato sage
- Carrot, chive, chèvre
- Brussels sprouts, blue cheese, bacon maple
- Za'atar, cauliflower
- Sesame, miso, sweet potato
- Beet, tart yogurt, dill
- Zucchini, sausage, tomato, basil
- Ginger, garlic, sesame oil, chile

Stocking Your Kitchen with Staples

If you want to make a habit of spontaneously going to the market and seeing what looks good, make sure your pantry staples are always well stocked. That way, when you get home, you can think of something delicious to make without having to head back out for necessities.

BAKING SHELF

— All-purpose flour
— Baking powder
— Baking soda
— Brown sugar
— Chocolate chips
— Cocoa powder
— Confectioners' sugar

— Cornstarch
— Dark chocolate
— Flaky sea salt
— Flavorings (e.g., vanilla beans, paste, or extract; almond extract; rose water; orange blossom water)

— Granulated sugar
— Old-fashioned rolled oats
— Semolina, polenta/ cornmeal, almond meal
— Simple decorations (e.g., sprinkles, dried rose petals, coconut flakes)

REFRIGERATOR

— Buttermilk
— Cream cheese
— Dijon mustard
— Feta in brine
— Grating cheese (e.g., Parmesan or pecorino)
— Heavy cream
— Hot sauce
— Jam

— Large eggs
— Lemons and/or limes (when they're not too expensive)
— Maple syrup
— Mayonnaise
— Melting cheese (e.g., Cheddar, Gruyère, Swiss)
— Milk

— Sesame oil
— Soy sauce
— Unsalted butter
— Vinegar
— Worcestershire sauce
— Yogurt (plain or Greek)

FREEZER

— Bread loaves and/or pita
— Chicken breasts and thighs
— Corn, peas, carrots, spinach, berries, sliced peaches, and other quality frozen fruits and vegetables

— Ginger, frozen (buy two or three big pieces, peel, mince in the food processor, place 1 Tbsp blobs on a flexible cutting board, freeze them, and store in a freezer bag for up to 2 months)
— Ground beef, turkey, or vegetarian meat alternative

— Miso paste (scoopable while frozen)
— Salmon fillets
— Sesame seeds
— Stock, homemade
— Sweetened condensed milk in a tube (squeezable while frozen)
— Tortillas, corn and/or flour

PANTRY

- Anchovies
- Beans
- Diced tomatoes
- Extra-virgin olive oil
- Honey and/or molasses
- Kosher and/or sea salt (optional)
- Lentils (red and/or brown)
- Neutral high-smoke-point oil (I use canola oil for frying and avocado for everything else)
- Nuts

- Olives (especially bright green Castelvetranos and oil-cured black olives)
- Onions and garlic
- Pasta
- Pomegranate molasses
- Rice, quinoa, bulgur, or other favorite grains
- Spices, dried herbs, and spice blends
  Most used: anise, dried basil, bay leaf, black pepper, cardamom, cinnamon, dried cilantro, coriander seed, cumin seed, dried dill, fennel, garlic powder, ginger, dried mint, mustard, dried oregano, paprika, dried parsley, dried rosemary, rubbed sage, sumac, thyme, turmeric, za'atar
  Nice to have: celery seed, fenugreek seed, nigella, onion flakes, poppy seed, saffron
- Stock cubes
- Table salt (see page 197)
- Tahini
- Tomato paste

Being Flexible While Shopping in Season (and out of Season)

Skillful seasonal cooks don't follow rules stringently. We celebrate high-quality, reasonably priced, in-season produce, and we use what's most practical.

The produce lists in this book's base recipes are meant to make your life easier when planning a menu, so that you know what to expect when you go to the farmers' market, or what to seek out for the best quality when you go to the supermarket. But they don't apply to every situation and region.

The produce lists are mostly relevant to regions that experience all four seasons—if you live in a warmer area, you may be able to find most produce just about any time of the year. Many seasonal ingredients are available year-round even in temperate climates, and you should feel free to use something even if it's technically "out of season."

But don't forget about the opportunity cost. For instance, you'll find quality carrots in supermarkets any time of the year, but Swiss chard is sometimes poor quality in the middle of winter. So if you have the option, go for the Swiss chard while it's at its best. But do whatever makes the most sense for you. There is no shame in eating something that's technically "out of season."

On the other hand, eating local, organic produce and reducing our meat and dairy consumption is often a good environmental move. But remember the bigger picture: The personal decisions we make about the food we eat is one very small part of our environmental stewardship. Electing leaders who prioritize environmental justice is the most significant thing we can do to help reduce climate change's impact on our most vulnerable communities.

PREPARING
INGREDIENTS SIMPLY

These are my favorite ways to prepare a single piece of produce
with few additional ingredients, no serious recipes necessary.
Don't forget to season everything you make with salt, and taste as you go.

Beets
Roast, peel, slice, and
serve with garlicky yogurt
and dill.

Broccoli
Make a classic broccoli
slaw with my Creamy
Vinaigrette (page 89),
dried cranberries, toasted
sliced almonds, and
minced red onion.

Cabbage
Make a spicy coleslaw
(see page 183).

Carrots
Grate and make a simple
slaw flavored with cumin,
mint, and parsley (see
page 89).

Celeriac
Thinly julienne and dress
with mayo, Dijon mus-
tard, fresh lemon juice,
capers, tarragon or chives
(either fresh or dried), and
black pepper for a celeriac
rémoulade.

Cherries
Pit, sprinkle with sumac,
and serve with shortcakes
and whipped cream.

Corn
Grill on an outdoor grill
or gas stove (see page 141)
and slather with butter and
homemade seasoning (see
page 190).

Cucumbers
Cut into 1 in [2.5 cm]
rounds, salt somewhat
generously, let sit for
30 minutes, strain, and
dress with chili garlic oil,
sesame oil, dried garlic
flakes, and a little bit of
rice wine vinegar.

Eggplant
Char, peel away the
charred bits (never scoop),
mash, drizzle with a good
amount of fresh lemon
juice and tahini, sprinkle
generously with parsley,
add a little garlic, and
enjoy some baba ganoush.

Fennel Bulbs
Make a super pared-down
version of the slaw on
page 87.

Fiddlehead Ferns and Asparagus
To prep them, first boil the fiddlehead ferns for 5 to 15 minutes, then discard the water. Then sauté prepped fiddlehead ferns or fresh asparagus, and squeeze lemon over them.

Figs
Serve raw with fresh goat cheese and balsamic reduction on a whole-wheat cracker.

Green Beans
Place in a very hot pan with no oil, and dry-roast until charred and blistered.

Morels or Chanterelles
Beer-batter (see page 179) and deep-fry.

Okra
Halve lengthwise, coat in a thin layer of oil, and roast on a baking sheet at 475°F [245°C] for 15 to 20 minutes. For extra slime, place them cut-side down before roasting. For no slime, place them cut-side up. Serve with a squeeze of lemon.

Parsnips
Sauté in butter (see page 97) and sprinkle with a whisper of cinnamon.

Peas
Turn the smashed pea crostini on page 107 into a full-size piece of ricotta toast for breakfast. Remember to add the lemon at the last minute and not during the mashing stage.

Radishes
Slice into wedges and set on a plate with some feta and a huge heap of your favorite leafy herbs such as basil and cilantro for a Persian sabzi khordan platter (see the photo on page 90).

Ramps
Place on a very hot grill for about 2 minutes until wilted and charred, squeeze a little lemon juice over the top, and serve with seared steak.

Rhubarb
Make a fool. Whip some cream to soft peaks and swirl spoonfuls of chilled Rhubarb Compote (page 241) into the whipped cream.

Squash and Pumpkins
Roast with fresh lime juice and cumin (see page 182).

Sweet Potatoes
Use the dressing on page 154 to make miso sweet potato bites (see the headnote on page 153).

Swiss Chard
Slice thinly to make a simple slaw (pare down the one on page 85).

Tomatillos
Hull several and place on a broiler tray with one whole stemmed jalapeño and a quartered white onion. Broil until blistered and slightly softened. Place in a blender with some cilantro, garlic, and fresh lime juice and blend until completely puréed to make salsa verde.

Tomatoes
Slow-roast in the oven until syrupy (see page 113).

Zucchini Blossoms
Stuff with the ravioli filling on page 209, dip in the batter on page 179, and deep-fry.

BREAKFAST

Frittatas

A frittata can be all about the eggs, all about the produce, or somewhere in between. You'll find the whole gamut in this section's seasonal variations, but this base recipe is most inspired by Persian kuku sabzi, which usually includes a bit of dried fruit, a ton of herbs, and enough egg to hold it all together.

Use the recipe on page 27 to create your own herby frittata. For a traditional spring kuku sabzi, skip the produce and add more fresh leafy herbs (2 cups [80 g] any combination of chopped chive, cilantro, dill, basil, or parsley), use ¼ cup [20 g] dried barberries for the dried fruit, skip the cheese, replace the onion with 2 or 3 chopped green onions, and add ½ cup [50 g] chopped walnuts to the egg mixture.

For an herby summer frittata, go crazy with basil and throw in all your favorite farmers' market produce. And in the fall and winter, instead use a more modest amount of thyme, sage, and rosemary for a cozy vibe.

Preparing your produce is super simple: If you're using vegetables that need only a brief sauté (as in the first column on page 26), do so before throwing them in with the eggs. Or if you're using a starchier produce from the second column that needs a bit longer to cook, panfry your thinly sliced pieces in a shallow layer of oil, working in batches (see the Winter Frittata recipe on page 30 for the technique). You can even include ingredients from both columns, as long as you work in batches.

Make Your Own Frittata Grid

Ingredients to swap in for the base recipe on the facing page

DRIED FRUIT

+ Raisins
+ Sultanas
+ Dates
+ Barberries
+ Chopped dried apricots
+ Chopped dried figs
+ Chopped dried plums

SPICES

+ Baharat blend
+ Paprika
+ Cumin
+ Coriander
+ Cinnamon
+ Fennel seeds

HERBS

+ **Leafy**
  Cilantro, dill, parsley, chives, basil
+ **Woody**
  Thyme, rosemary, sage, oregano

CHEESE

+ Crumbled goat cheese
+ Feta
+ Shredded Cheddar
+ Gruyère
+ Jarlsberg
+ Or any of your favorites

SEASONAL PRODUCE

Sauté for 2 to 3 minutes	Sauté for 7 to 10 minutes (or panfry; see the Winter Frittata recipe on page 30 for the technique)
Summer	
Diced tomato, corn kernels, green beans, sliced zucchini, sliced bell peppers, minced hot peppers, eggplant slices, chopped Swiss chard, sliced okra	
Fall	
Late-season summer veggies in early fall (all of the above), plus diced tomatillos, sliced celery, small broccoli or cauliflower florets, chopped blanched broccoli rabe, chanterelles, thinly sliced fennel or leeks	Thinly sliced carrots, firm-fleshed squash (e.g., butternut), pumpkin or sweet potatoes
Winter	
Chopped kale (or other hearty greens), chopped blanched broccoli rabe, thinly sliced fennel, thinly sliced leeks, small broccoli or cauliflower florets	Thinly sliced carrots, firm-fleshed squash (e.g., butternut), pumpkin or sweet potatoes
Spring	
Small broccoli or cauliflower florets, blanched and peeled fava beans (see page 98), asparagus, shell peas, snow peas, snap peas, chopped ramps, thinly sliced spring onions, shaved cabbage, morels, sliced celery	Thinly sliced carrots or sweet potatoes
Anytime	
Frozen corn, frozen green beans, frozen peas, thinly sliced mushrooms, wrung-out spinach (do not sauté)	Thinly sliced potatoes

Frittatas

Makes 4 to 6 servings

6 large eggs
Salt
Olive oil
¼ cup [40 g] dried fruit (optional)
½ medium onion, minced (90 g)
1 garlic clove, crushed through a press, plus
    more as needed
1 to 2 tsp spices
1 to 5 cups [150 to 550 g] prepared vegetables
    (see grid on facing page)
1 cup [40 g] chopped leafy herbs, or 2 tsp
    chopped woody herbs
½ to ⅔ cup [45 to 100 g] shredded or crumbled
    cheese (optional)

Beat the eggs in a medium mixing bowl, season with about ½ tsp of salt, and set aside.

Preheat the broiler. Preheat a nonstick broiler-safe 10 in [25 cm] sauté pan or skillet on the stove over medium heat for a few minutes until moderately hot.

Add about 2 tsp oil and swirl to coat. If using dried fruit: Sauté for no longer than 2 minutes, just until the fruit puffs up and/or caramelizes slightly. Remove with a slotted spoon and place in the bowl with the eggs.

Add the onion to the pan, season with a pinch of salt, and cook for 5 minutes, stirring every minute or so, until softened and slightly golden around the edges. Add the garlic and spices and cook, stirring constantly, for 1 minute more. Add to the bowl of eggs.

Increase the heat to medium-high, add about 1 tsp oil and your favorite veggies to the pan, and season with salt. If you're using a lot of vegetables (or if you're not sure if they'll finish cooking through at the same time), work in batches, transferring them to the bowl with the eggs as they finish cooking. If you're using any thinly sliced starchy vegetables from the second column, panfry them in a shallow amount of oil using the Winter Frittata technique on page 30, then discard any excess oil.

Once the veggies have browned and cooked through, add them to the bowl of eggs (or set aside a handful to sprinkle on top before broiling, if you want them to show).

Add the herbs and cheese (if using) to the bowl of eggs and stir to combine.

Lower the heat to medium, add about 1 tsp oil, and swirl to coat. Pour in the egg mixture and let it sit for 2 to 3 minutes. Once it's set on the bottom but still very runny, add any reserved produce and place it under the broiler. Broil until the whole thing is set and golden brown on top (depending on your broiler, this could take between 30 seconds and 5 minutes). Serve, in slices, right from the pan to keep it warm, or loosen the edges and slide it onto a plate.

Summer Frittata

Zucchini, Tomatoes, Herbs, Manchego Cheese, Caramelized Raisins

This is my favorite frittata to make with everything you can find in a farmers' market in the middle of summer. Feel free to sub in your

favorite summer veggies in place of the zucchini and tomatoes—eggplant, bell peppers, or yellow squash would all work just as wonderfully. You can also replace the parsley and cilantro with basil, chives, and/or a little bit of dill.

6 large eggs
Salt
Olive oil
¼ cup [38 g] golden raisins or sultanas
1 small onion, minced (90 g)
1 garlic clove, crushed through a press
½ tsp paprika
½ tsp ground black pepper
½ tsp ground coriander
¾ cup [90 g] ¼ in [6 mm] sliced zucchini
¾ cup [110 g] halved cherry tomatoes
½ cup [20 g] chopped fresh cilantro
½ cup [20 g] chopped fresh parsley
½ cup [45 g] shredded Manchego cheese

Beat the eggs in a medium mixing bowl, season with about ½ tsp of salt, and set aside.

Preheat the broiler. Preheat a nonstick broiler-safe 10 in [25 cm] sauté pan or skillet on the stove over medium heat for a few minutes until moderately hot.

Add about 2 tsp of oil and swirl to coat. Sautée the raisins for no longer than 2 minutes, just until they puff up and caramelize slightly. Remove with a slotted spoon and place in the bowl with the eggs.

Add the onion to the pan, season with a pinch of salt, and cook for 5 minutes, stirring every minute or so, until softened and slightly golden around the edges (slightly longer for any mushrooms). Add the garlic, paprika, black pepper, and coriander and cook, stirring constantly, for 1 minute more. Add to the bowl of eggs.

Increase the heat to medium-high, add about 1 tsp of oil, and add the zucchini and tomatoes. Season with a pinch of salt, sauté for 2 minutes, and then add them to the bowl of eggs. Add the

cilantro, parsley, and Manchego to the eggs and stir to combine.

Lower the heat to medium, add about 1 tsp of oil, and swirl to coat. Pour in the egg mixture and let it sit for about 2 minutes. Once it's set on the bottom but still very runny, place it under the broiler. Broil until the whole thing is set and golden brown on top (depending on your broiler, this could take between 30 seconds and 5 minutes). Serve, in slices, right from the pan to keep it warm, or loosen the edges and slide it onto a plate.

Fall Frittata

Dates, Feta, Chives, Cinnamon

If you're from Iran (or very familiar with Persian food), I probably don't need to tell you how amazing dates and eggs are together. When a Persian friend first told me about this particular dish, I had a hard time even wrapping my head around what it might taste like. But after that first bite, the clouds parted, and it was love.

Dates are harvested in the late summer and throughout the fall—if you're lucky enough to find some fresh ones on the stem, just enjoy them on a cheeseboard or on their own. Dried dates, on the other hand, are available year-round, so this dried date frittata is technically in season any time.

6 large eggs
Salt
1 Tbsp unsalted butter
10 Medjool dates, halved lengthwise and pitted (150 g)
3 Tbsp [26 g] crumbled feta
1 Tbsp chopped fresh chives
Pinch of cinnamon

Beat the eggs in a medium mixing bowl, season with about ½ tsp of salt, and set aside.

Preheat the broiler. Preheat a nonstick broiler-safe 10 in [25 cm] sauté pan or skillet on the stove over medium heat for a few minutes until moderately hot.

Add the butter to the pan and swirl to coat. Add the dates cut-side down. Let cook for about 2 minutes, just until slightly caramelized and softened. Transfer to a plate with a slotted spoon.

Add the eggs to the pan, mix them around to scramble for only 1 minute, then immediately remove from the heat while they're still very runny. Arrange the dates cut-side down on the surface of the runny eggs. Gently press them down to embed them slightly.

Place the pan under the broiler. Broil until the whole thing is set and the dates' tops have caramelized slightly (keep an eye on it, as it can take as little as 30 seconds).

Top the cooked frittata with the feta and chives and evenly sprinkle with just a pinch of cinnamon. Serve right from the pan to keep it warm, or loosen the edges and slide it onto a plate.

Winter Frittata

Potatoes, Onion, Garlic, Black Pepper

Tortilla de patatas is popular in Spain as well as many countries that were previously under Spanish occupation, such as the Philippines. While you can enjoy it at any temperature (and truly, at any time of the year, since potatoes are available year-round), I personally love it chilled, which makes for an even easier breakfast. Prep your week's breakfasts on Sunday night to start every day off right with a cold slice and a hot cup of coffee.

If you're using another starchy vegetable (sweet potato, firm-fleshed squash or pumpkin—see the chart on page 26) in this or another frittata, prepare them with the technique in the following recipe. Squash and pumpkin tend to take slightly longer to fry, so test them as you go (poke with a butter knife or fork).

6 large eggs
Salt
¼ tsp freshly ground black pepper
¼ cup [55 g] extra-virgin olive oil
2 large peeled russet potatoes, sliced ⅛ in [3 mm] thick (510 g)
½ medium onion, minced (90 g)
1 garlic clove, crushed through a press

Beat the eggs in a medium mixing bowl, season with about ½ tsp of salt, add the pepper, and set aside.

Preheat the broiler. Line a plate with paper towels. Preheat a nonstick broiler-safe 10 in [25 cm] sauté pan or skillet on the stove over medium heat for a few minutes until moderately hot.

Add the oil and swirl to coat. Add about a quarter of the potatoes in an even layer. Fry for about 2 minutes on the first side, then flip and cook for 2 minutes on the other side. Once they're tender throughout and very light brown, transfer to the prepared plate and continue working in batches until they're all cooked through.

Remove most of the oil from the pan if there is still a lot left, leaving about 1 Tbsp. Add the onion, season with a pinch of salt, and cook for 5 minutes, stirring every minute or so, until softened and slightly golden around the edges. Add the garlic and cook, stirring constantly, for 1 minute more.

Return the fried potatoes to the pan and fold together with the onions just to combine. Smooth out into an even layer and pour the eggs over the potatoes. Use a fork to very gently prod the potatoes in a few spots to make sure the egg settles all the way to the bottom. Let it sit for 2 to 3 minutes. Once it's set on the bottom but still very runny, place it under the broiler. Broil until the whole thing is set and golden brown on top (depending on your broiler, this could take between 30 seconds and 5 minutes). Serve, sliced, right from the pan to keep it warm, or loosen the edges and slide it onto a plate.

Spring Frittata

Asparagus, Goat Cheese, Dill, Dukkah

Persian kuku sabzi is an important part of spring New Year festivities (see page 27 for a recipe). Like classic kuku, any good spring frittata is usually packed with herbs. Feel free to include your favorite spring produce here—most spring flavors go wonderfully with dill, especially when there's a little creamy cheese in the mix.

10 untrimmed asparagus spears (200 g)
6 large eggs
Salt
Olive oil
½ medium onion, minced (90 g)
3 garlic cloves, crushed through a press
1 Tbsp Dukkah (page 151), plus more for garnish
⅔ cup [25 g] chopped dill
⅔ cup [100 g] crumbled goat cheese

Use a vegetable peeler to shave thin pieces of asparagus. Grip the asparagus by the woody end and hold it down on the cutting board. Peel along the asparagus away from the hand that's holding it. Once you've peeled as much as you can, snap off the last bit and discard the woody stem. You'll end up with about 2 cups [130 g] ribbons.

Beat the eggs in a medium mixing bowl, season with about ½ tsp of salt, and set aside.

Preheat the broiler. Preheat a nonstick broiler-safe 10 in [25 cm] sauté pan or skillet on the stove over medium heat for a few minutes, until moderately hot.

Add about 2 tsp of oil and swirl to coat. Add the onion, season with a pinch of salt, and cook for 5 minutes, stirring every minute or so, until softened and slightly golden around the edges. Add the garlic and cook, stirring constantly, for 1 minute more. Add to the bowl of eggs.

Increase the heat to medium-high, add about 1 tsp of oil, and add most of the asparagus. Season with a pinch of salt. Cook for about 3 minutes, stirring frequently, until the asparagus has turned bright green and softened slightly, then add them to the bowl of eggs. Add the dukkah, dill, and goat cheese to the eggs and fold together gently.

Lower the heat to medium, add about 1 tsp of oil, and swirl to coat. Pour in the egg mixture and let sit for 2 to 3 minutes. Once it's set on the bottom but still very runny, top with the remaining asparagus ribbons and place it under the broiler. Broil until the whole thing is set and golden brown on top (depending on your broiler, this could take between 30 seconds and 5 minutes).

Top with a little extra dukkah before serving. Serve right from the pan to keep it warm, or loosen the edges and slide it onto a plate.

Shakshuka

Shakshuka is one of my favorite Middle Eastern and North African egg dishes, and there are a ton of delicious regional variations—sometimes tiny meatballs are added (see page 38); sometimes other vegetables are thrown into the tomato sauce (see page 35, or add some sautéed eggplant to the tomato sauce to make something similar to a Tunisian shakshuka)—but they all have a few things in common:

1. There's got to be a tomato sauce. Whether it's chunky, soupy, or thick is up to the cook.

2. The eggs (an essential component) must always be poached directly in the tomato sauce, never fried separately and added in later. This enrobes the egg whites in flavorful sauce and gives them just the right texture.

This base recipe follows these rules closely, and if you stick with it, you'll yield a classic shakshuka with a bit of your own pizazz. But if you want to go further afield to make something that's more shakshuka inspired, feel free to experiment with polenta or greens in place of tomato sauce (see pages 37 and 39 for instructions).

Make Your Own Shakshuka Grid

Ingredients to swap in for the base recipe on the facing page

SPICES

+ Baharat blend
+ Paprika
+ Cumin
+ Coriander
+ Cinnamon
+ Fennel seeds

HERBS

+ **Leafy**
  Cilantro, dill, parsley, chives, basil
+ **Woody**
  Thyme, rosemary, sage, oregano

CHEESE

+ Crumbled goat cheese
+ Feta
+ Parmesan
+ Pecorino Romano
+ Or any of your favorites

SEASONAL PRODUCE

Summer

Corn kernels, green beans, sliced zucchini, sliced bell peppers, minced hot peppers, eggplant slices, chopped Swiss chard, sliced okra

Fall

Late-season summer veggies in early fall (all of the above), plus diced tomatillos, sliced celery, small broccoli or cauliflower florets, chopped blanched broccoli rabe, chanterelles, thinly sliced fennel, thinly sliced leeks

Winter

Chopped kale (or other hearty winter greens), chopped blanched broccoli rabe, thinly sliced fennel, thinly sliced leeks, small broccoli or cauliflower florets

Spring

Small broccoli or cauliflower florets, blanched and peeled fava beans (see page 98), asparagus, shell peas, snow peas, snap peas, chopped ramps, thinly sliced spring onions, shaved cabbage, morels, sliced celery

Anytime

Frozen corn, frozen green beans, frozen peas, thinly sliced mushrooms, wrung-out spinach (do not sauté)

Shakshuka

Makes 4 servings

2 Tbsp [30 g] unsalted butter or olive oil
Up to 2 cups [up to 240 g] prepared vegetables
   (see grid on facing page)
Salt
3 garlic cloves, crushed through a press
1 tsp spices (optional)
One 14½ oz [410 g] can diced tomatoes
   (see Note)
4 large eggs
2 Tbsp crumbled feta (optional)
Chopped fresh cilantro or parsley,
   for garnish (optional)
Pita bread or toast, for serving

Place a sauté pan or skillet over medium-high heat and add the butter or oil. Once hot, add the veggies, season with salt, and sauté for 2 to 3 minutes, just until they soften (longer for any mushrooms).

Lower the heat to medium and add the garlic and spices. Cook, stirring, for about 30 seconds, and then add the diced tomatoes. Cook, stirring, for 3 minutes, just until the tomato sauce thickens slightly.

Break the eggs into the tomato sauce from about 2 in [5 cm] above (to make sure they sink in). Season with salt and top with feta (if using). Immediately cover and cook for about 4 minutes for runny egg yolks, or 5 minutes for soft-set, custardy, slightly runny egg yolks.

Check the eggs by poking the white near the yolk with a knife and gently poking the yolk with your finger. The whites should not ooze, and the yolks should feel jiggly. If the whites are not set, continue cooking them, covered, checking every 45 seconds to see if they are done.

Garnish with some chopped cilantro or parsley (optional) and serve immediately with bread on the side.

Note: See the summer variation for instructions on using fresh tomatoes instead of a can of diced tomatoes.

Summer Shakshuka

Corn, Fresh Tomatoes, Green Beans, Cilantro

This shakshuka is poached in one of my favorite summer staples: succotash! This northeastern Native American dish has been adopted and adapted over the years, but the essential features remain the same: It must contain corn, it often includes tomatoes, and it usually includes green beans. I often take a note from Jessica B. Harris's succotash recipe and add some okra in place of some or all of the green beans. Simply slice the okra into ½ in [13 mm] rounds and sauté it along with the corn and/or green beans until softened slightly. You won't be disappointed either way.

2 Tbsp [30 g] unsalted butter
1 cup [140 g] corn kernels
1 cup [100 g] green bean pieces
2 cups [360 g] chopped fresh tomatoes
3 garlic cloves, crushed through a press
4 large eggs

2 Tbsp crumbled feta
Handful fresh cilantro leaves, for garnish
Pita bread or toast, for serving

Place a sauté pan or skillet over medium-high heat and add the butter. Once it melts, add the corn and green beans and season with salt. Cook, stirring occasionally, for about 3 minutes, until the corn is lightly browned and the green beans are slightly softened. Lower the heat to medium and add the tomatoes and garlic. Cook, stirring, for 3 to 5 minutes, just until the tomatoes break down a bit.

Make four indentations in the sauce with the back of a spoon and break an egg into each. Season with salt and top with the feta. Immediately cover and cook for about 4 minutes for runny egg yolks, or 5 minutes for soft-set, custardy, slightly runny egg yolks.

Check the eggs by poking the white near the yolk with a knife and gently poking the yolk with your finger. The whites should not ooze, and the yolks should feel jiggly. If the whites are not set, continue cooking them, covered, checking every 45 seconds to see if they are done.

Garnish with cilantro and serve with pita bread on the side.

Fall Shakshuka

Polenta, Mushrooms,
Kale, Parmesan Cheese

Eggs poached in polenta or grits is always a crowd-pleaser. Just remember to use enough liquid whenever you're making grits or polenta, whether you plan to poach eggs in it or not. Porridges have a tendency to become rubbery as they cool, but they stay silky when you use enough liquid and a good bit of fat. Silky is the

perfect consistency for poaching eggs, so in this case, it's a win-win.

2 Tbsp [30 g] unsalted butter
2½ cups [200 g] sliced cremini or button mushrooms
Salt
2¼ cups [45 g] chopped kale leaves
4¼ cups [1 kg] stock
½ cup [115 g] heavy cream
¾ cup [120 g] polenta (not instant)
Freshly ground black pepper
4 large eggs
½ cup [45 g] coarsely grated Parmesan cheese
Louisiana-style hot sauce, for serving

Place a large sauté pan or skillet over medium-high heat and add the butter. Once the butter melts, add the mushrooms and season with salt. Cook, stirring occasionally, until shrunken and browned, about 8 minutes. Add the kale and cook, stirring frequently, until any juices have evaporated. Transfer the veggies to a plate.

Add the stock to the pan and increase the heat to high. Once simmering, stir in the cream and polenta, season with salt and ¼ tsp pepper, and lower the heat to medium.

Let the mixture return to a simmer, then turn the heat to low and cook, uncovered, stirring occasionally, until it starts to thicken (3 to 10 minutes, depending on your polenta).

As soon as the polenta begins to thicken, increase the heat to medium-low and sprinkle on the mushrooms and kale. Immediately drop in the eggs from about 4 in [10 cm] above the polenta while it is still hot and liquid. The eggs should not sit on top of the polenta, but nestle in while remaining slightly visible (if you wait too long, they will not sink in at all). Season with salt, sprinkle Parmesan around them, cover, and let cook without disturbing for 3 minutes. Make sure the pan is evenly heated so the eggs cook through.

After 3 minutes, inspect the eggs by gently poking the whites and yolks. If the whites are still clear, cover and cook for another 1 to 2 minutes. If some are cooking faster than others, move the pan so the heat source is closer to the ones that are underdone. Once the whites are opaque but slightly runny, remove from the heat and let them rest, covered, for about 3 minutes before serving with a sprinkling of pepper and hot sauce.

Winter Shakshuka

Crushed Tomatoes, Petite Meatballs, Pomegranate Molasses

These cute little meatballs are inspired by Iraqi ras asfour. They're traditionally served in a tomato stew, and the idea is to make the meatballs as teeny-tiny as possible. The evocative name literally means "birds' heads" in Arabic, which gives them a very "you're so cute, I could eat you up" vibe.

For the meatballs
8 oz [225 g] ground beef
2 tsp pomegranate molasses (see Note)
¼ cup [35 g] finely diced onion
2 Tbsp raisins
1 garlic clove, crushed through a press
1 tsp baharat (or your favorite spice blend; see Note)
¼ tsp salt

For the tomato sauce
2 Tbsp olive oil
¼ cup [35 g] finely diced onion
1 garlic clove, crushed through a press
One 14½ oz [410 g] can diced tomatoes
Salt
4 large eggs

Pomegranate molasses, for garnish (optional)
Pita bread or toast, for serving

To make the meatballs: In a large mixing bowl, combine the ground beef, pomegranate molasses, onion, raisins, garlic, and baharat and mix until well combined. Shape into about 25 tiny meatballs. Sprinkle them evenly with salt. Set aside.

To make the tomato sauce: Place a large sauté pan or skillet over medium heat for a couple of minutes until moderately hot, and then add the olive oil, onion, and garlic. Stir for about 2 minutes, just until softened slightly. Add the diced tomatoes and bring to a simmer. Cook for about 5 minutes, stirring occasionally, until the sauce thickens slightly. Taste and adjust the seasoning if needed.

Place the meatballs into the sauce, evenly spaced, lower the heat to medium-low, cover, and cook for 3 minutes, just to give the meatballs a head start.

Nudge some meatballs out of the way, make four indentations in the sauce with the back of a spoon, and break an egg into each. Sprinkle a pinch of salt over each egg and immediately cover. Cook for about 4 minutes for runny egg yolks, or 5 minutes for soft-set, custardy, slightly runny egg yolks.

Check the eggs by poking the white near the yolk with a knife and gently poking the yolk with your finger. The whites should not ooze, and the yolks should feel jiggly. If the whites are not set, continue cooking them, covered, checking every 45 seconds to see if they are done.

Serve immediately (optionally, with a little drizzle of pomegranate molasses), with bread on the side.

Notes: You can find pomegranate molasses in most Middle Eastern markets, as well as supermarkets with a large international aisle.

If you can't find it, leave it out and finish with a squeeze of lemon juice.

Baharat means "spices" in Arabic but usually refers to a blend of spices. You can find baharat in Middle Eastern markets, but if you can't find a blend, make this simplified version: ¼ tsp ground cumin, ¼ tsp ground coriander, ¼ tsp paprika, ¼ tsp freshly ground black pepper, and a pinch of cinnamon.

Spring Shakshuka

Ramps or Green Onions, Spinach, Feta

This recipe for eggs poached in greens (inspired by Persian nargesi esfenaj) can be easily adapted to include whatever green things you'd like. Ramps, green onions, spinach, arugula, kale—you name it. If you're using fresh greens (instead of frozen), just make sure you sauté them for 2 to 3 minutes, until they soften and shrink down and any excess liquid cooks off.

One 8 oz [225 g] container frozen spinach, thawed
3 Tbsp [45 g] unsalted butter
2 cups [100 g] coarsely chopped ramps or green onions
Salt
3 garlic cloves, crushed through a press
4 large eggs
¼ cup [35 g] crumbled feta
Freshly ground black pepper
Pita bread or toast, for serving

Lightly wring out the spinach so that it is no longer dripping wet (you should end up with about 2 cups [165 g]).

Place a sauté pan or skillet over medium-high heat and add 2 Tbsp of the butter. Once it melts, add the ramps and season with salt. Cook,

stirring occasionally, for about 4 minutes, just until softened and shrunk down slightly.

Lower the heat to medium and add the spinach, garlic, and the remaing 1 Tbsp of butter. Stir for about 1 minute, just to warm it through.

Make four indentations in the greens with the back of a spoon and break an egg into each. Season with salt and top with the crumbled feta. Immediately cover and cook for about 4 minutes for runny egg yolks, or 5 minutes for soft-set, custardy, slightly runny egg yolks.

Check the eggs for doneness by poking the white near the yolk with a knife and gently poking the yolk with your finger. The whites should not ooze, and the yolks should feel jiggly. If the whites are not set, continue cooking them, covered, checking every 45 seconds to see if they are done.

Sprinkle with a little black pepper and serve immediately with bread on the side.

Breakfast Carbs

Everyone should have a perfect recipe for fluffy pancakes, delicately chewy crêpes, crispy waffles, and eggy French toast. These base recipes are everything you could ever need, but it's always nice to throw a little seasonal produce on top.

To feed a crowd, I love making one or two breakfast carbs, and then setting the table with whatever else I've got on hand: seasonal produce, a syrup or two, even some savory toppings. Every base recipe in this section (pancakes, crêpes, waffles, and French toast) can go with either sweet or savory toppings at any time of the year. Feel free to include any of your other favorite breakfast carbs—all of the following toppings go wonderfully with everything from hashbrowns to oatmeal (whether sweet or savory!).

Sweet toppings are usually comprised of a syrup or sweetener and some seasonal produce. It's also nice to include something creamy, something crunchy, and a little shaker or pinch bowl of complementary spices.

For savory, I usually like to include a veggie sautéed with lots of onion and garlic, a few poached or fried eggs, crunchy bacon (see page 49), and even some chopped herbs (sparingly use woody ones such as thyme, rosemary, sage, and oregano). The key here is not to skimp on the garlic and onion.

Sweet Toppings

Ingredients to top the following base recipes for pancakes, crêpes, waffles, or French toast

SWEETENERS

+ Sweetened condensed milk
+ Honey
+ Maple syrup
+ Jam or compote
+ Date syrup
+ Molasses
+ Brown sugar
+ Nutella
+ Confectioners' sugar

CREAMY THINGS

+ Cream cheese
+ Mascarpone
+ Ricotta
+ Yogurt
+ Whipped cream
+ Butter
+ Vegan Tahini Cream (page 48)

CRUNCHY THINGS

+ Toasted coconut flakes
+ Sprinkles
+ Honeycomb candy chunks
+ Candied, toasted, or raw nuts

SPICES

+ Cinnamon
+ Ground ginger
+ Cloves
+ Cardamom
+ Fennel
+ Anise

COMBINATIONS

+ Roasted red grapes, mascarpone, sliced almonds
+ Apple, cardamom, maple syrup, toasted coconut
+ Blood orange supremes, ricotta, walnuts, brown sugar
+ Strawberries, sumac, cinnamon, sweetened condensed milk, pistachios

SEASONAL FRUIT

Summer

Sliced or whole berries (blueberry, strawberry, raspberry, gooseberry, blackberry), pitted whole cherries and sliced stone fruit (peach, plum, nectarine, apricot), roasted grapes (see page 62) or halved raw grapes, whole stemmed currants, sliced Anjou pears, sliced figs

Fall

Sliced Bosc/Bartlett/Anjou pears, thinly sliced apples (or applesauce), sliced pitted plums, pomegranate arils, sliced figs, roasted peeled chestnuts (see page 62), roasted grapes (see page 62) or halved raw grapes, late fall sliced persimmons or Persimmon Pudding Compote (page 49)

Winter

Citrus supremes, sliced Bosc/Bartlett/Anjou pears, roasted peeled chestnuts (see page 62), sliced persimmons or Persimmon Pudding Compote (page 49)

Spring

Sliced pitted sour plums, Rhubarb Compote (page 241), late spring sliced strawberries, halved or sliced loquats

Anytime

Frozen berries (thaw by macerating overnight with some sugar in the refrigerator, and use the liquid as a syrup), sliced bananas, passion fruit pulp, sliced mango, sliced kiwi

Savory Toppings

Ingredients to top the following base recipes for pancakes, crêpes, waffles, or French toast

HERBS

+ Cilantro
+ Dill
+ Parsley
+ Chives
+ Basil
+ Thyme
+ Rosemary
+ Sage
+ Oregano

COMBINATIONS

+ Buttered corn and chives
+ Butter-sautéed mushrooms with extra garlic
+ Spinach with basil
+ Bacon, egg, and green onion (see page 49)

TO SAUTÉ

Place a sauté pan or skillet over medium heat and let it preheat for a couple of minutes. Add 1 Tbsp of oil or 2 Tbsp of butter, followed by 1 small chopped onion or 1 small bunch green onions, chopped, and season with salt. Cook, stirring occasionally, for about 5 minutes, just until softened. Add 8 to 12 thinly sliced medium garlic cloves. Continue cooking while stirring constantly for another 1 to 2 minutes. Once the garlic slices have very lightly browned, add about 2 cups [about 240 g] of prepped seasonal vegetables and continue to cook for another 3 to 4 minutes while stirring occasionally. Most vegetables are done once they've softened/wilted and/or are lightly golden, but mushrooms will take a bit longer. Top with any herbs at the table.

SEASONAL PRODUCE (TO SAUTÉ)

Summer

Diced tomato, corn kernels, green beans, sliced zucchini, sliced bell peppers, minced hot peppers, eggplant slices, chopped Swiss chard, sliced okra

Fall

Late-season summer veggies in early fall (from the yellow box above), plus diced tomatillos, sliced celery, small broccoli or cauliflower florets, chopped blanched broccoli rabe, chanterelles, thinly sliced fennel, thinly sliced leeks

Winter

Chopped kale (or other hearty winter greens), chopped blanched broccoli rabe, thinly sliced fennel, thinly sliced leeks, small broccoli or cauliflower florets

Spring

Small broccoli or cauliflower florets, blanched and peeled fava beans (see page 98), asparagus, shell peas, snow peas, snap peas, chopped ramps, thinly sliced spring onions, shaved cabbage, morels, sliced celery

Anytime

Frozen corn, frozen green beans, frozen peas, thinly sliced mushrooms, wrung-out spinach (do not sauté)

Pancake Base Recipe

Makes 12 to 16 pancakes

2 cups [260 g] all-purpose flour
2 tsp baking powder
¼ tsp baking soda
1 tsp salt
2 cups [480 g] buttermilk, at room temperature (see Note)
2 large eggs, at room temperature
2 Tbsp granulated sugar
3 Tbsp [45 g] unsalted butter, melted
Cold butter, for greasing the pan

Combine the flour, baking powder, baking soda, and salt in a medium mixing bowl. Whisk or sift together until it is lump-free. Set aside.

Combine the buttermilk, eggs, sugar, and melted butter in another medium mixing bowl. Whisk until completely smooth.

Preheat a griddle, cast-iron skillet, or non-stick sauté pan or skillet over medium heat for a few minutes. It should be hot enough for a drop of water to sizzle off in about 10 seconds, but not so hot the water dances. Adjust the heat as necessary.

Once the griddle is just about heated, pour the wet ingredients over the dry ingredients. Stir together just until there are no longer any pockets of dry flour. Do not overmix and don't worry if it's a little lumpy.

Use a cold stick of butter like a big paint-brush and swipe a light layer of butter onto the pan. Immediately drop ¼ to ⅓ cup [65 to 80 g] half-ladlefuls of batter onto the pan, leaving enough room for each to spread and expand. Let sit until several bubbles break the surface and make a few little craters that do not disappear, 3 to 4 minutes. Flip and cook the second side for another 2 to 3 minutes. Try not to flip them more than once. Work in batches and feel free to keep them warm in the oven at 200°F [95°C]. Leftover pancakes freeze well.

Note: If you don't have buttermilk, make a substitute by stirring together one part plain yogurt with one part milk (e.g., 1 cup [240 g] yogurt plus 1 cup [240 g] milk to make 2 cups [480 g] buttermilk substitute). If you use Greek yogurt, use about one part yogurt to three parts milk (e.g., ½ cup [120 g] Greek yogurt plus 1½ cups [360 g] milk to make 2 cups [480 g] buttermilk substitute).

Crêpe Base Recipe

Makes 10 to 20 crêpes

3 Tbsp [45 g] unsalted butter
6 large eggs, at room temperature
2 Tbsp granulated sugar (omit for savory)
½ tsp salt
½ tsp vanilla extract (omit for savory)
1½ cups [195 g] all-purpose flour
2 cups [480 g] milk
Cold butter, for greasing the pan

Place the butter in a microwave-safe medium mixing bowl. Cover and microwave just until it melts, 30 seconds to 1 minute.

Add the eggs, sugar (if using), salt, and vanilla (if using) to the bowl and whisk until completely combined. Add the flour and whisk together until completely lump-free (but stop before it gets gluey). Gradually add the milk, whisking as you pour it in. (If you'd rather use a blender, add the melted butter, eggs, sugar, salt, vanilla, flour, and milk to a blender and run until the batter is completely combined and lump-free.) Set aside.

Place a nonstick sauté pan or skillet over medium-high heat and let it preheat for a few minutes. Once the pan is hot, swipe a stick of butter across the surface; it should immediately sizzle for just a few seconds and then will start to brown and quiet down without burning (if the butter burns, your heat is too high, and if the sizzling goes on for a long time, the heat is too low). As soon as the butter goes on, hold the pan in one hand and pour on about ⅓ cup [80 g] of batter (more or less, depending on how wide your pan is) and immediately tilt the pan circularly to coat it evenly in a thin layer.

Let your crêpe cook for about 1 minute on the first side, then flip and cook for another 30 seconds on the other side. Repeat with the remaining batter.

Waffle Base Recipe

Makes about 10 waffles

2 cups [260 g] all-purpose flour
2 tsp baking powder
1 tsp salt
⅛ tsp baking soda
1½ cup [360 g] buttermilk (see Note, page 44)
2 large eggs
7 Tbsp [100 g] butter, melted
¼ cup [50 g] granulated sugar
Cooking spray (optional)

Combine the flour, baking powder, salt, and baking soda in a medium mixing bowl. Whisk or sift together until it is lump-free. Set aside.

Combine the buttermilk, eggs, butter, and sugar in another medium mixing bowl. Whisk together until it's completely smooth.

Preheat your waffle maker.

Pour the wet ingredients over the dry ingredients. Stir together just until there are no longer any pockets of dry flour, but do not overmix. It's okay if it is a little lumpy.

Once your waffle maker has completely preheated, spray with cooking spray (feel free to skip if your waffle maker is nonstick). Follow your machine's directions, pouring the required amount into the center, closing, and letting it cook for the recommended time. My waffle maker doesn't get super hot, so I cook mine at the highest setting for 6 minutes. Every waffle maker is different, so use your own judgment. Your waffles are done once they're deeply golden brown and crisp on the outside and fluffy on the inside.

French Toast Base Recipe

Makes 8 pieces

¾ cup [180 g] whole milk
2 large eggs
1 Tbsp granulated sugar
½ tsp salt
Eight ½ in [13 mm] slices stale sourdough bread (see Note)
Cold butter, for greasing the pan

Combine the milk, eggs, sugar, and salt in a medium mixing bowl. Beat together until smooth.

Set a large plate or two next to the milk mixture. Place a couple of bread slices in the liquid and let them float for about 30 seconds on one side, then flip and let them soak for another 30 seconds on the other. Remove once they are soft, letting some of the excess drip away for about 5 seconds—don't let them soak in the liquid any longer, or they will get soggy. Transfer the soaked pieces to the plates and let them rest in a single layer for 2 to 20 minutes.

Once your bread pieces are soaked and resting, preheat a nonstick or cast-iron sauté pan or skillet over medium heat. Once hot, swipe a stick of butter across the surface. The butter should sizzle and then go quiet, but it should not smoke (adjust the heat as necessary). Place two or three slices of bread on the buttered pan. Let cook for about 3 minutes per side, just until they are cooked all the way through and golden brown on the outside. Repeat with the remaining bread slices.

Note: If the bread slices are rock-hard, they will need to soak for much longer.

Summer Pancakes

Buttermilk Pancakes with Peaches, Fennel Seeds, Maple Syrup, Pistachios

For the most tender and fluffy buttermilk pancakes, just remember that less is more. Don't overmix the batter. Whisk the wet ingredients as much as you'd like, and sift the dry ingredients together to your heart's content, but once you pour them together and start combining, be sure to stir with purpose and restraint. Once your perfectly mixed batter hits the skillet or griddle, try not to flip them more than once. Helicopter flipping will make your pancakes spread and collapse.

1 recipe Pancake Base (page 44)
3 ripe peaches, pitted and sliced into wedges
Maple syrup
Finely ground pistachios
Whole or ground fennel seeds

Prepare the pancakes as instructed. Top your pancakes with fresh peach slices, maple syrup, pistachios, and a little pinch of fennel seed (whole or ground). If you don't love fennel, a dusting of cinnamon is a lovely alternative. Or use another idea from the toppings grids (pages 42 and 43).

Fall Crêpes

Crêpes with Bosc Pears, Cardamom, Sweetened Condensed Milk, Walnuts

My aunty Masy makes crêpes using just one bowl, and ever since learning her technique, my blender has been relegated to morning smoothie duty. If you were to just dump all your crêpe ingredients together in one bowl and give them a whisk, you'd never get all the lumps out, but using this technique, you can make lump-free crêpes using just one bowl.

1 recipe Crêpes Base (page 44)
½ cup [60 g] finely chopped walnuts
Pinch of cardamom
3 ripe Bosc pears, sliced into wedges
Sweetened condensed milk, for drizzling

Prepare the crêpes as instructed. Stir together the walnuts and cardamom, just so they're lightly scented.

Top or fill each crêpe with a few slices of pear, drizzle with sweetened condensed milk, and top with the cardamom walnuts. Or use another idea from the toppings grids (pages 42 and 43).

Winter Waffles

Buttermilk Waffles with Tahini Cream,
Persimmon Pudding Compote,
Sesame Seeds

While persimmons are really best enjoyed perfectly ripe on their own, persimmon pudding is a lovely alternative, especially if you've got a tree with a bumper crop and you're looking for ideas of delicious ways to put your persimmons to use. This super simple compote is inspired by the flavors of classic persimmon pudding (cinnamon, ginger, nutmeg) and turns them into a charming topping for waffles and all your other favorite breakfast carbs.

1 recipe Waffles Base (page 45)
Tahini Cream, for topping (recipe follows)
Persimmon Pudding Compote, for topping
 (optional; recipe follows)
Sesame seeds, for sprinkling

Prepare the waffles as instructed. Top each waffle with a drizzle of Tahini Cream, a spoonful of Persimmon Pudding Compote (or use another idea from the base recipe, page 45), and a big pinch of sesame seeds and serve.

Tahini Cream

⅓ cups [85 g] tahini
¼ cup [60 g] water
1 Tbsp date molasses or honey

Whisk together the tahini, water, and molasses. The mixture will look broken and runny at first but will come together into a creamy sauce after a minute or two.

Persimmon Pudding Compote

2 firm-ripe Fuyu persimmons, cut into ¼ in [6 mm] slices

2 Tbsp fresh lemon juice

2 Tbsp water

2 Tbsp brown sugar

1 tsp cinnamon

1 tsp dried ginger

Big pinch of salt

Pinch of nutmeg

Place the persimmon slices in a saucepan with the lemon juice, water, brown sugar, cinnamon, ginger, salt, and nutmeg. Bring to a simmer over medium heat, cover, turn the heat to low, and continue cooking for about 10 minutes. Give it a stir once or twice while it cooks, and stop once the persimmons soften significantly and begin to break down into a sauce (similar to apple pie filling). Store in an airtight container in the refrigerator for a few days, or freeze for up to 3 months.

Spring French Toast

French Toast with Fried Green Onions, Eggs, Bacon, Garlic

I love crusty sourdough for both sweet and savory French toast. It holds up to a moderately long soak, which means it gets a little extra custardy once it hits the pan. Whether you're making your toast savory (as with this recipe) or sweet, just be sure to leave in the small amount of sugar, which helps things caramelize. If you're going in a different direction with sweet toppings, try adding 1 tsp vanilla extract and 1 tsp cinnamon, ½ tsp rose water and ¼ tsp cardamom, or 1 tsp orange blossom water to the milk.

1 recipe French Toast Base (page 45)

8 to 12 pieces regular-cut bacon (200 to 300 g)

Neutral oil, such as canola or avocado

4 large eggs

Salt

3 green onions, or 2 small spring onions, thinly sliced

3 garlic cloves, crushed through a press

Freshly ground black pepper

Prepare the French toast as instructed. Preheat your oven to 400°F [205°C].

Place the bacon on a rimmed baking sheet in a single layer. Bake for about 17 minutes, just until it's crisp-chewy and browned (thick-cut will take a couple of minutes longer; thin bacon will take a bit less time).

Using a neutral oil, fry your eggs in a non-stick sauté pan or skillet following your favorite technique.

Remove the fried eggs from the pan and set aside. Remove all but 1 Tbsp of oil from the pan. Add the green onions and garlic to the still-hot pan and stir over medium heat for about 2 minutes. Season with salt and pepper.

Serve the French toast topped with the bacon, fried eggs, onion, and garlic, or use another idea from the toppings grids (pages 42 and 43).

Refrigerator Jam

Use homemade jam to top pancakes, crêpes, French toast, or waffles (see page 42), use it to fill turnovers (see page 252), or spread it on crostini (see page 102). In the late spring through summer, use my stone fruit or berry jam method, and in the fall and early winter, use my pome butter method. From about midwinter through early spring, try a Citrus Curd instead (page 239).

Feel free to mix and match fruits within each category, add whatever flavorings you'd like, and tinker with the fruit-to-sugar ratio, as some fruits that have a lot of pectin don't need as much sugar. Less sugar means that your jam won't keep as long.

Stone Fruit or Berry Jam

For this method, stick with soft and sweet things like berries, pitted cherries, and pitted sliced stone fruits. This is the kind of jam you'd use for most late spring and summer fruits. Stone fruit and berries go great with a little rose water and orange blossom water, or leave it plain and let the fruit speak for itself.

3⅔ to 4½ cups [450 g] sliced stone fruit or
    berries
1 Tbsp water
⅛ tsp salt
2¼ cups [450 g] granulated sugar
1 to 2 Tbsp lemon juice (optional)

Set a plate in the freezer for later.

Place your fruit in a large saucepan with the water and salt, and place over medium-low heat until they break down a bit (about 5 minutes), then pour in the sugar and continue cooking at a simmer while stirring occasionally. Add a little lemon juice toward the end of the cooking process (if your fruit is already quite acidic, you might not need any).

Once your jam has visibly thickened, start testing it: Drip a little drop on the frozen plate. If it sets up into a jammy texture and ripples when you nudge it, it's ready. The amount of time varies from one fruit to another, but you can count on at least 5 minutes after adding the sugar. Larger batches take longer than smaller batches. Make sure it cools completely before using, and store in the refrigerator for at least a few days (or a couple of weeks if you use the full amount of sugar), or you can freeze it for up to 6 months.

Pome Fruit Butter

"Pome" is the name of the apple, pear, and quince family; they tend to be in season in the fall and early winter and work great with a more apple butter–like process. Poach them in syrup until some of the liquid cooks off and the fruit becomes super soft, smash the pieces, and let the liquid continue to reduce until they reach your desired texture and a pinkish-brown hue. Pome butter goes great with cinnamon, cardamom, and all your favorite warm spices.

3½ cups [825 g] water
4 cups [450 g] ½ in [13 mm] peeled diced
    apples/pears or ¼ in [6 mm] peeled diced
    quince (see Note)
1½ cups [300 g] granulated sugar
⅛ tsp salt
2 Tbsp lemon juice
½ tsp lemon zest (optional)

Set a plate in the freezer for later.

Add the water, fruit, sugar, and salt to a large saucepan and bring to a simmer over medium-high heat. Turn the heat down to medium-low to maintain a low boil. Let simmer uncovered for about 90 minutes, until much of the liquid cooks off and the fruit softens significantly.

After 90 minutes, smash the fruit chunks with a potato masher or the back of a fork until they're completely falling apart. Once you smash them, cook them for another 25 to 30 minutes. Keep an eye on the heat (gradually turn it all the way to low), stir often, and make sure the bottom isn't scorching. The jam is done once the fruit has dissolved completely, turned brown or pink, and a little drop sets up to the texture of jam when dripped onto the frozen plate.

Once it's done, add the lemon juice and zest (if using) and continue simmering for another 2 minutes. Transfer to one or two clean jars to cool and then store in the refrigerator for a few weeks or the freezer for up to 6 months.

Note: Coring apples is easy, but take extra care when coring quince and pears. Peel, slice in half, scoop out the seeds and pithy bits, and then scrape the core with a spoon to get rid of the gritty inner layer. Once you've scraped away about ⅛ in [3 mm], you'll notice a subtle change in texture. The stuff scraped away should be gritty and have little hard bits in it, and the rest of the quince or pear flesh should be smoother. This will take a little more effort for quince, as pears are already quite soft.

SALADS

Garden Salads

At its best, a garden salad holds your attention as much as the juicy burger you're serving alongside it. At its worst, it's a last-minute attempt to work some veggies into the meal. The difference between these two scenarios is not determined by time or effort, but by getting a little creative and treating your ingredients with care.

First, treat your greens well and use them in moderation. While a simple side salad of greens and your favorite dressing is often just the thing you need to flesh out a dinner, I usually prefer a more modest amount of greens to make room for lots of other produce.

Second, choose your components: Start with two or three of your favorite fruits and vegetables. If you go the sweet and savory route and you're unsure whether two disparate ingredients would go nicely together, simply taste a bite of the two together and decide from there.

Don't forget to include something crunchy (besides the produce), as well as something rich and creamy (unless the dressing you've chosen is already very rich and creamy). You can also add some pickles if you need a little extra tanginess, or some protein if you want to turn it into more of a main. None of these categories are mutually exclusive, and this is more a rule of thumb than a formula, but it's hard to go wrong if you follow it.

Finally, make sure you mix up or buy a good dressing, and choose the right one for your salad—it should be rich but not heavy, tangy but not too acidic, and it should complement the salad's ingredients. For instance, if your salad is on the rich side, make sure you choose something on the tangy side; if your salad is super light and refreshing, try a creamy dressing.

Make Your Own Salad Grid

Ingredients to swap in for the base recipe on page 59

SEASONAL PRODUCE

Leaves	Savory Produce	Sweet Produce
Summer Stemmed Swiss chard, purslane, watercress	Fresh or slow-roasted tomatoes (see page 113), blanched green beans, grilled or thinly shaved raw zucchini/summer squash, leafy herbs (parsley, cilantro, mint, dill, chives), bell pepper chunks, minced hot peppers, grilled eggplant, diced cucumber, boiled halved new potatoes	Sautéed, grilled, or raw sweet corn kernels, stone fruit (sliced peaches, plums, nectarines, apricots), sliced figs, whole or sliced berries, pitted cherries, raw or slow-roasted grapes (see page 62), bite-size melon pieces, sliced Anjou pear
Fall Massaged kale leaves (see page 62), arugula, spinach, iceberg, watercress, endive, frisée	Sautéed Brussels sprouts, pickled or roasted okra (see page 21), thinly sliced sautéed fennel or leeks, roasted squash or pumpkin, sautéed chanterelles, roasted sweet potatoes	Sliced Bosc/Bartlett/Anjou pears, plum slices, pomegranate arils, sliced figs (early fall), roasted peeled chestnuts (see page 62), persimmon chunks (late fall)
Winter Massaged kale leaves (see page 62), radicchio, romaine, endive, frisée	Sautéed Brussels sprouts, thinly sliced sautéed fennel or leeks, roasted sweet potatoes, raw/shredded or sautéed carrots or parsnips, shredded or boiled beets, roasted squash, roasted cauliflower or broccoli	Persimmon chunks (early winter), sliced Bartlett/Anjou/Bosc pears, citrus supremes (orange, grapefruit, tangerine)
Spring Spring greens, arugula, spinach, iceberg, radicchio, watercress, endive, frisée, romaine	Roasted cauliflower or broccoli, raw/shredded or sautéed carrots or parsnips, whole blanched and peeled fava beans (see page 98), sliced radishes, fresh blanched peas/snap peas/snow peas, prepped fiddlehead ferns (see page 21), sliced celery, sautéed ramps, steamed or sautéed asparagus, sautéed morels, chopped or whole herbs, chopped green onions	Sliced strawberries (late spring), sliced Anjou pears, sliced loquats
Anytime You can find excellent-quality romaine, iceberg, and kale year-round.	Sautéed mushrooms, sautéed or blanched frozen corn, blanched frozen peas, roasted or steamed potatoes	Dried fruit cut into bite-size pieces (be careful not to use too much dried fruit), jammy caramelized onions (see page 132), vacuum-sealed roasted chestnuts

DRESSINGS

+ Garlicky Steakhouse Dressing (page 62)
+ Sumac Lemon Dressing (page 61)
+ Citrus Poppy Dressing (page 64)
+ Blue Cheese Dressing (page 65)
+ Buttermilk Dressing (page 85)
+ Chili Sesame Dressing (page 87)
+ Honey Mustard Vinaigrette (page 88)
+ Lemon Orange Vinaigrette (page 88)
+ Avocado Lime Mint Sauce (page 151)
+ Herby Yogurt Sauce (page 155)
+ Pesto (page 227)
+ Creamy Vinaigrette (page 89)

CRUNCHY

+ Croutons (see page 69)
+ Poppy Seed Crackers (page 63)
+ Pita chips (see page 61)
+ Sliced or slivered almonds
+ Coarsely chopped walnuts
+ Ground or chopped pistachios
+ Whole pepitas
+ Tortilla chips
+ Toasted coconut flakes
+ Parmesan cheese crisps
+ Whole pecans
  (for extra richness, place nuts in a moderately hot pan with ½ tsp oil over medium heat and cook, stirring constantly, for about 3 minutes)

RICH AND CREAMY

+ Crumbled blue cheese
+ Sliced Brie
+ Grated pepper Jack
+ Sliced fresh mozzarella (or mozzarella pearls)
+ Crumbled feta
+ Shaved Manchego cheese
+ Crumbled chèvre
+ Any other cheese you love
+ Sliced or diced avocado
+ Sliced banana

PROTEINS

+ Grilled or sautéed chicken
+ Sliced hard-boiled eggs
+ Black beans
+ Cannellini beans
+ Pinto beans
+ Chickpeas
+ Edamame
+ Lentils
+ Charcuterie
+ Sliced medium-rare seared steak
+ Crispy bacon
+ Poached or seared salmon
+ Anchovies
+ Deep-fried tofu
+ Seared tuna

PICKLES

+ Pickled Red Onions (page 79)
+ Torshi (page 192)
+ Olives
+ Capers
+ Cornichons
+ Peperoncini
+ Pickled okra
+ Pickled beets
+ Pickled radishes
+ Kimchi
+ Marinated artichoke hearts

If you want to reduce the acidic intensity of your pickles, rinse them before adding them to the salad (they'll still be quite acidic, but their flavor won't permeate the entire salad quite so much).

TO ESTIMATE

The volume of your salad should be: half greens plus half vegetables plus a few generous handfuls of other stuff. Add the dressing gradually to make sure you don't use too much.

NOTE

Always salt your dressings to taste—slaw dressings can be used for garden salads, but you should add a touch less salt when using them in a garden salad.

Garden Salads

Makes 6 servings

1 head greens (225 g)
Dressing of choice
4 to 6 cups [600 g] seasonal produce
   (a combination of sweet and savory, see grid
   on page 56)
1 to 2 cups [100 to 200 g] crunchy things
½ to ¾ cup [about 100 g] rich/creamy things
10 to 20 oz [285 to 565 g] protein (optional)
½ cup [50 g] pickles (optional)

Prepare your greens: If you're using a pre-washed and bagged variety, they're already prepped. Otherwise, separate the leaves, place them in a very clean sink or giant bowl, and submerge them in cold water. Swish the greens around (as if you're shampooing hair), then hold them to the side of the bowl or sink and drain. Refill the bowl or sink, swish the greens around again, pause for a minute or so to let the dirt and grit settle to the bottom, and this time *lift* the greens out of the water. Place the greens in a salad spinner to dry them completely. Or, if you don't have a salad spinner, spread them out in a single layer on a very clean towel, gently roll the towel up, and gently shake it up and down. Line a container with another clean towel (or a few paper towels), fill with the greens, and store in the refrigerator (heartier greens can keep for weeks this way).

Dress your greens first: Add the greens to a large mixing bowl and top with about ¼ cup [60 g] of dressing—taste and add more as you go, and remember you can always add more, but it's difficult to subtract. Toss the greens with the dressing until evenly coated.

Throw in any ingredients that aren't delicate (produce, crunchy things, rich/creamy things, pickles), top with a little more dressing, and give it just a few more tosses. Move to a serving or salad bowl (or just another large mixing bowl); transferring it to another bowl is optional, but it lets the little bits wind up mostly on top.

If you're using anything particularly delicate (such as citrus supremes, very ripe fruit slices, extremely crumbly cheese), sprinkle them on top, but don't toss it together.

Top with any big protein pieces (whole salmon fillets or sliced steak) and garnish with any reserved ingredients.

Summer Salad

Watermelon Fattoush

Pita chips and sumac are the heart of any good fattoush. The way I make my pita chips varies, depending on the season. When it's freezing outside, I usually like to toast them in the oven, but in the middle of summer, I much prefer roasting them in a pan instead. It requires a tiny bit more attention, but it's so worth not heating up the house.

This salad is very adaptable, but if you want to keep with the fattoush concept, remember to always opt for very crunchy and refreshing produce (e.g., iceberg would be a more appropriate choice than spring greens, and substituting

radishes would work much better than substituting cauliflower), and don't skip the sumac or pita chips. To turn it into a more classic fattoush, simply replace the watermelon with extra tomato and cucumber and leave out the feta.

1 large thin pita, or 1½ medium pocket pitas

2 tsp neutral oil, such as avocado or canola

Salt

8 oz [225 g] outer leaves from 1 medium head romaine, cut into bite-size pieces

1 tomato, cut into bite-size pieces, or 10 halved cherry tomatoes (180 g)

2 slices watermelon, cut into bite-size pieces and rinds discarded (240 g)

2 Persian cucumbers, cut into bite-size pieces (180 g)

1 green bell pepper, seeded and cut into bite-size pieces (150 g)

⅔ cup [90 g] crumbled feta

½ cup [30 g] chopped green onion, or ¼ small red onion, thinly sliced

1 cup [25 g] coarsely chopped fresh parsley

1 cup [20 g] coarsely chopped fresh mint

Sumac Lemon Dressing (recipe follows)

Make the pita chips: Cut the pita into bite-size triangles and place in a sauté pan or skillet over medium heat. Drizzle with the neutral oil and sprinkle with a pinch of salt. Toss gently every few seconds for a couple of minutes, and then lower the heat to medium-low. Cook for about 15 minutes, giving them a toss every couple of minutes until they're dry and crunchy. Increase the heat if they're not toasting quickly enough, but keep a close eye on them and be careful not to let them burn. (Alternatively, coat in the olive oil, place on a baking pan, sprinkle with a pinch of salt, and bake at 350°F [180°C] for 12 to 14 minutes.)

Place the romaine in a salad bowl or mixing bowl. Top with the tomato, watermelon, cucumber, bell pepper, feta, green onion,

parsley, and mint, reserving some of the herbs for garnish (you can make it ahead up to this point and leave it in the refrigerator for a couple of hours).

When you're ready to serve, top with the pita chips, drizzle with the dressing, and gently toss everything together. Garnish with the reserved herbs and serve.

Sumac Lemon Dressing

¼ cup [60 g] fresh lemon juice

¼ cup [55 g] extra-virgin olive oil

3 Tbsp [20 g] sumac

½ tsp freshly ground black pepper

Salt

Combine the lemon juice, extra-virgin olive oil, sumac, black pepper, and about ¼ tsp of salt in a small mixing bowl or jar. Whisk or shake again right before drizzling.

Fall Salad

Massaged Kale, Roasted Grapes, Chestnuts, Pecorino Romano Cheese, Green Olives, Garlicky Steakhouse Dressing

When I lived in Hong Kong, I used to visit South Korea in the fall. I'd bundle up in a big wool coat and spend the day wandering around the markets, eating my weight in seafood, enjoying the chilly weather and golden ginkgo trees, and eventually I'd magically stumble upon a vendor selling roasted chestnuts. I'd peel and eat them out of the brown paper bag, shoving the husks in my jacket pockets. While we wouldn't return home to quite as many chestnut vendors in muggy Hong Kong, our local convenience stores always had my favorite snack: roasted and peeled chestnuts in commercially sealed red packets.

So choose your own adventure—roast fresh ones and peel them carefully one by one in a romantic celebration of autumn, or simply head to your local Asian market for a couple of bags of roasted and peeled ones for an easy shortcut any time.

This salad is also a good jumping-off point for your own inspired seasonal swaps. Replace the grapes with another sweet ingredient (for instance, throw in some pear slices, or top with citrus supremes right before serving), replace the chestnuts with something starchy, satisfying, and a little sweet (roasted potatoes, sweet potatoes, or squash are a lovely substitute), and leave everything else as is.

3½ cups [560 g] whole red or black grapes
1 tsp neutral oil, such as avocado or canola
Salt
9 oz [255 g] kale leaves from about 1½ large or 2 medium bunches
Garlicky Steakhouse Dressing (recipe follows)
20 chestnuts, roasted and peeled (see Note) (160 g peeled)
⅓ cup [50 g] pitted and halved Castelvetrano olives
Pecorino romano cheese, for sprinkling (can substitute Parmesan)

Roast your grapes: Preheat the oven to 350°F [180°C]. Cut any large grapes in diagonal halves, coat the grapes in a thin layer of the oil, sprinkle with a pinch of salt, and spread out evenly on a rimmed baking sheet with any halved grapes cut-side up. Roast for 35 to 60 minutes (depending on their size) until concentrated and syrupy but not dry.

Place the kale in a large mixing bowl and top with about two-thirds of the dressing. Wash your hands very well and massage the dressing into the leaves, just until they lose some of their crinkliness and become velvety.

Top the kale leaves with the roasted grapes, peeled chestnuts, and olives, top with more dressing, and shave some pecorino on top (about ¼ cup [20 g]), using a vegetable peeler. Serve immediately, but note that the leftovers keep beautifully for a day or two in the refrigerator.

Note: To roast and peel fresh chestnuts: Preheat your oven to 425°F [220°C]. Bring a small pot of water to a boil. Use a serrated knife to carefully score a line into the flat side of each chestnut. Once the water comes to a boil, blanch them for 1 minute and then drain. Transfer the chestnuts to a baking sheet and roast for about 20 minutes. Let them cool so you can handle them, and then peel away their outer husks. If they fight you, give them a little squeeze until they make a crackling sound.

Garlicky Steakhouse Dressing

⅓ cup [75 g] mayonnaise
½ cup [30 g] finely grated pecorino romano or Parmesan cheese
3 Tbsp [45 g] fresh lemon juice, or 2 Tbsp (30 g) red wine vinegar plus 1 Tbsp (15 g) water
3 garlic cloves, crushed through a press
2 tsp Worcestershire sauce
2 tsp Dijon mustard
½ tsp freshly ground black pepper
Salt

Combine the mayo, pecorino, lemon juice, garlic, Worcestershire sauce, mustard, black pepper, and about ¼ tsp of salt in a small bowl or jar. Whisk or shake again before drizzling.

Winter Salad

Radicchio, Citrus, Avocado, Salmon, Poppy Seed Crackers, Citrus Poppy Dressing

Right when the weather is gloomiest, we can always count on lemons, oranges, and grape-fruits to bring some much-needed sunshine into our lives. This salad is nothing short of a citrus fest, with a lemon-orange poppy seed dressing and lots of orange and grapefruit supremes.

Feel free to mix and match whatever sweet citrus you've got on hand for the zests and the supremes. Just be sure to use only lemon juice in the dressing. (Citrus flavor is most concentrated in its zest, which richly flavors the dressing with-out diluting it.)

2 to 4 salmon fillets (280 to 560 g)
Salt
½ tsp neutral oil, such as avocado or canola
1 medium radicchio head, torn into bite-size pieces (225 g)
Citrus Poppy Dressing (recipe follows)
1 grapefruit, supremed (160 g) (see Note)
1 orange, supremed (115 g)
1 avocado, sliced (200 g)
Poppy Seed Crackers (recipe follows)

Place a nonstick or cast-iron sauté pan or skillet over medium-high heat for a couple of minutes.

Season your salmon with about ¼ tsp of salt. Once the pan is hot, add the oil to the pan, swirl to coat, and add the salmon. Let it cook for about 5 minutes, undisturbed, and flip once it's nicely browned. Let it continue cooking for

about 5 minutes on the other side, and remove once it's opaque all the way through. Let it cool for at least a few minutes.

Place the radicchio in a salad bowl or mixing bowl. Top with some of the dressing and toss together until the leaves are evenly coated. Top with the grapefruit and orange supremes (leaving behind any juices that have collected), avocado, crackers, and salmon and drizzle with some extra dressing. Serve without tossing.

Note: Supreming is simply cleanly carving the peel away, and then freeing citrus segments from their membranes. To do so, slice off the stem end so that you can see the flesh peeking through a little. Do the same with the base end. Rest the citrus on one of the flat ends so it's stable. Rest your knife where the white pith meets the flesh at the top, and angle your knife down and away so that it carves away a strip of peel from the top of the citrus to the bottom, exposing the flesh. Repeat in slightly overlap-ping strips until almost all of the white pith is gone and the citrus flesh is completely exposed. Flip it to rest it on the other flat side, and carve any remaining white bits that you missed on the bottom. Once the flesh is completely exposed, turn the citrus so it's on its side, and carefully slice down the side of each membrane to loosen each segment. Reserve the freed segments and discard the rest. Throughout the process, always cut away from your hands in case the knife slips.

Poppy Seed Crackers

These crackers are a wonderful addition to any salad, and you can easily get creative with the seeds you choose to sprinkle on. For this recipe, poppy seeds work great, but you can also try sesame, cumin, cracked coriander, or even an everything bagel seasoning if you're making these crackers for another salad.

¾ cup [100 g] all-purpose flour
½ cup [115 g] lukewarm water
3 Tbsp [40 g] extra-virgin olive oil
½ tsp instant yeast
¼ tsp salt
1 Tbsp poppy seeds
Flaky sea salt or kosher salt, for sprinkling

Combine the flour, water, oil, yeast, and salt in a medium mixing bowl. Stir together for 1 to 2 minutes until very smooth and gluey. Cover and let sit in a warm corner of your kitchen until it's bubbly (about 1 hour).

Preheat the oven to 350°F [180°C] and line a baking sheet with parchment paper.

Pour the batter into the center of the parchment and use an offset spatula to spread it into an even wafer-thin layer, about 11 by 15 in [28 by 38 cm]. Top with the poppy seeds and sprinkle on about ⅛ tsp sea salt.

Bake for about 30 minutes, until golden brown all over with a couple of paler spots. Let cool completely and then break into shards. Store in an airtight container for up to 3 days.

Note: This also works as a sourdough discard cracker. Start with 115% hydrated starter. Measure out about ½ cup [115 g] of stirred starter and combine with ⅓ cup [50 g] of all-purpose flour, ¼ cup [60 g] of water, 3 Tbsp [40 g] of extra-virgin of olive oil, and ¼ tsp of salt. Stir together and proceed with the recipe from the rising step. It may take longer than 1 hour to become bubbly.

Citrus Poppy Dressing

3 Tbsp [45 g] fresh lemon juice
3 Tbsp [40 g] extra-virgin olive oil
1 Tbsp honey
2 Tbsp poppy seeds
1 tsp lemon zest (from about 1 lemon)
½ tsp orange zest
1 garlic clove, crushed through a press
¼ tsp freshly ground black pepper
¼ tsp salt

Combine the lemon juice, olive oil, honey, poppy seeds, lemon zest, orange zest, garlic, pepper, and salt in a small mixing bowl or jar. Whisk or shake again immediately before using.

Spring Salad

Romaine Heart Wedges, Radishes, Asparagus, Bacon, Chives, Blue Cheese Dressing

Spring has few sweet treats, and while dried fruit is a lovely option for a sweet and savory salad, sometimes it's nice to just embrace the zesty, fresh character of the season.

You can change things up here to include romaine hearts, or even iceberg lettuce, and you don't have to limit yourself to asparagus. Try substituting fiddlehead ferns (see page 21) and/or sautéed morels. In the later summer months, go for watermelon, cucumber, and tomato with a sprinkling of sumac. For fall, try pomegranate arils and apple slices, and for winter try steamed squash or pumpkin. Just keep the toppings light, refreshing, and minimal, and don't be shy with the dressing.

4 heads baby romaine (650 g)
6 strips bacon, cut into ½ in [13 mm] pieces (150 g)
16 asparagus spears, trimmed (200 g)
Salt

Blue Cheese Dressing (recipe follows)
⅓ cup [50 g] blue cheese crumbles
3 to 5 thinly sliced radishes (80 g)
Chives, for sprinkling

Trim any brown bits from the romaine stems. Slice the romaine heads down the middle, from stem to tips. Slice each half lengthwise again so that you end up with 16 wedges.

Place the bacon in a cold sauté pan or skillet and set over medium heat. Once it starts sizzling audibly (after about 2 minutes), lower the heat to medium-low and continue to cook until crisp-chewy, stirring occasionally (about 12 minutes after sizzling).

Remove the crispy bacon from the pan and set aside. Discard all but about 1 Tbsp of fat and place the pan back over medium heat. Add the asparagus, season with a pinch of salt, and cook, stirring occasionally, until they're bright green and softened slightly, 3 to 4 minutes.

Place the romaine wedges on a big serving plate or bowl, top with the dressing, asparagus, bacon, blue cheese crumbles, sliced radishes, and chives and serve immediately.

Blue Cheese Dressing

½ cup [120 g] buttermilk
¼ cup [60 g] mayonnaise
1 Tbsp fresh lemon juice
⅓ cup [50 g] blue cheese crumbles
⅓ cup [15 g] finely chopped chives
¼ tsp freshly ground black pepper
¼ tsp salt

Combine the buttermilk, mayonnaise, lemon juice, blue cheese crumbles, chives, pepper, and salt in a medium mixing bowl. Stir together, breaking up any big chunks of blue cheese with your spoon against the side of the bowl.

Panzanella

Tuscan panzanella, a chopped salad featuring stale bread as its star, is my favorite way to use up a lot of leftover bread on its last leg. But our house goes through bread so quickly, I most often make panzanella by turning fresh bread into crunchy croutons in the oven. The following recipe is written for fresh bread, but you can absolutely make it with stale bread.

Just remember that there is a big difference between stale bread and dried-out bread. If you seal bread up in an airtight container, after a few days it'll start to *taste* dry, even though it still has quite a lot of moisture locked in there. Heating stale bread just makes that water more available, and thereby makes the bread taste much better, even after we toast it and intentionally dry it out further. On the other hand, bread that's been left to sit out for days and is hard as a rock needs to be lightly spritzed with water and left to rehydrate for a few minutes before toasting.

Classic panzanella usually includes tomato and basil, but there are a couple of things to pay attention to if you're getting creative with other ingredients. The bottom line is to always be aware of the moisture level. In order to achieve a chewy-firm (but not soggy) texture, add some juicy produce but try not to overdo it, especially when it comes to things like citrus supremes. If you're using a lot of high-moisture produce, do not add any water to the dressing. Also be sure to place any extremely delicate and/or high-moisture things (such as citrus supremes or creamy cheese) on top instead of mixing them in.

Make Your Own Panzanella Grid

Ingredients to swap in for the base recipe on the facing page

BREADS

+ Rye
+ Baguette
+ Crusty whole wheat
+ Multigrain
+ Sourdough
+ Bagels
+ Ciabatta

Stay away from more delicate enriched breads such as challah, brioche, and sliced sandwich bread.

HERBS

+ **Leafy**
  Cilantro, dill, parsley chives, basil, mint
+ **Woody**
  Thyme, rosemary, sage, oregano
+ **Dried**
  Use up to one-third of the volume of fresh herbs called for if using dried

TO ESTIMATE

The croutons should make up about one-third of the volume of the salad, and the produce should make up about two-thirds. Add the dressing gradually to make sure you don't overdo it.

TIP

If some of your produce is extremely juicy and delicate (e.g., citrus supremes), use no more than a large handful of that particular ingredient, combine it with some less juicy things, and carefully fold it in or set it on top.

SEASONAL PRODUCE

Medium-moisture produce (Add 1 Tbsp of water to the dressing if you're using a lot of produce from this column.)

High-moisture produce (Don't add water to the dressing if using a lot of produce from this column.)

Summer

Medium-moisture produce	High-moisture produce
Grilled or fresh corn kernels, grilled or blanched green bean segments, quartered figs, blueberries, gooseberries, whole pitted cherries, thinly sliced bell peppers, minced hot peppers, roasted okra (see page 21)	Halved cherry tomatoes, grilled zucchini or eggplant, sliced stone fruit, sliced cucumbers, berries or grapes

Fall

Medium-moisture produce	High-moisture produce
Roasted okra (see page 21), pomegranate arils, thinly sliced fennel, roasted squash or pumpkin, quartered figs, roasted carrots, parsnips, or beets, sliced apple or celery, roasted broccoli or cauliflower, chestnuts (see page 62), sautéed chanterelles, sautéed broccoli rabe	Sliced plums, halved grapes, sliced pears, ripe persimmons

Winter

Medium-moisture produce	High-moisture produce
Thinly sliced radicchio or fennel, roasted carrots, parsnips, or beets, roasted squash, pumpkin, or sweet potato, roasted cauliflower florets, sautéed kale or collards, clementine segments	Ripe persimmons, supremed citrus, sliced pears

Spring

Medium-moisture produce	High-moisture produce
Roasted broccoli or cauliflower florets, sliced radishes, roasted carrots, parsnips, or beets, blanched fava beans (see page 98), sautéed asparagus, sautéed ramps, sautéed leeks, prepped fiddlehead ferns (see page 21), blanched peas, sliced celery, sautéed morels	Sliced strawberries (late spring), sliced Anjou pears

Anytime

Medium-moisture produce	High-moisture produce
Sautéed mushrooms, sliced olives, frozen corn	Sliced mango

Panzanella

Makes 6 servings

8 oz [225 g] loaf crusty bread

Cooking spray or olive oil

4 to 6 cups [500 to 800 g] prepared produce,
a combination from one or both columns on
the facing page

½ cup [65 g] crumbled or shredded cheese
(optional)

½ to 1⅓ cups [20 to 55 g] chopped fresh leafy
herbs, or 2 tsp minced fresh woody herbs

⅓ cup [70 g] extra-virgin olive oil

2 Tbsp red wine vinegar

1 Tbsp water (optional)

1 garlic clove, crushed through a press

1 tsp mustard (optional)

¼ tsp freshly ground black pepper or your
favorite spice

¼ to ½ tsp salt

Preheat the oven to 325°F [165°C].

Cut the bread into ¾ in [2 cm] cubes and spread out on a baking sheet. Spray lightly with cooking spray or drizzle with a little olive oil and bake for about 15 to 20 minutes, just until dried out and lightly browned. Transfer to a large mixing bowl.

Set aside anything delicate that will fall apart once mixed in, such as citrus supremes, particularly ripe stone fruit, or very creamy feta. Place the rest of the prepared produce in the bowl with the bread, and top with the cheese and herbs, reserving some herbs for garnish. Set aside.

Decide whether you should add water to the dressing: If you're using a lot of high-moisture produce from the second column on the facing page, you won't need to; if you're using a lot of medium-moisture produce from the first column, you will. Combine the olive oil, red wine vinegar, water (if using), garlic, mustard (if using), black pepper, and salt in a small mixing bowl. Whisk together until completely combined.

Pour the dressing over the salad and toss together until evenly coated. Garnish with any delicate produce or any reserved herbs, let it sit for about 5 minutes, and then serve.

Summer Panzanella

Baguette, Tomatoes, Nectarines,
Corn, Jalapeño, Cilantro, Basil

If you're just learning how to combine sweet and savory produce, this is a great place to start. Switch out the nectarines for another stone fruit (e.g., apricots or peaches), and trade the cilantro and basil for any combination of chives, parsley, and fresh mint (if you're using mint, try combining it with parsley if you don't want it to become overpowering). Tomato and corn are simultaneously sweet and savory, so they make a nice bridge for other flavors.

8 oz [225 g] crusty baguette

Cooking spray or olive oil

2 ears corn

1 pt [300 g] cherry tomatoes, halved

3 nectarines, cut into ½ in [13 mm] slices

1 seeded, ribbed, and minced jalapeño

¼ cup [10 g] chopped fresh cilantro

¼ cup [10 g] chopped fresh basil

⅓ cup [70 g] extra-virgin olive oil

2 Tbsp red wine vinegar

1 garlic clove, crushed through a press

1 tsp mustard

¼ tsp freshly ground black pepper

¼ to ½ tsp salt

Preheat the oven to 325°F [165°C].

Cut the bread into ¾ in [2 cm] cubes and spread out on a baking sheet. Spray lightly with cooking spray or drizzle with a little olive oil and bake for about 15 minutes, just until dried out and lightly browned. Transfer to a large mixing bowl.

Heat your grill to high. Place the corn cobs directly on the grates and let cook for 1 to 2 minutes per side, just until their surface is about 50 percent charred. Once they are cool enough to handle, slice the corn off the cobs. (Alternatively, blanch them for 1 minute in boiling water, or simply rinse the cobs well and use the kernels raw if they're super fresh.) You'll end up with about 1½ cups [210 g].

Place the corn, tomatoes, nectarines, and jalapeño in the bowl with the bread and top with the cilantro and basil, reserving some produce and herbs for garnish. Set aside.

Combine the olive oil, red wine vinegar, garlic, mustard, black pepper, and salt in a small mixing bowl. Whisk together until completely combined.

Pour the dressing over the salad and toss everything together until evenly coated. Garnish with any reserved herbs and veggies, let it sit for about 5 minutes, and then serve.

Fall Panzanella

Sourdough, Clementines, Kale, Squash, Sage, Pomegranate Arils

This particular panzanella is a great jumping-off point: Change out the kale for whatever hearty winter greens you've got (mustard greens or thinly sliced Brussels sprouts both work great). Anything somewhat starchy will work wonderfully in place of the squash (try roasting sweet potatoes or parsnips instead). And if it's not fall or early winter and you're having trouble finding reasonably priced pomegranates, use dried cranberries for a little acidity and a pop of color.

8 oz [225 g] sourdough loaf

Cooking spray or olive oil

2½ cups [330 g] ¾ in [2 cm] butternut squash wedges, from ½ small squash

Salt

5 cups [100 g] stemmed and chopped kale, from a small bunch

1¼ cups [175 g] seedless clementine segments (from 3 or 4 clementines)

2 tsp minced fresh sage, or 1 tsp ground sage

⅓ cup [70 g] extra-virgin olive oil

2 Tbsp red wine vinegar

1 Tbsp water

1 garlic clove, crushed through a press

1 tsp mustard

¼ tsp freshly ground black pepper

½ cup [65 g] pomegranate arils

Preheat the oven to 325°F [165°C].

Cut the bread into ¾ in [2 cm] cubes and spread out on a baking sheet. Spray lightly with cooking spray or drizzle with a little olive oil and bake for about 15 minutes, just until dried out and lightly browned.

Once your bread has toasted, transfer it to a medium mixing bowl (but don't wash the baking sheet) and increase the oven temperature to 450°F [230°C].

Place the squash on the baking sheet and drizzle with about 1 tsp olive oil. Use your hands to coat evenly and then season lightly with a pinch of salt. Roast for 10 to 15 minutes, until the squash is tender and turning brown in spots. Place the kale in a pile on the squash. Drizzle the kale with another 1 tsp of olive oil, coat evenly, and season lightly with another pinch of salt. Place back in the oven for about 2 minutes, until the kale is wilted and charred in spots. Remove from the oven and let cool to room temperature on the pan.

Place the kale and squash in the bowl with the bread and top with the clementines and sage. Set aside.

Combine the olive oil, red wine vinegar, water, garlic, mustard, black pepper, and ¼ to ½ tsp of salt in a small mixing bowl. Whisk together until completely combined.

Pour the dressing over the salad and toss everything together until evenly coated. Garnish with the pomegranate arils, let it sit for about 5 minutes, and then serve.

Winter Panzanella

Rye, Oranges, Roasted Sweet Potatoes, Castelvetrano Olives, Feta, Red Onion

While you can use any orange in this salad, I particularly love using Cara Caras here. Their super-sweet flavor goes so nicely with buttery Sicilian green olives, feta, and crunchy red onion. You can find oranges just about any time of year, but they're at their peak in the middle of winter, and Cara Caras in particular are hard to find out of season. If you just like olives to a medium degree, stick with Castelvetranos (even if you don't love olives, they're one of the mildest). But

if you'd like to dial up the olive flavor, feel free to use those super shriveled oil-cured black olives here instead. Just be sure to pop the orange supremes on top *after* tossing, so they don't fall apart.

8 oz [225 g] seedless rye loaf

Cooking spray or olive oil, for coating the bread cubes

2 medium sweet potatoes, peeled and cut into ½ in [13 mm] wedges (425 g)

Salt

2 big handfuls arugula (85 g)

½ small red onion, cut into small dice or thinly sliced (45 g)

⅓ cup [70 g] extra-virgin olive oil

2 Tbsp red wine vinegar

1 garlic clove, crushed through a press

1 tsp mustard

½ tsp orange zest

¼ tsp freshly ground black pepper

2 oranges, supremed (see Note on page 63) and strained (180 g)

½ cup [70 g] crumbled feta

⅓ cup [45 g] pitted halved Castelvetrano or Sicilian green olives

Preheat the oven to 325°F [165°C].

Cut the bread into ¾ in [2 cm] cubes and spread out on a baking sheet. Spray lightly with cooking spray or drizzle with a little olive oil and bake for about 15 minutes, just until dried out.

Once your bread has toasted, transfer it to a medium mixing bowl (but don't wash the baking sheet) and increase the oven temperature to 425°F [220°C].

Coat the sweet potato in a light layer of oil and season with a pinch of salt. Place on the baking sheet and roast for about 10 minutes, until cooked through and browned.

Place the roasted sweet potato, arugula, and red onion in the bowl with the bread. Set aside.

Combine the olive oil, red wine vinegar, garlic, mustard, orange zest, black pepper, and ¼ to ½ tsp salt in a small mixing bowl. Whisk together until completely combined.

Pour the dressing over the salad and toss everything together until evenly coated. Top with the orange supremes, feta, and olives, let it sit for about 5 minutes, and then serve.

Spring Panzanella

Everything Bagel Crisps, Favas, Baby Arugula, Dill, Chives

Bagels are one of my favorite breads to use in a panzanella—they're so dense that they don't easily become soggy, so they're ideal if you're using a lot of juicier produce. They also work with light and crinkly spring greens for a nice contrast in texture. You can always use other spring greens here, or even thinly chopped kale in the middle of winter.

Favas are the true star of this dish—they're available for a short period in the spring, but luckily they're available frozen anytime. You can also substitute another zesty, green spring vegetable, such as fiddlehead ferns or asparagus (see page 21), in their place. See page 98 for fava bean preparation instructions.

2 everything bagels (225 g)
Cooking spray or olive oil
1¼ cups [200 g] shelled fava beans
3 big handfuls baby arugula (140 g)
⅔ cup [25 g] chopped dill
⅔ cup [25 g] chopped chives
⅓ cup [70 g] extra-virgin olive oil
2 Tbsp red wine vinegar
1 Tbsp water
1 garlic clove, crushed through a press

1 tsp mustard
¼ tsp freshly ground black pepper
¼ to ½ tsp salt

Preheat the oven to 325°F [165°C].

Cut the bagels into ¾ in [2 cm] cubes and spread out on a baking sheet. Spray lightly with cooking spray or drizzle with a little olive oil and bake for about 15 minutes, just until dried out and lightly browned. Transfer to a medium mixing bowl.

Bring a small pot of water to a simmer. Add the fava beans and let them simmer for 1 minute. Drain and rinse with cold water. Peel the membranes away with a paring knife (make a little slit, and then pop the bean out of the membrane).

Place the favas in the bowl with the bagel cubes and top with the arugula, dill, and chives, reserving some favas and arugula and herbs for garnish. Set aside.

Combine the olive oil, red wine vinegar, water, garlic, mustard, black pepper, and salt in a small mixing bowl. Whisk together until completely combined.

Pour the dressing over the salad and toss everything together until evenly coated. Garnish with the reserved herbs and veggies, let sit for about 5 minutes, and then serve.

Bean Salads

A bean salad is not just a garden salad with some beans thrown in—the beans should be the star of the show. Because the salads in this section are so bean-centric, they can be a little unwieldy, which is why it's important to prepare your ingredients properly. Try to cut your produce so it's about the size of your beans or include some wispy greens so the beans have somewhere to nest.

Skim through the seasonal variations for some flavor inspiration and a few extra ways to change things up, or try the base recipe for an easily adaptable classic. You can mix and match just about anything in the grid (page 76) and wind up with a delicious salad.

Make Your Own Bean Salad Grid

Ingredients to swap in for the base recipe on the facing page

BEANS

+ Black
+ Navy
+ Cannellini
+ Butter
+ Chickpea
+ Fresh favas
+ Lima
+ Black-eyed peas
+ Whole lentils (not split)
+ Red kidney (or literally any other bean you'd like)

PICKLES

+ Torshi (Middle Eastern pickled fall vegetables; page 192)
+ Pickled Turnips (page 81)
+ Pickled Red Onions (page 79)
+ Pickled Carrots and Daikon Radishes (page 195)

HERBS

+ **Leafy**
  Cilantro, dill, parsley, chives, basil, mint
+ **Woody**
  Thyme, rosemary, sage, oregano

TO ESTIMATE

Don't add all the dressing in at once; add it gradually to taste (make a bit more if you think you prepped too many vegetables). Adjust everything so that it's a little tangy, rich, and very flavorful. Be careful not to add way too many greens—add more like 5 cups of denser things like romaine lettuce, and 8 to 10 cups (or 4 to 5 big handfuls) of lighter things like spinach.

SEASONAL PRODUCE

Produce	Greens
Summer	
Fresh or slow-roasted tomatoes (see page 113); blanched or sautéed chopped green beans; sautéed sliced zucchini/summer squash; diced bell peppers; minced hot peppers; grilled sliced eggplant (sliced after grilling); diced cucumbers; corn kernels	Purslane, watercress, thinly sliced Swiss chard
Fall	
Roasted okra (see page 21), thinly sliced raw or sautéed fennel or leek, diced roasted squash or pumpkin, sautéed chanterelles	Arugula; spinach; watercress; frisée; thinly sliced/shaved kale, Brussels sprouts, or cabbage
Winter	
Thinly sliced raw or sautéed fennel or leeks, raw/grated carrots/parsnips/beets, diced roasted squash or pumpkin	Arugula; spinach; watercress; frisée; thinly sliced/shaved kale, Brussels sprouts, or cabbage
Spring	
Raw/grated carrots/parsnips/beets, sliced radishes, blanched peas/snow peas/snap peas, sliced celery, sautéed ramps, steamed or sautéed chopped asparagus, sautéed morels	Spring greens, arugula, spinach, watercress, frisée
Anytime	
Sautéed mushrooms, sliced avocado, frozen corn	Thinly sliced kale, spinach, and cabbage

Bean Salads

2 cups [300 g] prepared produce, or 5 to
   10 cups [300 g] chopped greens (or half of
   each, see grid on facing page)
Two 15 oz [425 g] cans beans, drained and
   rinsed
¼ to ⅔ cup [25 to 65 g] pickles (optional)
½ to ¾ cup [20 to 30 g] chopped leafy herbs, or
   1 Tbsp chopped woody herbs
2 to 3 Tbsp extra-virgin olive oil
1 to 2 Tbsp vinegar (see Note)
1 garlic clove, crushed through a press
2 tsp mustard (optional)
¼ tsp freshly ground black pepper
¼ tsp salt

Set the produce and/or greens, beans, pickles
(if using), and herbs in a large mixing bowl.
Reserve a few pickles and herbs for garnish. Set
the bowl aside.

In a small mixing bowl, whisk together the
oil, vinegar, garlic, mustard (if using), pepper,
and salt. Pour over the salad. Toss together,
garnish, and enjoy.

Note: If including pickles or anything else
tangy, cut back to 1 Tbsp vinegar. Otherwise,
use 2 Tbsp.

Summer Bean Salad

Canellinis, Dill, Basil, Tomatoes, Cucumbers

Mollie Katzen's "Just White Beans" is the salad I
make when I have nothing but pantry ingredients
available. While it's indeed just white beans, it
has a lot of aromatic Mediterranean-inspired
flavor from all the dill, basil, and garlic. It's perfect
on its own, but I also love building a Moosewood-
inspired white bean salad with some of my
favorite seasonal produce layered in. In the
summer, I add tomatoes and cucumbers (as you
see here). In the colder months, I use dried herbs
and whatever seasonal roasted produce I've got;
few things clash with such simple ingredients.
Asparagus, cauliflower, pumpkin, asparagus—
you name it!—are all perfect here.

3 Tbsp [40 g] extra-virgin olive oil
2 Tbsp red wine vinegar
1 garlic clove, crushed through a press
2 tsp mustard
¼ tsp freshly ground black pepper
¼ tsp salt
Two 15 oz [425 g] cans cannellini beans, drained
   and rinsed
½ pt [150 g] cherry tomatoes, halved
1 large or 2 small Persian cucumbers, cut into
   ½ in [13 mm] half-moons (150 g)
2 Tbsp chopped dill, or 2 tsp dried dill
1 small bunch basil (30 g leaves), or 1 Tbsp dried
   basil

Combine the olive oil, vinegar, garlic, mustard, pepper, and salt in a large mixing bowl

and whisk together. Add the beans, tomatoes, cucumbers, and dill.

Coarsely tear the basil with clean hands (don't worry if it bruises in spots), add to the bowl, toss everything together, and serve.

Fall Bean Salad

Black Beans, Cabbage, Lime, Chipotle, Cilantro, Red Onions

The ingredients in this bean salad-slaw hybrid are all cool-weather staples, so you can make it as is with local in-season ingredients just about any time from fall through spring, but it's especially fun to change things up in the dog days of summer. For a more summery vibe, simply replace some of the cabbage with halved cherry tomatoes and grilled corn (see page 141) and replace the chipotle with a minced jalapeño (seeded and deribbed). You can also skip the pickled red onions or replace them with 2 thinly sliced green onions. And don't forget to freeze any extra chipotles in separate blobs on a parchment-lined flexible cutting board, and then store in a freezer bag for months.

3 Tbsp [45 g] mayonnaise or Greek yogurt
2 Tbsp fresh lime juice
1 tsp lime zest (from about 1 lime)
1 Tbsp minced chipotle in adobo sauce
1 garlic clove, crushed through a press
½ tsp salt
Two 15 oz [425 g] cans black beans, drained and rinsed
5 cups [325 g] thinly shredded red cabbage (from about ¼ large head)
¾ cup [30 g] chopped fresh cilantro leaves
¼ cup [30 g] Pickled Red Onion, drained (recipe follows)

Combine the mayonnaise, lime juice, lime zest, chipotle, garlic, and salt in a large mixing bowl and whisk together. Add the black beans, cabbage, and most of the cilantro and red onion and toss everything together. Garnish with the reserved cilantro and red onion and serve.

Pickled Red Onions

1 large red onion, thinly sliced (240 g)
½ cup [115 g] water
½ cup [115 g] red wine vinegar
1½ tsp salt
1 tsp granulated sugar

Place the onions in a clean heatproof glass container or jar.

Combine the water, red wine vinegar, salt, and sugar in a small saucepan over high heat. As soon as it comes to a simmer, pour over the onions in the jar. Make sure they're fully submerged, let cool for a few minutes, then cover and store in the refrigerator. While they're tasty after an hour or two, they're best the next day, and they keep for weeks.

Winter Bean Salad

Gigantes with Nestled Feta

This recipe is not technically a salad, but it takes all the ingredients you'd find in a bean salad and bakes them together in a comforting casserole, inspired by Greek gigantes plaki. While you can skip the feta to make this a traditional vegan version of gigantes, the little pockets of soft and spreadable feta are a delight.

3 Tbsp [40 g] extra-virgin olive oil
1 medium onion, chopped (180 g)

1 Tbsp minced or pressed garlic

2 carrots, cut into ¼ in [6 mm] slices (140 g)

Salt

1 tsp granulated sugar

2 tsp dried thyme

1 tsp dried oregano

¼ tsp red pepper flakes, plus more as needed

½ tsp freshly ground black pepper

Two 14½ oz [410 g] cans diced tomatoes

Three 15 oz [425 g] cans butter beans, drained and rinsed

¼ cup [10 g] chopped fresh dill fronds, or 1½ Tbsp dried dill

1 cup [40 g] chopped fresh parsley leaves (reserve some for garnish)

7 oz [200 g] feta, cut into about 12 large cubes

Heat a 10 to 12 in [25 to 30 cm] steep-sided ovenproof sauté pan or skillet over medium heat for a few minutes, then add the olive oil, followed by the onion, garlic, carrots, and about ¼ tsp of salt. Cook, stirring occasionally, for 10 to 15 minutes, until the onions and carrots are softened (lower the heat to low if they start to caramelize).

Add the sugar, thyme, oregano, red pepper flakes, black pepper, and diced tomatoes, and bring up to a simmer. Once simmering, lower the heat to medium-low and cook, uncovered, stirring occasionally, for 20 to 25 minutes, just until it forms a very thick sauce.

Preheat the oven to 425°F [220°C] while the sauce is simmering.

Taste the sauce and adjust the seasoning. Stir in the butter beans and remove from the heat. Add most of the dill and parsley. Distribute all but one of the feta cubes evenly over the surface of the beans. Gently push down the cubes so that they nestle in, then gently nudge some beans back over the feta cubes to make sure they're not showing. Crumble the remaining cube of feta on top and bake for 25 to 30 minutes, just until the exposed feta is browned and the whole thing is heated through. Garnish with the reserved herbs and serve.

To make ahead: Make the sauce, cut the feta into cubes, and prep the rest of the ingredients. When you're ready to bake, heat the sauce back up in the pan with a couple tablespoons of water. Fold in the beans, dill, and parsley and proceed with the recipe.

Spring Bean Salad

Chickpeas, Pickled Turnips and Beets, Spinach, Za'atar Labneh Balls

For a brightly colored and easy brunch, toast your favorite sourdough, heap a messy pile of this salad on top, smash the labneh balls down slightly, and crush a few of the chickpeas with the back of a fork.

This recipe is ideal for making the components a day or two ahead and letting time do all the work for you. But if you're more in the mood for bean salad *now*, start with the turnips to let them marinate for just an hour or two and simply sub fresh goat cheese for the labneh. The results will be different but delicious.

If you do choose to make your own labneh for this recipe, just be sure to start with plain, unstrained yogurt. Commercial Greek yogurt has already been strained and made to taste delicious, and if you try to strain it further, it will become unpleasantly chalky. Plain yogurt is the ideal starting point when you're straining it yourself at home.

2 Tbsp extra-virgin olive oil

1 Tbsp balsamic vinegar

½ cup [20 g] chopped fresh parsley leaves

1 garlic clove, crushed through a press

¼ tsp freshly ground black pepper

¼ tsp salt

4 big handfuls fresh spinach (200 g)

Two 15 oz [425 g] cans chickpeas, drained and rinsed

½ cup [70 g] Pickled Turnips and Beets, patted dry (recipe follows)

1 batch Za'atar Labneh Balls (recipe follows)

In a small mixing bowl, stir together the oil, vinegar, parsley, garlic, black pepper, and salt.

Put the spinach, chickpeas, and turnips in a medium mixing bowl. Give the dressing another stir, pour over the chickpeas, and fold to coat them evenly. Add the za'atar labneh balls, give it one or two very gentle folds, being careful not to smash the labneh balls, and transfer to a serving bowl. Serve immediately.

Za'atar Labneh Balls

1½ cups [360 g] plain unstrained yogurt

3 Tbsp [25 g] za'atar

Line a fine-mesh sieve with a clean tea towel and suspend it over a large measuring cup or bowl. Place the yogurt in the lined sieve, fold the towel over the top, and place a small bowl or plate on top to hold it in place. Place a heavy book on top of the bowl or plate to weight it down. Refrigerate for about 24 hours.

The yogurt should give off a little more than ¾ cup [200 g] of whey and shrink down to about ⅔ cup [160 g] of labneh, about as thick as cream cheese. Once it's done draining, discard the whey or save it for another purpose.

Scoop a level teaspoonful of the labneh, plop it in the za'atar, roll it around until evenly coated, and then roll it gently in your hands into a smooth ball. Set aside and repeat with the remaining labneh. You should end up with 30 to 35 balls.

Pickled Turnips and Beets

1 turnip, peeled and sliced into ⅛ in [3 mm] thick pieces (170g)

1 small beet, peeled and sliced into ⅛ in [3 mm] thick pieces (80 g)

2 garlic cloves, halved

¾ cup [175 g] water

¼ cup [60 g] red wine vinegar

1½ tsp salt

1 tsp whole black peppercorns

Nest the turnips, beets, and garlic in a heatproof glass container or pint jar.

Combine the water, red wine vinegar, salt, and black peppercorns in a small saucepan over high heat. As soon as it comes to a simmer and the salt dissolves, pour over the turnips. Make sure they're fully submerged, let cool, then cover and store in the refrigerator. They're ready to eat after 24 hours and they'll keep for weeks.

Slaws

Slice or grate crunchy vegetables into a voluminous pile, toss everything in a creamy dressing, and you've made a fabulous slaw. By increasing the surface area of the produce, the dressing coats absolutely everything and permeates every bite. But because slaws are more dressed than your average garden salad, always opt for very crunchy, hearty veggies.

If you're looking for opportunities to hone your knife skills, a slaw can be good practice. But if you're more interested in getting dinner on the table quickly, you can use a food processor to prep most vegetables. Use the grater attachment for things like carrots and beets, and use the slicer attachment for things like cabbage and fennel. Don't bother washing the bowl of the food processor between ingredients, and get everything done in one fell swoop to cut down on dishes. For Swiss chard and other less compact hunks of produce, slice them thinly the old-fashioned way.

Most slaw ingredients are cold-weather crops with very long shelf lives, so they're usually readily available year-round but especially in-season in cooler weather. I tend to make more garden salads in the summer and slaws in the winter, but you can make either any time of year. Additionally, good-quality Swiss chard is available in the summer (see page 85 for notes on using Swiss chard).

Make Your Own Slaw Grid

Ingredients to swap in for the base recipe on the facing page

DRESSINGS

+ Buttermilk Dressing (page 85)
+ Chili Sesame Dressing (page 87)
+ Honey Mustard Vinaigrette (page 88)
+ Lemon Orange Vinaigrette (page 88)
+ Creamy Vinaigrette (page 89)

LEAFY HERBS

+ Cilantro
+ Dill
+ Parsley
+ Chives
+ Basil
+ Mint

TO ESTIMATE

Keep in mind that certain things are more voluminous than others (e.g., a cup of carrots weighs almost twice as much as a cup of cabbage, so you should use more cabbage than you think). Make a little extra dressing and add it gradually, tasting as you go to make sure you don't use too much or too little.

ESSENTIAL PRODUCE, AVAILABLE YEAR-ROUND

Very Thinly Sliced

Cabbage, kale, collards, broccoli, cauliflower, fennel, celery, apples

Grated or Julienned

Carrots, beets, parsnips, celeriac, kohlrabi

SEASONAL ACCENT PRODUCE

Summer

Grilled (see page 141) or blanched corn kernels, halved grapes, halved cherry tomatoes, thinly sliced bell peppers, thinly sliced cucumbers, minced hot peppers (use with moderation)

Fall

Halved grapes, whole pomegranate arils

Spring

Thinly sliced radishes, thinly sliced asparagus

Anytime

Dried fruit (use with moderation), sautéed frozen corn, rinsed and strained capers, sliced olives

Slaws

Makes 6 servings

Buttermilk Dressing (recipe follows, or choose another dressing from this section)

Up to ½ cup [75 g] finely diced onion, or 1¼ cups [75 g] thinly sliced green onion

5 to 10 cups [600 g] shredded/grated/thinly sliced produce

Up to 1 cup [150 g] accent produce (optional)

⅓ to ¾ cup [40 to 90 g] chopped nuts (optional)

½ cup [20 g] chopped fresh leafy herbs, or 2 tsp dried herbs (optional)

Put the dressing in a small mixing bowl and whisk in the onion.

Put the shredded/grated/sliced produce, accent produce, chopped nuts, and herbs in a large mixing bowl. Pour the dressing over and toss together (add the dressing gradually and taste as you go if you're not weighing your produce).

Buttermilk Dressing

For a dairy-free dressing (or just for a lighter-tasting alternative), feel free to use the Creamy Vinaigrette on page 89 in place of this one. Both this recipe and the Creamy Vinaigrette are extremely versatile and will work with most flavors.

½ cup [120 g] buttermilk

¼ cup [60 g] mayonnaise

1 Tbsp red wine vinegar

1 garlic clove, crushed through a press

¼ tsp freshly ground black pepper

½ tsp salt

Combine the buttermilk, mayonnaise, vinegar, garlic, pepper, and salt in a small mixing bowl or jar and shake until emulfsified. Whisk or shake again right before drizzling.

Summer Slaw

Chard, Cucumbers, Red Grapes, Toasted Almonds, Chili Sesame Dressing

Swiss chard is one of the few greens that thrives in hot weather. But unlike hearty cold weather greens and vegetables, it wilts a bit more readily in the kitchen, so you should never pair it with a super creamy or heavy dressing. It makes a refreshing summer treat paired with this Chili Sesame dressing, which was inspired by Taipei's Din Tai Fung's chilled cucumber salad.

2 small Persian cucumbers, unpeeled and thinly sliced (150 g)

1 cup [160 g] red grapes, halved

¼ tsp salt

1 bunch Swiss chard (300 g)

1 cup [60 g] thinly sliced green onions

1 tsp neutral oil, such as avocado or canola

½ cup [50 g] sliced almonds

Chili Sesame Dressing (recipe follows)

Place the cucumbers and grapes in a medium mixing bowl. Sprinkle with the salt and toss together well. Set aside for 30 minutes.

Chiffonade the Swiss chard leaves and stems (stack and tightly roll about half the clean and dry leaves, then thinly slice to make skinny

strips; repeat with the remaining leaves). Place in a large mixing bowl with the green onions.

Place a saucepan over medium heat. Once hot, add the oil and almonds. Stir constantly for about 3 minutes until they are golden brown. Transfer to a bowl to cool.

Once the cucumbers and grapes have given up about 1 Tbsp of liquid, drain them well (set in a sieve for about 2 minutes) and return to the mixing bowl with the Swiss chard, reserving some for garnish. Add the almonds, reserving a handful for garnish. Drizzle on the dressing, toss together, transfer to a serving bowl, and garnish with the reserved almonds, cucumbers, and grapes.

Chili Sesame Dressing

1 Tbsp garlic chili oil
1 Tbsp rice vinegar
2 tsp sesame oil
½ tsp soy sauce
1 tsp dried garlic flakes
½ tsp granulated sugar

Combine the chili oil, vinegar, sesame oil, soy sauce, garlic flakes, and sugar in a small mixing bowl or jar and shake until emulsified. Whisk or shake again right before drizzling.

Fall Slaw

Fennel, Apples, Pomegranate Arils, Fennel Seeds, Parsley, Parmesan Cheese, Honey Mustard Vinaigrette

Thinly sliced fennel is one of my favorite ways to add a lot of crunch to a salad. But sometimes, its subtle anise flavor can get overshadowed by competing flavors, so I usually like to throw in a little fennel seed to highlight it. If you have only ground fennel, rather than fennel seeds, feel free to use that in place of the whole fennel seeds sprinkled on at the end—just be sure to use a little less, to taste.

2 fennel bulbs, thinly sliced (350 g)
2 Granny Smith apples, unpeeled and thinly sliced (225 g)
½ onion, very thinly sliced (60 g)
¾ cup [100 g] pomegranate arils
½ small bunch parsley, stemmed (20 g leaves)
⅔ cup [50 g] Parmesan cheese shaved with a vegetable peeler
Honey Mustard Vinaigrette (recipe follows)
1 tsp whole fennel seeds
Small handful chopped fennel fronds (optional)

Combine the sliced fennel, apples, and onion in a large mixing bowl. Add the pomegranate arils, parsley leaves, and Parmesan, reserving a little bit of each for garnish. Pour on the mustard vinaigrette, toss together, and garnish with the reserved toppings, whole fennel seeds, and fennel fronds (if using).

Honey Mustard Vinaigrette

3 Tbsp [40 g] extra-virgin olive oil

2 Tbsp mustard

2 Tbsp apple cider vinegar

1 Tbsp honey

1 large garlic clove, crushed through a press

¼ tsp freshly ground black pepper

½ tsp ground fennel seed (optional; see Note)

Salt (see Note)

Combine the oil, mustard, vinegar, honey, garlic, black pepper, fennel seed, and salt in a small mixing bowl or jar and shake until emulsified. Whisk or shake again right before drizzling.

Notes: You can optionally omit the fennel seed if using this dressing in another recipe.

Use about ½ tsp of salt for slaw and ¼ tsp for a garden salad.

Winter Slaw

Shredded Beets, Red Cabbage, Walnuts, Lemon Orange Vinaigrette

This slaw is so deceptively simple—it looks like just a bunch of shredded beets and cabbage—but it's absolutely bursting with citrusy flavor from the lemon orange vinaigrette. If you've got a lot of other vegetables around (or if you're not the world's biggest fan of beets), you can throw in some grated carrots, very thinly sliced celery, and/or grated parsnips instead.

Lemon Orange Vinaigrette (recipe follows)

½ cup [75 g] finely diced red onion

2 large or 4 small raw beets, peeled (300 g)

¼ head red cabbage (300 g)

¾ cup [75 g] coarsely chopped walnuts

Lemon and orange zest, for garnish

Combine the vinaigrette with the red onion in a medium mixing bowl and set aside.

Set up your food processor with the shredder attachment. Use the fitted plastic tamper to send the peeled beets safely through the feed tube. Cut the beets into smaller chunks if they will not fit whole. Transfer the shredded beets to a large mixing bowl but don't wash the food processor.

Replace the shredder attachment with the slicer attachment. Use the plastic tamper to send the cabbage through the feed tube. Transfer the sliced cabbage to the mixing bowl with the beets.

Add the walnuts to the mixing bowl, reserving some for garnish. Drizzle on the dressing, toss together, move to a serving bowl, and garnish with the zest and the reserved walnuts.

Lemon Orange Vinaigrette

3 Tbsp [40 g] extra-virgin olive oil

3 Tbsp [45 g] fresh lemon juice

1 Tbsp honey

1½ tsp orange zest

1 tsp lemon zest

1 garlic clove, crushed through a press

¼ tsp freshly ground black pepper

½ tsp salt

Combine the oil, lemon juice, honey, orange zest, lemon zest, garlic, black pepper, and salt in a small mixing bowl or jar and shake until emulsified. Whisk or shake again right before drizzling.

Spring Slaw

Shredded Carrots, Sliced Cauliflower,
Mint, Parsley, Cumin, Dates, Pistachios,
Creamy Vinaigrette

You can find cool-weather crops like cauliflower
and carrots at year-round farmers' markets,
but once it gets a tiny bit warmer out you'll also
start to find some early-season spring herbs
such as mint. Mint is a perennial that grows like
a weed, and it's usually one of the first things to
pop back up in an herb garden once winter is
safely behind us. This slaw is the perfect thing
to celebrate that mid-spring moment, but these
ingredients are normally very easy to find in the
supermarket just about any time of the year,
so feel free to make it whenever. It is also apt
before the first frost later in the fall, when there
are plenty of cauliflower heads at the farmers'
market and your out-of-control accidental mint
garden is waiting for its pre-winter harvest.

½ small head cauliflower, thinly sliced (200 g)
5 to 6 carrots, grated (400 g)
1 heaping cup [70 g] finely sliced green onion
⅓ cup [10 g] chopped fresh mint
¼ cup [10 g] chopped fresh parsley
½ cup [70 g] chopped pitted dates
2 Tbsp ground pistachios
½ tsp ground cumin
Creamy Vinaigrette (recipe follows)

Combine the cauliflower, carrots, green onion,
mint, parsley, dates, pistachios, and cumin
(reserve some pistachios and herbs for garnish)
in a large mixing bowl. Top with the vinaigrette
and toss together. Garnish with the reserved
pistachios and herbs.

Creamy Vinaigrette

3 Tbsp [40 g] extra-virgin olive oil
3 Tbsp [45 g] fresh lemon juice
2 Tbsp mayonnaise
1 garlic clove, crushed through a press
½ tsp freshly ground black pepper
Salt (see Note)

Combine the olive oil, lemon juice, mayonnaise,
garlic, black pepper, and salt in a small mixing
bowl or jar and shake until emulsified. Whisk or
shake again right before drizzling.

Notes: Use about ½ tsp of salt for slaw and
¼ tsp for a garden salad.
  To make this vegan, simply use vegan mayo.
Or, if you are not vegan but hate mayo, you can
substitute 2 Tbsp Greek yogurt—just be sure
to also cut back slightly on the lemon (to taste),
and shake it right before using, as it will not
emulsify as much.

APPETIZERS
& SIDES

Hummus

You can't go wrong topping hummus simply with a drizzle of olive oil and sprinkling of za'atar, but I love throwing on my favorite seasonal produce whenever I've got a little extra on hand. The key is to treat one or two complementary vegetables like a little salad, tossing them with a bit of salt and red wine vinegar or lemon. Their flavor and crunch provide a welcome contrast to the smooth and creamy hummus, and it's easy to change things up depending on what's at the market and in your fridge. I normally make a big batch of hummus, divide and freeze it, and eventually pop a small batch in the fridge to thaw overnight when I've got a bit of leftover produce to use up.

When it comes to presentation, take a note from my mom and grandmother, who taught me to spread hummus on a plate, use the back of a spoon to make little dips across the surface, and pool it with olive oil. A plate affords more surface area than a bowl, which means more room for toppings.

Make Your Own Hummus Grid

Ingredients to swap in for the base recipe on the facing page

EXTRA TOPPINGS

+ **Your favorite spices**
  Za'atar
  Baharat blend
  Paprika
  Black pepper
  Sumac
+ Sesame seeds
+ Pistachios
+ Toasted slivered almonds
+ Raisins sautéed in butter
  for 1 to 2 minutes
+ Pepitas
+ Walnuts
+ Hazelnuts
+ Toasted pine nuts
+ Fresh and dried herbs
+ Tiny meatballs in tomato sauce
  (see page 38)

SEASONAL PRODUCE (CHOOSE ONE OR TWO)

Veggies	Greens
Summer	
Fresh or slow-roasted tomatoes (see page 113), blanched green beans, grilled zucchini/summer squash, leafy herbs (parsley, cilantro, mint, dill, chives), bell pepper chunks, minced hot peppers, grilled eggplant, diced cucumbers, boiled halved new potatoes	Stemmed Swiss chard, purslane, watercress
Fall	
Sautéed or roasted Brussels sprouts, pickled or roasted okra (see page 21), thinly sliced raw or sautéed fennel or leeks, roasted or steamed squash, pumpkin, sautéed chanterelles or sweet potatoes	Massaged kale (see page 62), arugula, spinach, watercress, frisée
Winter	
Sautéed or roasted Brussels sprouts, thinly sliced sautéed fennel or leeks, roasted sweet potatoes, raw/shredded or sautéed carrots or parsnips, raw/shredded or boiled beets, roasted squash or pumpkin, roasted cauliflower or broccoli	Massaged kale (see page 62), radicchio, romaine, frisée
Spring	
Roasted cauliflower or broccoli, raw shredded/sautéed sliced carrots or parsnips, fava beans (see page 98), sliced radishes, blanched shelled peas/snap peas/snow peas, prepped fiddlehead ferns (see page 21), sliced celery, sautéed ramps, sautéed asparagus, sautéed morels, herbs	Spring greens, arugula, spinach, iceberg, radicchio, watercress, endive, frisée, romaine
Anytime	
Sautéed mushrooms, sautéed or blanched frozen corn, blanched frozen peas, roasted or steamed potatoes	You can find quality romaine, iceberg, and kale year-round.

Hummus

Makes 2 small plates of hummus

1 garlic clove, or 1½ tsp garlic powder
3 or 4 ice cubes (80 g; see Note)
Two 15 oz [425 g] cans chickpeas, rinsed and
    drained
⅓ cup [80 g] fresh lemon juice
⅓ cup [85 g] tahini
Salt
1½ cups seasonal produce (200 g for most
    things, or 50 g for greens)
½ to 1 tsp red wine vinegar or fresh lemon juice
Extra-virgin olive oil, for drizzling
Extra toppings
Pita and/or crudités, for serving

Put the garlic in the bowl of a food processor
fitted with the blade attachment. Pulse until it's
finely chopped.

Add the ice cubes to the food processor, followed by the chickpeas and lemon juice. Blend
until the ice cubes break into small pieces and
melt completely and the chickpeas smooth out.

Add the tahini, season with salt, and continue
blending until completely combined.

Prep your vegetables according to the chart
on the facing page, season with salt, and toss in
a little vinegar.

Spread the hummus evenly on one large or
two small plates, dip the back of a spoon across
the surface to create little dimples, top with oil,
the prepped produce, and extra toppings, and
serve with pita and/or crudités.

Note: If you don't have any ice cubes on hand,
you can use ⅓ cup [80 g] of water instead.

Summer Hummus

Grilled Sweet Corn, Cilantro, Basil

While I'm not much of a gardener, I usually have a
few pots of basil, parsley, and dill on my balcony
every summer, and they end up defining the
dishes that come out of my summertime kitchen.
This hummus is topped simply with grilled sweet
corn and herbs, but its five humble ingredients
pack a delightful punch and crunch. Feel free
to replace the cilantro and basil with any other
leafy herbs you've got on hand.

2 ears corn
¼ cup [10 g] chopped fresh basil
¼ cup [10 g] chopped fresh cilantro, plus more
    for garnish
1 tsp red wine vinegar
Pinch of salt
Pinch of freshly ground black pepper
1 batch Hummus Base Recipe
Extra-virgin olive oil, for drizzling

Grill the corn over a gas range or outdoor grill
until charred. Slice the corn off the ears.

Mix the corn with the basil, cilantro, vinegar,
salt, and pepper.

Spread the hummus evenly on one large or
two small plates, dip the back of a spoon across
the surface to create little dimples, and top with
oil, the corn mixture, a sprinkling of pepper,
and a little more cilantro.

Fall Hummus

Steamed Kabocha Squash, Pepitas, Feta, Harissa

Roasted squash is all well and good, but steaming enhances its characteristic custardy texture. I almost always turn to the microwave for steaming, but feel free to use a stove-top steamer if that's your preference. This hummus is a great way to use up a bit of leftover squash from another recipe, but if you've bought a whole squash specially for this recipe, simply cut off as much as you need and then store the leftovers wrapped tightly in the refrigerator for a few days.

7 oz [200 g] kabocha squash, sliced ¼ in [6 mm] thick
Pinch of salt
½ tsp red wine vinegar
¼ cup [55 g] olive oil
1 Tbsp harissa, or as needed
1 batch Hummus Base Recipe (page 95)
¼ cup [35 g] raw pepitas
¼ cup [35 g] crumbled feta

Put the squash slices in a microwave-safe bowl, sprinkle with salt, add water to a depth of ¼ in [6 mm], cover with a microwave-safe plate, and steam for about 5 minutes, until tender and slightly translucent (depending on the strength of your microwave). Drain and toss with the vinegar.

In a small mixing bowl, whisk together the olive oil and harissa.

Spread the hummus evenly on one large or two small plates, dip the back of a spoon across the surface to create little dimples, and top with the squash, pepitas, crumbled feta, and harissa oil.

Winter Hummus

Sautéed Parsnips, Pistachios, Dried Mint

Dried herbs are usually discussed in terms of seasonality and strength. For instance, the standard wisdom states that in the winter, when many fresh herbs are out of season, you should use about 1 tsp dried in place of 1 Tbsp fresh in cooked dishes.

But in addition to differences in strength, dried herbs also don't tend to taste anything like their fresh counterparts. But that's not always a bad thing, and can be an opportunity to introduce a totally distinct flavor. Dried mint, for instance, has a bit more earthiness and lacks the zestiness of fresh. So whenever you're worried about making something taste like an after-dinner mint, dried is your friend. It's one of my favorite ingredients to add depth to both sweet and savory dishes, and I love that it's always in season and on hand in my pantry.

2 Tbsp unsalted butter
2 parsnips, peeled and cut into ½ in [13 mm] diagonal slices (200 g)
¼ tsp salt
1 batch Hummus Base Recipe (page 95)
Extra-virgin olive oil, for drizzling
Fresh lemon juice
Finely ground pistachios
Dried mint

Line a plate with paper towels.

Place the butter in a sauté pan or skillet over medium heat. Once it melts, add the parsnips along with the salt and cook for about 10 minutes, stirring occasionally, until caramelized and very tender. Remove to the lined plate.

Spread the hummus evenly on one large or two small plates, dip the back of a spoon across the surface to create little dimples, and top with oil, sautéed parsnips, a squeeze of lemon juice, a generous sprinkling of pistachios, and a pinch of dried mint.

Spring Hummus

Favas, Sautéed Garlic Oil, Sesame Seeds

Fava beans come in an edamame-like pod, which becomes tough and inedible as they grow. You'll most often find mature favas, which need a little prep work. For a shortcut, buy frozen favas, which are already shelled (and often peeled) and available year-round. Or track down some super young fresh favas early in the season. They're the soft-shell crabs of the vegetable world—coarsely chop them whole and sauté. I learned about these from chef Abeer Najjar's mom, who has a talent for sifting through piles at markets and finding the young tender ones.

¼ cup [55 g] extra-virgin olive oil, plus more for garnish

1 Tbsp minced or pressed garlic

1⅓ cups [200 g] shelled, blanched, and peeled fava beans (see Note)

1 Tbsp toasted sesame seeds, plus more for garnish

Salt

1 batch Hummus Base Recipe (page 95)

Heat the oil in a sauté pan or skillet over medium-low heat for a couple of minutes. Once it's moderately hot, add the garlic and let gently cook for about 2 minutes. Add the favas and cook for 2 minutes more. Add the toasted sesame seeds, season with salt, stir together, and remove from the heat.

Spread the hummus evenly on one large or two small plates, dip the back of a spoon across the surface to create little dimples, and top with the favas and garlic oil, plus a little extra olive oil and sesame seeds.

Note: To shell, blanch, and peel fava beans: First, peel away the tough outer shell. Bring a pot of water to a boil over high heat. Blanch the shelled beans for just 1 minute to make them easier to slip out of their skins. Boiling them any longer makes them mushy and difficult to peel. Immediately shock them in ice water to halt the cooking. To peel, focus your attention on the edge of a bean, pinch the membrane between the side of your index finger and the side of a paring knife held with your thumb, and tweeze away a patch. Pop the bean through the little hole you created, and repeat with the others. Discard the membranes.

Crostini

Crostini make everything from weeknight dinners to special occasions a little extra lovely. Even when I'm trying to branch out for a dinner party, I usually make room for one or two of these on the menu, because even if all else fails, the crostini will be a hit. You can also use these recipes as a jumping-off point for a fancy breakfast toast or snack—for breakfast, try selecting a few subtler flavors, such as ricotta with figs, almonds, honey, and a little basil.

Most crostini combine a little something sweet, savory, crunchy, rich, and herby in one bite, but this formula isn't a hard-and-fast rule. I like to change things up slightly, depending on the season. I keep my spring crostini on the savory side, while I love adding a little extra sweetness to my winter crostini. Summer crostini are all about the combination of sweet and herby, and fall is when I go a little crazy with pickling, emphasizing crunch and tang.

When coming up with your own concept, imagine you're standing in front of a cheeseboard and ask yourself: What would I put together in one bite? Start with the cheese and the produce and consider what else is needed to complement and highlight their flavors and textures. Feel free to use the following list of ingredients for ideas. The base recipe yields a cheese and vegetable crostini, but you can feel free to take it in a different direction. While there are thousands of lovely combinations, not every possibility is a winner—but since there's no real cooking involved, it's a perfect opportunity to experiment with combining flavors a little more bravely than usual.

Make Your Own Crostini Grid

Ingredients to swap in for the base recipe on page 104

CHEESE/SAVORY

+ Brie
+ Aged Cheddar
+ Ricotta
+ Chèvre
+ Cream cheese
+ Manchego

Just about any cheese will work here, especially the kind you'd place on a cheeseboard. If you're pairing a very strong cheese with a subtly flavored fruit or vegetable (e.g., Roquefort with persimmon), use the lesser amount of cheese in the base recipe to keep it from becoming overpowering.

Also feel free to add some extra savoriness with charcuterie, anchovies, smoked salmon, flaked seared salmon (see page 63), or sardines. But be careful when pairing fish with fruit. It's possible to do, but much harder to pull off than pairing fruit with charcuterie.

NUTS AND SEEDS

+ Pecans
+ Walnuts
+ Hazelnuts
+ Pine nuts
+ Pepitas
+ Sesame seeds
+ Sliced almonds
+ Chopped pistachios

Nuts and seeds can be toasted or served raw. Toasting will intensify their crunch and nuttiness, but you'll lose some of their subtler flavors, so it depends on the effect you're going for.

SEASONAL PRODUCE

Summer

Grilled or raw corn kernels, thinly sliced tomatoes or slow-roasted tomatoes (see page 113), sautéed green bean segments or zucchini/summer squash rounds, sliced grilled or raw peaches/plums/nectarines/apricots/Anjou pears (see Summer Crostini, page 104, for grilling instructions), halved or quartered figs or strawberries, whole mulberries, blueberries, raspberries, pitted cherries, fire-roasted red peppers or eggplant, thinly sliced cucumbers or melon, whole roasted grapes, halved raw grapes

Fall

Sliced plums, pears, or persimmons, pickled or grilled okra, pomegranate arils, thinly sliced raw or caramelized fennel, thinly sliced steamed squash or pumpkin, halved or quartered figs, butter-sautéed thinly sliced carrots or parsnips, boiled and thinly sliced beets, thinly sliced apples, raw or roasted grapes (see page 62), roasted and peeled chestnuts (see page 62), sautéed chanterelles

Winter

Sliced plums, pears, or persimmons (for a note on ripeness and varieties, see Note on page 107), thinly sliced raw or caramelized fennel, sautéed thinly sliced leek (white and light green parts only), butter-sautéed thinly sliced carrots or parsnips, boiled and thinly sliced sliced beets, thinly sliced steamed squash or pumpkin, citrus supremes

Spring

Butter-sautéed thinly sliced carrots or parsnips, halved or quartered strawberries, thinly sliced radishes, peeled and blanched fava beans (see page 98), steamed asparagus, ramps, sautéed leeks, whole blanched peas, smashed peas (see page 107), thick-sliced Anjou pears, sliced loquats, watercress, baby greens, sautéed morels

Anytime

Dates, raisins, dried figs, dried apricots, dried cranberries (cut back on the quantity if you're using dried fruit), thinly sliced mangos, butter-sautéed frozen corn, jammy caramelized onions (see page 132), oil-preserved roasted red peppers, olives, capers, smashed avocados with lime juice, Pickled Red Onions (page 79)

SWEET

+ Balsamic reduction
+ Pomegranate molasses
+ Jam
+ Preserves
+ Marmalade
+ Quince paste
+ Mango chutney
+ Cranberry sauce
+ Honey

HERBS

+ **Leafy**
  Cilantro, parsley, basil, dill, mint, chives
+ **Woody**
  Oregano, thyme, sage, rosemary

If you're using leafy herbs, feel free to go a little over the top, but be sure to practice restraint if you're using woody herbs. When fresh basil isn't in season, store-bought pesto works wonderfully.

Crostini

Makes 30 small crostini

One 10½ oz [300 g] baguette, cut into thirty ½ in
[13 mm] slices
Olive oil, for brushing
5 to 7 oz [140 to 200 g] cheese, broken into bite-
size chunks or slices
14 oz [400 g] seasonal produce, prepared
according to the grid (see page 102)
Something sweet, for topping
¼ cup [35 g] nuts or seeds (optional)
Up to 1 cup [40 g] leafy herbs, or 2 to 4 Tbsp
[10 g] woody herbs
Sea salt (optional)

Toast the bread slices (using a countertop
toaster, broiler, toaster oven, or grill) until
golden brown, brush lightly with olive oil,
and set aside on a plate. Top each toast with a
slice or swipe of cheese, one or two pieces of
produce, a drizzle or swipe of something sweet,
a sprinkling of nuts or seeds, and a few herbs.
Finish with a tiny pinch of sea salt, if desired.

Summer Crostini

Aged Cheddar Cheese, Grilled Peaches,
Honey, Pine Nuts, Basil

I make some version of this for just about every
summertime party I throw, and I usually serve
them along with a couple of fiddlier canapés, like
painstakingly stuffed and fried croquettes, or
teeny-tiny blini. But no matter the competition,
these disarmingly simple crostini win guests
over every single time.

If you're making these ahead for a party, you
can grill the peaches a day in advance and store
them in the fridge. You can even skip the grilling
step, opting for toasted bread and ripe peaches,
or use a culinary torch to give each slice a little
char before topping. If possible, look for a Cheddar or similar cheese with tiny visible crystals
(such as Red Leicester), but just about any Cheddar will do with in-season ripe peaches.

One 10½ oz [300 g] baguette, cut into thirty ½ in
[13 mm] slices
Olive oil, for brushing, and for coating the
peaches
3 just-ripe yellow peaches, pitted and
quartered (see Note)
7 oz [200 g] aged Cheddar cheese, broken into
bite-size chunks or slices
¼ cup [35 g] lightly toasted pine nuts
1 bunch basil (40 g leaves)
Honey, for drizzling
Sea salt (optional)

Preheat your grill to high heat.
Brush each bread slice with a very light layer
of oil on each side. Place on the grill for 1 to
2 minutes on each side, with the grill lid open,
just until very slightly charred and golden
brown. Transfer to a plate and leave the grill on.
Brush the peach quarters with a light layer of
olive oil. Place on the grill cut-side down with
the grill lid open. Once one cut side has charred
(after 1 to 2 minutes), tip it over to give the other
cut side a chance to char (another 1 to 2 minutes).

Remove from the grill before they get a chance to soften (no more than 4 minutes total). Slice each peach chunk into two or three pieces.

Top each toast with a piece of Cheddar, a few pine nuts, a few basil leaves, a piece of peach, and a drizzle of honey. Finish with a tiny pinch of sea salt, if desired. Serve immediately.

Note: The peaches should not be overripe or mushy. If your peaches are on the ripe side, simply skip the grilling and serve them raw.

Fall Crostini

Brie, Pomegranate Arils,
Pecans, Marmalade

This crostini is a lifesaver during the holidays, especially Thanksgiving, but the ingredients are usually available well into winter. It's festive and elegant, and the components also work when used separately on a simple grazing board: Place a big wheel of Brie in the center, place a cute jar of marmalade on one side, fan out some crackers and bread slices on the other, and fill in the gaps with your favorite charcuterie, pecans, pomegranate arils, and a few orange twists. Also feel free to swap the baguette for mini blini (as pictured) if you've got a bunch around from all that holiday entertaining.

One 10½ oz [300 g] baguette, cut into
   thirty ½ in [13 mm] slices
Olive oil, for brushing
7 oz [200 g] Brie
⅓ cup [45 g] whole pecans
⅓ cup [105 g] orange marmalade
¾ cup [100 g] pomegranate arils (from 1 small
   pomegranate)
1 tsp orange zest
Sea salt (optional)

Toast the bread slices (using a countertop toaster, broiler, toaster oven, or grill) until golden brown, brush lightly with olive oil, and set aside on a plate.

Top each toast with a slice of Brie and a whole pecan. Smash the pecan into the Brie to slightly flatten everything. Top with a swipe of marmalade, a sprinkling of pomegranate arils, and a little orange zest. Finish with a tiny pinch of sea salt, if desired. Serve immediately.

Winter Crostini

Blue Cheese, Persimmons,
Pistachios, Balsamic

Persimmons are a wonderful surprise in the colder months. Suddenly, here comes a fruit that looks like a tomato and tastes like sunshine. They run a little on the pricey side, so I use them where they'll make a big impact, and when it comes to canapés, you need only three persimmons to feed a crowd.

One 10½ oz [300 g] baguette, cut into thirty ½ in
   [13 mm] slices
Olive oil, for brushing
5 oz [140 g] blue cheese
3 ripe Fuyu persimmons (see Note), sliced
Balsamic reduction, for drizzling (store-bought
   is fine)
¼ cup [40 g] ground pistachios
Dried mint (optional)
Sea salt (optional)

Toast the bread slices (using a countertop toaster, broiler, toaster oven, or grill) until golden brown, brush lightly with olive oil, and set aside on a plate.

Cut pieces from the blue cheese as you go, breaking it into chunks if it is crumbly, thin

slices if it is firm, or spreading if it is soft. Top each toast with a bit of blue cheese, a wedge of persimmon, a drizzle of balsamic reduction, a sprinkling of pistachios, and a tiny pinch of dried mint, if desired. Finish with a tiny pinch of sea salt, if desired. Serve immediately.

Note: Two persimmon varieties are widely available. Fuyus are the short and squat ones, and they don't need to be extremely ripe to enjoy—they should yield at least a little when gently squeezed, like a ripe peach. Hachiyas are the acorn-shaped ones, and they must be extremely ripe—they should feel almost like water balloons. If a Hachiya is underripe, or even only slightly ripe, it'll give you an unpleasantly astringent cottonmouth sensation. Leave either variety in a fruit bowl or paper bag and wait a few days for them to soften. Because Hachiyas need to be extremely ripe to enjoy, they are usually best eaten on their own, and just-ripe Fuyus are easier to incorporate into recipes (for instance, they hold their shape in a salad and don't give off too much moisture in a galette).

Spring Crostini

Smashed Peas, Nigella, Lemon, Mint

These crostini embrace the herby zestiness of spring. Just be sure to wait until the last minute to drizzle on the lemon, otherwise your peas will turn browner than you might like. If you wait until the last moment, they'll stay nice and bright green. You can use frozen peas for this recipe year-round, especially if you can't find already-shelled ones and don't feel like bothering to shuck them.

2¾ cups [400 g] shelled peas
1 Tbsp olive oil, plus more for brushing and drizzling
¼ tsp salt
One 10½ oz [300 g] baguette, cut into thirty ½ in [13 mm] slices
7 oz [200 g] ricotta
2 Tbsp fresh mint leaves
1 tsp nigella seeds
1 tsp lemon zest
Sea salt
Fresh lemon juice

Fill a small stockpot or large saucepan with water and bring to a boil. Blanch the peas in the boiling water for 1 to 2 minutes, until they turn a bit brighter green, then drain, immediately shock in ice water, and drain again. Transfer to a mixing bowl, add the oil and salt, and smash with the back of a fork or a potato masher, stopping as soon as half the peas are smashed.

Toast the bread slices (using a countertop toaster, broiler, toaster oven, or grill) until golden brown, brush lightly with olive oil, and set aside on a plate.

Top each toast with a swipe of ricotta, a generous spoonful of smashed peas, mint leaves, a drizzle of olive oil, and a sprinkling of nigella seeds, lemon zest, and sea salt. Finish with a squeeze of lemon juice immediately before serving.

Roasted Vegetables

To roast vegetables, you simply coat them in a light layer of oil and cook them in the oven. The goal is similarly straightforward: They should be softened on the inside and caramelized and a little charred on the outside, with lots of golden brown crispy bits. I usually throw on a tiny bit of cheese to help them get a little extra crispy caramelization—you can use almost anything you've got around.

As simple as roasting may be, there are two tricks to getting the best results:

1. Some fruits and vegetables roast better at a low temperature, and others at a high temperature, and you should not combine these two categories in the same batch.

2. If you're roasting a few different vegetables from one temperature category on the same pan, make sure they will all finish roasting at the same time. This works a little differently, depending on which category you're working with (see chart, page 110).

No matter what you're roasting, roasted foods desperately need acidity. You'll find a bunch of easy sauce ideas in the roasted vegetable variations following this base recipe, or stick with the Classic Vinaigrette (page 111). The sauces in this section have a bit less oil and more water than a dressing that you'd use for a salad, since the roasted produce is already coated in oil before roasting. A light dressing enlivens them with a little acidity rather than bogging them down.

Make Your Own Roasted Vegetables Grid

Ingredients to swap in for the base recipe on the facing page

CHEESE

+ Blue cheese
+ Parmesan
+ Cheddar
+ Feta
+ Chèvre
+ Or your favorite hard cheese

HERBS

+ **Leafy**
  Cilantro, parsley, basil, dill, mint, chives,
+ **Woody**
  Oregano, thyme, sage, rosemary

NUTS

+ Sliced almonds
+ Ground pistachios
+ Chopped walnuts
+ Chopped pecans
+ Roasted pepitas
+ Lightly toasted pine nuts

TO ESTIMATE

Don't crowd the pan. At each stage of roasting, your produce should fit in a single layer, with at least a small crevice of space between them (more space for higher-moisture ingredients); otherwise the vegetables will partially steam instead of roast. For larger quantities, work in batches.

NOTE

*A little persimmon, fig, corn, mushroom, or leek goes a long way. Combine these starred fruits and veggies with a couple others and don't be afraid to mix and match in general.

SEASONAL PRODUCE

Low-temperature produce (350°F [180°C])	High-temperature produce (500°F [260°C])
Summer	
Tomatoes halved along their equators (90 to 150 minutes), cherry tomatoes halved stem to end (50 minutes), whole grapes (35 to 60 minutes, depending on size)	Corn kernels*, green bean segments, halved figs*, coarsely sliced pepper, large-diced eggplant, large-diced zucchini/ summer squash
Fall	
Large-diced unpeeled tart apples (35 minutes), whole grapes (35 to 60 minutes, depending on size)	Halved figs*; okra halved lengthwise; thinly sliced fennel; large-diced squash, pumpkin, carrots, parsnips, or celery; broccoli or cauliflower florets; boiled large-diced beets; halved small or quartered large Brussels sprouts
Winter	
Just-ripe Fuyu persimmons* halved along their equators (1 hour)	Thinly sliced fennel; thinly sliced leeks*; large-diced carrots, squash, pumpkin, sweet potatoes; boiled large-diced beets; broccoli or cauliflower florets; radicchio wedges
Spring	
Spring produce tends to be fresh and snappy (rather than sweet and juicy), and usually does best with fast-roasting, or simply enjoying raw.	Thinly sliced leeks*, broccoli or cauliflower florets, whole trimmed asparagus, whole ramps, prepped fiddlehead ferns (see page 21), large-diced carrots or celery, radicchio wedges
Anytime	
Quartered mushrooms (35 minutes)	Frozen corn*, frozen peas, sliced mushrooms*, thinly sliced onions, large-diced potatoes

Roasted Vegetables

Makes 4 to 6 servings

Seasonal produce (see grid on facing page)
Neutral oil, such as avocado or canola, for roasting
Salt
Freshly ground black pepper
5 to 8 garlic cloves, thinly sliced
¼ to ⅓ cup [25 g] shredded or crumbled cheese (optional)
Classic Vinaigrette (recipe follows) or another favorite sauce
¼ cup [10 g] chopped fresh leafy herbs, or 1 Tbsp chopped fresh woody herbs (optional)
¼ cup [25 g] coarsely chopped nuts (optional)

If you're roasting any low-temperature produce, preheat the oven to 350°F [180°C]. If not, skip to the fourth paragraph.

Coat low-temperature produce in a light layer of oil, place on a rimmed baking sheet cut-side up (if applicable), and sprinkle with salt and pepper. Remember not to crowd the pan.

Roast for 30 minutes to 1 hour (see the Seasonal Produce chart on the facing page for time estimations), opening the door once or twice to allow the steam to escape. They're done once they've significantly shrunk and are very caramelized. Some juices may pool and caramelize on the pan, looking almost burnt—don't worry, that's a good thing! Transfer the low-temperature produce to a bowl but do not wash the baking sheet.

Raise the oven temperature to 500°F [260°C] or its highest setting. Coat high-temperature produce in a light layer of oil. Spread in an even layer on top of the caramelized juices/bits on the baking sheet (or just on a clean baking sheet) and sprinkle evenly with salt and pepper, the garlic, and the cheese. Again, don't crowd the pan.

Roast until the high-temperature produce caramelizes, chars in spots, and cooks through, 8 to 11 minutes. The cheese will set into a crispy frico as it cools slightly. Transfer to the bowl with the low-temperature produce (scrape up any cheese bits with a spatula), drizzle lightly with about one-third of the vinaigrette (serve with extra at the table), top with some herbs and/or nuts, and serve warm or at room temperature.

Classic Vinaigrette

¼ cup [55 g] extra-virgin olive oil
2 Tbsp water
1 Tbsp balsamic vinegar
2 tsp mustard
1 or 2 garlic cloves, crushed through a press
¼ tsp freshly ground black pepper
¼ tsp salt

Whisk together the olive oil, water, vinegar, mustard, garlic, pepper, and salt in a small mixing bowl or jar until emulsified. Whisk or shake again right before drizzling. See the seasonal variations for more sauce ideas.

Summer Roasted Vegetables

Slow-Roasted Tomatoes, Green Beans, Corn, Black Pepper, Cheddar Cheese, Italian Salsa Verde

Makes 6 to 8 servings

You don't need to do much to summer tomatoes to make them absurdly delicious, but it's nice to have a few tricks up your sleeve, especially toward the end of the season when you might be looking for some novelty. Slow-roasting at a low temperature transforms tomatoes into little self-contained bowls, in which their juices concentrate and become syrupy.

Serve these roasted veggies over cornbread with some fresh goat cheese, piled high next to pasta salad, or in a grilled chicken sandwich (brush the bread with a little salsa verde before filling).

5 to 7 vine-ripened tomatoes, halved along equators (800 g)
Neutral oil, such as avocado or canola
Salt
Freshly ground black pepper
2 big handfuls green beans, stemmed (250 g)
1 heaping cup [150 g] corn kernels, from about 1 ear
5 to 8 garlic cloves, thinly sliced
⅓ cup [35 g] shredded Cheddar cheese
Italian Salsa Verde (recipe follows)

Preheat the oven to 350°F [180°C].

Coat the tomato halves in a light layer of oil, place on a rimmed baking sheet cut-side up, and sprinkle with salt and pepper (about ¼ tsp salt and ¼ tsp pepper).

Roast for 90 to 150 minutes, opening the door once or twice to allow the steam to escape, until the tomatoes' juices concentrate and become syrupy.

Once the tomatoes are out of the oven, raise the temperature to 500°F [260°C] or its highest setting. Remove the tomatoes from the baking sheet but don't wash it.

Coat the green beans, corn, and garlic in a light layer of oil, and about ¼ tsp of salt and ¼ tsp of pepper. Spread in an even layer on top of the caramelized tomato juices and sprinkle evenly with the Cheddar.

Roast for about 9 minutes, until lightly charred and slightly softened. Transfer to a serving bowl with the tomatoes (or move the tomatoes back onto the baking sheet), top with about one-third of the salsa verde, and serve warm or at room temperature with extra salsa verde on the side.

Italian Salsa Verde

1 small bunch parsley, stemmed (40 g leaves)
1 or 2 garlic cloves
2 Tbsp rinsed and drained capers
⅓ cup [70 g] extra-virgin olive oil
1 Tbsp red wine vinegar
1 Tbsp water
Salt
¼ tsp freshly ground black pepper
Pinch of red pepper flakes (optional)

Put the parsley, garlic, capers, olive oil, vinegar, water, salt, black pepper, and red pepper flakes in the bowl of a food processor fitted with the blade attachment (or a blender with a tamper).

Pulse several times until everything is very finely chopped, almost puréed. You can also use a mortar and pestle or mince the produce finely by hand before combining with the oil and other ingredients.

Fall Roasted Vegetables

Brussels Sprouts, Apples, Blue Cheese, Maple Mustard Vinaigrette

Makes 6 servings

Apples are one of my favorite things to roast at a lower temperature. They're very high in moisture and prone to disintegration, so if you roast them too fast or cut them too large, they'll steam from the inside and explode into golden brown and delicious mush—a wonderful way to make applesauce, but not such a good way to make roasted apples. By roasting them more moderately, they dehydrate slightly while they cook through and caramelize.

3 Granny Smith apples, unpeeled and cut into large dice (450 g)
Neutral oil, such as avocado or canola
Salt
Freshly ground black pepper
20 large Brussels sprouts (500 g)
5 to 8 garlic cloves, thinly sliced
2 tsp maple syrup
¼ cup [35 g] crumbled blue cheese
¼ cup [25 g] coarsely chopped pecans
Maple Mustard Vinaigrette (recipe follows)

Preheat the oven to 350°F [180°C].

Coat the apple pieces in a light layer of oil, place on a rimmed baking sheet, and sprinkle with salt and pepper. Roast for about 35 minutes, opening the door once or twice to allow the steam to escape. They're done once they've significantly shrunk and are very caramelized. Do not disturb them until they've shrunk down, or they will fall apart.

Once the apples are out of the oven, raise the temperature to 500°F [260°C] or its highest setting. Transfer the apples to a bowl but do not wash the baking sheet.

Halve any small Brussels sprouts and quarter any large ones. Coat the Brussels sprouts and garlic in about 2 tsp of oil and the maple syrup. Season with ¼ tsp of salt and ¼ tsp of pepper. Spread in an even layer on top of the caramelized juices and bits on the baking sheet and sprinkle evenly with the blue cheese.

Roast for about 9 minutes, until the Brussels sprouts soften and char slightly. Transfer to the bowl with the apples, top with the pecans and about one-third of the vinaigrette, and serve warm or at room temperature with more vinaigrette at the table.

Maple Mustard Vinaigrette

¼ cup [55 g] extra-virgin olive oil
2 Tbsp water
1 Tbsp maple syrup
1 Tbsp balsamic vinegar
1 Tbsp mustard
1 or 2 garlic cloves, crushed through a press
¼ tsp freshly ground black pepper
¼ tsp salt

Combine the oil, water, maple syrup, vinegar, mustard, garlic, pepper, and salt in a small mixing bowl or jar and whisk or shake until emulsified. Whisk or shake again right before drizzling.

Winter Roasted Vegetables

Butternut Squash, Onions, Thyme, Walnuts, Caramelized Raisins, Feta, Tahini Yogurt Sauce

Makes 6 servings

One of my favorite simple pleasures is a bowl of roasted cauliflower topped with cumin, coriander seed, lemony tahini sauce, and cilantro (see photo on page 109). This roasted butternut squash recipe is a variation on that classic, but the fundamentals are the same. Whatever you do, don't skip the raisins here. I'm a strong believer that anyone who claims to hate raisins has just never had them roasted or sautéed before. If plain old packaged raisins are like stale Milk Duds, then roasted raisins are like homemade salted caramels.

1 small butternut squash, peeled and cut into
   ½ in [13 mm] chunks (700 g)
½ medium onion, thinly sliced (100 g)
Neutral oil, such as avocado or canola
¼ tsp salt
¼ tsp freshly ground black pepper
5 to 8 garlic cloves, thinly sliced
¼ cup [35 g] crumbled feta
3 tsp fresh thyme leaves
¼ cup [35 g] raisins
Tahini Yogurt Sauce (recipe follows)
¼ cup [25 g] coarsely chopped walnuts

Preheat the oven to 500°F [260°C] or its highest setting.

Coat the squash and onion in a light layer of oil. Spread in an even layer on a rimmed baking sheet and sprinkle evenly with the salt, pepper, garlic, feta, and 1½ tsp of the thyme.

Roast for about 11 minutes, just until they soften and caramelize in spots. Once they're cooked through, sprinkle the raisins on top and roast for about 1 minute more, until they look a little puffier and slightly caramelized (be careful not to let them burn).

Transfer everything to a bowl, drizzle lightly with a couple of spoonfuls of the tahini sauce, top with the walnuts and the remaining 1½ tsp of thyme, and serve warm or at room temperature with extra tahini sauce on the side.

Tahini Yogurt Sauce

¼ cup [60 g] Greek yogurt
2 Tbsp tahini
2 Tbsp water
1 Tbsp fresh lemon juice
Pinch of salt

Combine the yogurt, tahini, water, lemon juice, and salt in a small mixing bowl and whisk until it forms a creamy sauce.

Spring Roasted Vegetables

Asparagus, Spring Onions, Pecorino Romano Cheese, Olives, Green Goddess Dressing

Makes 4 to 6 servings

This flavor-packed spring veg roast will snap you out of your winter hibernation. It looks like an absolute forest of green onions and asparagus before it goes in the oven, but with this many green onions, it's okay to crowd the pan since they're mostly air. As everything deflates, those zesty green flavors intensify, especially when topped with an herby green goddess dressing at the table. A little goes a long way, and the whole dish is lovely served with something mellow, such as red quinoa and grilled chicken.

2 bunches asparagus, trimmed and split lengthwise if thick (250 g)

2 small bunches green onions (250 g), halved lengthwise

Neutral oil, such as avocado or canola

Pinch of salt

Pinch of freshly ground black pepper

5 to 8 garlic cloves, thinly sliced

⅓ cup [30 g] coarsely grated pecorino romano cheese

10 Castelvetrano olives, pitted and sliced

Green Goddess Dressing (recipe follows)

Fresh chives or dill, for garnish (optional)

Preheat the oven to 500°F [260°C] or its highest setting.

Coat the asparagus and green onions in a light layer of oil. Spread in an even layer on a rimmed baking sheet, sprinkle evenly with the salt and pepper, and add the garlic and cheese. The pan will look more crowded than usual, but don't sweat it.

Roast for about 9 minutes, just until the asparagus is bright green and tender and the onions have wilted and charred in spots. Transfer to a bowl, add the olives, drizzle lightly with a couple of spoonfuls of the dressing, top with chives (if using), and serve warm or at room temperature with extra dressing at the table.

Green Goddess Dressing

1 small bunch fresh chives (15 g)

⅓ cup [15 g] packed fresh dill fronds

1 or 2 garlic cloves

½ cup [120 g] Greek yogurt

3 Tbsp [45 g] mayonnaise

2 tsp red wine vinegar

¼ tsp salt, plus more if needed

Put all the ingredients in a food processor or blender. Blend until smooth and light green with dark green flecks. Taste and adjust the seasoning if needed.

Au Gratin

Combine seasonal produce with cheese and cream, top it with bread crumbs, bake until golden brown and meltingly tender, and you've got a perfect gratin. Most vegetables need to be sliced very thin to yield the perfect texture for this dish—this can be a fun opportunity to work on your knife skills, or a good excuse to break out the food processor. Simply put the slicer attachment in place, use the fitted tamper to send whole vegetables through the feed tube safely, and slice away.

Produce is added to the dish at two different stages, depending on the vegetable at hand:

1. Sauté vegetables must be added to the pan after the onion, to give them a chance to get a little golden and wilted, and shouldn't make up the bulk of the vegetables in the dish, lest your gratin turn out soggy. Mix and match with a low-moisture vegetable or two.

2. Low-moisture vegetables should be added right into the mixing bowl raw.

Use a total of 2¼ lb [1 kg] of produce from the chart on page 120, plug it into the right part of the recipe, and your gratin will have a perfect texture. Mix and match between categories, but be sure to include at least 24½ oz [700 g] of low-moisture vegetables (i.e., no more than 10½ oz [300 g] sauté vegetables). Or if you don't have a scale, check out my notes on estimating on page 120.

Cook times will vary, but most gratins will cook to perfection in 60 to 75 minutes. Keep an eye on it and remove it from the oven once the whole thing is bubbly and any excess moisture has cooked off. Since we're shooting for tender and cheesy, you don't have to stress about overcooking anything—it's best to err on the side of a little too crispy.

Make Your Own Au Gratin Grid

Ingredients to swap in for the base recipe on the facing page

HERBS AND SPICES

+ Up to 1 cup [40 g] fresh chopped basil, parsley, cilantro, dill, or chives
+ 1 Tbsp fresh rosemary
+ 2 Tbsp fresh thyme
+ 1 to 2 tsp dried herbs
+ 1 to 2 tsp of your favorite ground spices

CHEESE

+ Gruyère
+ Crumbled chèvre
+ Cheddar
+ Any other cheese you'd stir into a béchamel sauce

TO ESTIMATE

The unbaked gratin should fill a 10 in [25 cm] cast-iron skillet just to the top after tamping down, and the cream should be about 1 in [2.5 cm] below the vegetables.

NOTE

Sauté vegetables need to be sautéed after the onion, in batches. Use no more than 10½ oz [300 g]. Low-moisture vegtables can be added right into the mix, as is.

SEASONAL PRODUCE (EITHER 1 KG LOW-MOISTURE VEGETABLES OR A COMBINATION OF 700 G LOW-MOISTURE VEGETABLES AND 300 G SAUTÉ VEGETABLES)

Sauté vegetables	Low-moisture vegetables
Summer	
Thinly sliced bell peppers	Corn kernels or green bean segments (use both in moderation with thinly sliced potatoes)
Fall	
Thinly sliced fennel, cabbage, or celery; chopped kale or collards	Thinly sliced pumpkin, squash, parsnips, or carrots; small broccoli or cauliflower florets; halved or quartered Brussels sprouts
Winter	
Thinly sliced fennel, cabbage, celery, or leeks (white and light green parts only); chopped kale or collards	Thinly sliced pumpkin, squash, parsnips, sweet potatoes, or carrots; small broccoli or cauliflower florets
Spring	
Thinly sliced fennel, cabbage, celery, or leeks (white and light green parts only)	Small broccoli or cauliflower florets, whole peas (use peas in moderation, paired with another vegetable)
Anytime	
Thinly sliced onions	Thinly sliced potatoes, frozen corn, frozen peas (use corn and peas in moderation, paired with another vegetable)

Au Gratin

Makes 8 servings

Extra-virgin olive oil
1 medium onion, thinly sliced (180 g)
Salt
2¼ lb [1 kg] seasonal produce (see grid on facing page)
1½ cups [345 g] heavy cream
Herbs and spices (optional)
2¼ cups [225 g] grated cheese
1 Tbsp minced or pressed garlic
½ tsp freshly ground black pepper
¼ cup [25 g] bread crumbs

Preheat the oven to 375°F [190°C].

Heat a 10 or 12 in [25 or 30 cm] cast-iron skillet (or another deep, wide ovenproof sauté pan) over medium heat. Once it's hot, add about 1 Tbsp of oil, followed by the onion and ¼ tsp of salt. Cook for about 10 minutes, stirring occasionally, until tender. Transfer the onions to a medium mixing bowl. Add about another 1 Tbsp of oil to the pan along with any vegetables from the sauté column. Once they're softened and/or wilted, transfer them to the mixing bowl with the onions. Remove the pan from the heat but do not wash it.

Add the heavy cream, vegetables from the low-moisture column (which can be added right in without pre-cooking), herbs, spices, cheese, garlic, black pepper, and ½ tsp of salt to the mixing bowl and stir together.

Scoop the mixture into the pan; use your hands to gently tamp it down so it's in an even, compact layer and as submerged as possible in the cream. If it's extremely full, be sure to place a baking sheet under it to catch any drips.

Put the bread crumbs in a small mixing bowl, drizzle with 1 tsp of olive oil and a pinch of salt, mix to coat, and sprinkle on top of the gratin.

Bake for 65 to 75 minutes, until the whole thing is golden brown and bubbly and there is no longer runny liquid pooling. Let cool for at least 10 minutes before serving.

Summer Gratin

Zucchini, Tomatoes, Spinach, Basil, Cheddar Cheese

For high-moisture produce such as zucchini/summer squash, tomato, and spinach, we've got to depart from the standard gratin formula. Frozen spinach needs to be thawed and wrung out, and zucchini and tomatoes need to be salted, pressed, and drained before adding them to the cream mixture, otherwise the whole gratin will end up soupy. While it takes a few minutes of waiting and multitasking, it's super easy, and the resulting melt-in-your-mouth gratin speaks for itself. I love serving this gratin at parties, almost as you would a veggie dip, with a loaf of sliced crusty bread next to it. If you've got fresh spinach you want to use up, just steam it, let it cool, and wring it out so that you end up with about 1 packed cup [135 g].

3 zucchini, cut into ⅛ in [3 mm] slices (450 g)
1⅔ cups [250 g] cherry tomatoes, halved
Salt

Extra-virgin olive oil
1 medium onion, thinly sliced (180 g)
1½ cups [345 g] heavy cream
9 oz [255 g] frozen spinach, thawed and wrung
    out
1 small bunch basil, stemmed (30 g leaves)
2¼ cups [225 g] grated Cheddar cheese
1 Tbsp minced or pressed garlic
½ tsp freshly ground black pepper
¼ cup [25 g] bread crumbs

Put the zucchini and tomatoes in a medium mixing bowl and season them evenly with about 1 tsp of salt. Let sit for 30 minutes, until juices have gathered in the bottom of the bowl. Press the zucchini and tomato against the side of the bowl to wring them out a bit, drain well, and discard the juices. Give them a little squeeze to make sure they're not still holding on to a lot of liquid before proceeding.

Preheat the oven to 375°F [190°C].

Heat a 10 or 12 in [25 or 30 cm] cast-iron skillet (or another deep ovenproof sauté pan or skillet) over medium heat. Once it's hot, add about 1 Tbsp of oil, followed by the onion and ¼ tsp of salt. Cook for about 10 minutes, stirring occasionally, until tender. Transfer the onions to the bowl with the zucchini and tomatoes.

Add the cream, spinach, basil, Cheddar, garlic, pepper, and more salt (as needed) to the mixing bowl and stir together.

Scoop the mixture into the pan; use your hands to gently tamp it down so it's in an even, compact layer and as submerged as possible in the cream. If it's extremely full, be sure to place a baking sheet under it to catch any drips.

Put the bread crumbs in a small mixing bowl, drizzle with 1 tsp of olive oil and a pinch of salt, mix to coat, and sprinkle on top of the gratin.

Bake for about 65 to 75 minutes, until the whole thing is golden brown and bubbly. Let cool slightly before serving.

Fall Gratin

Kale, Sweet Potatoes, Sage, Gruyère

Gratins love starchy produce, which is abundant in the colder months, and they're the perfect thing to warm your kitchen and stick to your ribs. This one is just as indulgent as any potato gratin, but it's a smidge lighter with the inclusion of sweet potatoes and kale.

Extra-virgin olive oil
1 medium onion, thinly sliced (180 g)
Salt
1 bunch kale, stemmed (130 g leaves)
1½ cups [345 g] heavy cream
4 medium sweet potatoes, peeled and thinly
    sliced (830 g)
1 tsp dried sage
2½ cups [225 g] grated Gruyère
1 Tbsp minced or pressed garlic
½ tsp freshly ground black pepper
¼ cup [25 g] bread crumbs

Preheat the oven to 375°F [190°C].

Heat a 10 or 12 in [25 or 30 cm] cast-iron skillet (or another deep ovenproof sauté pan or skillet) over medium heat. Once it's hot, add about 1 Tbsp of olive oil, followed by the onion. Season with ¼ tsp of salt and cook over medium heat for about 10 minutes, stirring occasionally, until tender. Transfer to a medium mixing bowl.

Add half of the kale to the still-hot pan, season with a pinch of salt, and cook, stirring occasionally, until it wilts and any juices evaporate, about 3 minutes. Repeat with the remaining kale. Transfer to the mixing bowl, remove the pan from the heat, and do not wash the pan.

Add the heavy cream, sweet potatoes, sage, Gruyère, garlic, pepper, and ½ tsp of salt to the mixing bowl and stir together.

Scoop the mixture into the pan; use your hands to gently tamp it down so it's in an even, compact layer and as submerged as possible in the cream. If it's extremely full, be sure to place a baking sheet under it to catch any drips.

Put the bread crumbs in a small mixing bowl, drizzle with 1 tsp of olive oil and a pinch of salt, mix to coat, and sprinkle on top of the gratin.

Bake for about 60 to 75 minutes, until the whole thing is golden brown and bubbly. Let cool slightly before serving.

Winter Gratin

Fennel, Potatoes, Caraway Seeds, Cheddar Cheese

Back when my grandmother was growing up on a farm in Syria, her family would make gubta mtumarta, an Assyrian cheese that's preserved with caraway seeds and buried in clay pots underground. It's one of the things she most missed when she got married and moved to Baghdad. Decades later, when I moved away from my family's home in Chicago, Ina Garten's potato fennel gratin was one of the first things I learned how to cook as an adult. Her recipe taught me the technique I've adapted in this section, where you bake lots of thinly sliced vegetables in a puddle of heavy cream and grated cheese. Here, I've included some caraway, an homage to my family's gubta.

Extra-virgin olive oil
1 onion, thinly sliced (180 g)
Salt
1 medium fennel bulb, thinly sliced (250 g)
1½ cups [345 g] heavy cream
4 russet potatoes, unpeeled and thinly sliced (750 g)
2 tsp whole caraway seeds

2¼ cups [225 g] grated Cheddar cheese
1 Tbsp minced or pressed garlic
½ tsp freshly ground black pepper
¼ cup [25 g] bread crumbs

Preheat the oven to 375°F [190°C].

Heat a 10 or 12 in [25 or 30 cm] cast-iron skillet (or another deep ovenproof sauté pan or skillet) over medium heat. Once it's hot, add about 1 Tbsp of olive oil, followed by the onion. Season with about ¼ tsp of salt and cook for about 10 minutes, stirring occasionally, until tender. Transfer the onions to a medium mixing bowl.

Add another 1 Tbsp of oil and the fennel to the still-hot pan. Once it's softened (about 10 minutes), transfer to the mixing bowl, remove the pan from the heat, and do not wash it.

Add the heavy cream, sliced potatoes, caraway seeds, Cheddar, garlic, pepper, and ½ tsp of salt to the mixing bowl and stir together.

Scoop the mixture into the pan; use your hands to gently tamp it down so it's in an even, compact layer and as submerged as possible in the cream. If it's extremely full, be sure to place a baking sheet under it to catch any drips.

Put the bread crumbs in a small mixing bowl, drizzle with 1 tsp of olive oil and a pinch of salt, mix to coat, and sprinkle on top of the gratin.

Bake for 60 to 75 minutes, until the whole thing is golden brown and bubbly. Let cool slightly before serving.

Spring Gratin

Carrots, Chives, Chèvre

Chives are one of the first herbs to grow in the spring, and you don't need to wait very long to start harvesting them. Every bit of chive that grows out of the ground is edible, and no energy is wasted on stalks and stems. So if you have a little herb garden on your balcony or windowsill, chives will make a big impression on your spring cooking. Likewise, while fresh goat cheese is available year-round, you'll find the best-quality fresh goat cheese at farmers' markets in the spring, when grass-fed goats are just starting their milk production. But rest assured, just about any chèvre will work in this recipe, including inexpensive generic supermarket brands that are available any time of the year.

Extra-virgin olive oil
1 medium onion, thinly sliced (180 g)
Salt
1½ cups [345 g] heavy cream
2¼ lb [1 kg] carrots, peeled and thinly sliced
½ cup [20 g] chopped chives
8 oz [225 g] chèvre, crumbled
1 Tbsp minced or pressed garlic
½ tsp freshly ground black pepper
¼ cup [25 g] bread crumbs

Preheat the oven to 375°F [190°C].

Heat a 10 or 12 in [25 or 30 cm] cast-iron skillet (or another deep ovenproof sauté pan or skillet) over medium heat. Once it's hot, add about 1 Tbsp of olive oil, followed by the onion. Season with about ¼ tsp of salt and cook for about 10 minutes, stirring occasionally, until tender. Transfer the onions to a medium mixing bowl.

Add the cream, carrots, chives, cheese, garlic, black pepper, and ½ tsp of salt (or as needed) to the mixing bowl and stir together.

Scoop the mixture into the pan; use your hands to gently tamp it down so it's in an even, compact layer and as submerged as possible in the cream. If it's extremely full, be sure to place a baking sheet under it to catch any drips.

Put the bread crumbs in a small mixing bowl, drizzle with 1 tsp of olive oil and a pinch of salt, mix to coat, and sprinkle on top of the gratin.

Bake for 60 to 75 minutes, until the whole thing is golden brown and bubbly. Let cool slightly before serving.

Focaccia

It's hard to go wrong with a plain sheet of focaccia, but seasonal produce adds a pop of flavor and color. Use the chart on page 128 to select your favorite produce to embed across the dough's surface, and don't be afraid to mix and match. For more inspiration, think of the kinds of vegetables and ingredients you'd find together in some of your favorite dishes (zucchini, oregano, caramelized onion; apple, blue cheese, thyme; pumpkin, sage, frozen corn . . . the possibilities are endless).

If you've got a stash of pesto, feel free to use it in place of the herbs, but be sure to also cut back on the olive oil in the dough to compensate for the extra richness. Simply replace the herbs with ½ batch [115 g] of the Pesto on page 227, and cut the oil in the dough back from ⅓ cup [70 g] to ¼ cup [50 g].

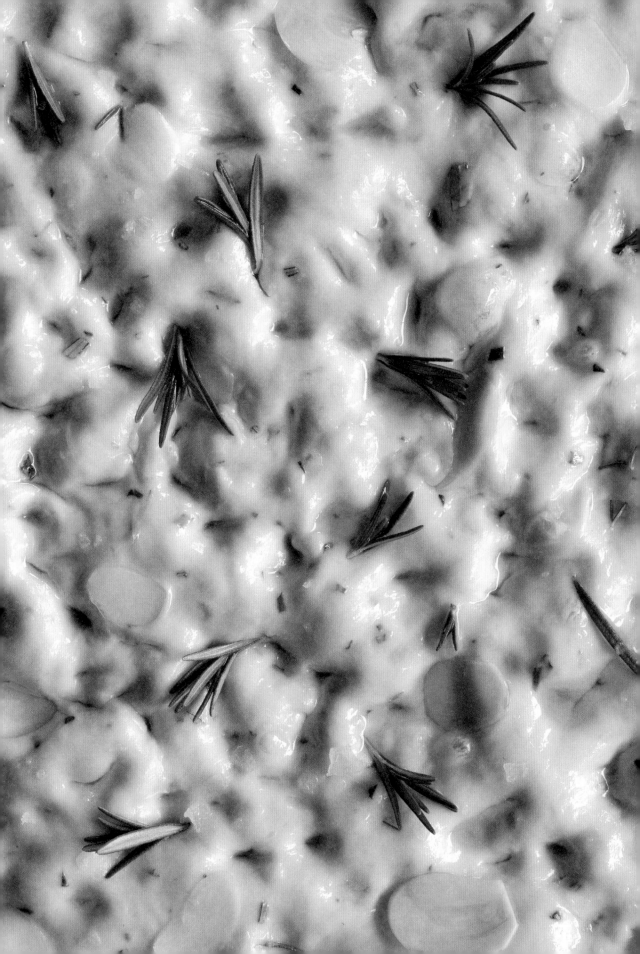

Make Your Own Focaccia Grid

Ingredients to swap in for the base recipe on the facing page

HERBS

+ **Leafy**
  Cilantro, dill, parsley, chives, basil
+ **Woody**
  Thyme, rosemary, sage, oregano

FLAVOR BOOSTERS

+ Jammy caramelized onions (see page 132)
+ Anchovies
+ Thinly sliced onion
+ Capers
+ Olives
+ Crumbled blue cheese
+ Red pepper flakes (a pinch)

You can use extra of any of these, especially caramelized onions and olives, but be careful not to overwhelm any other ingredients if you do.

TO ESTIMATE

Less is more, especially with high-moisture fruits and vegetables; avoid bogging down the dough, which will make it soggy and dense.

SEASONAL PRODUCE

Summer

Corn kernels, halved cherry tomatoes, green bean segments, thinly sliced zucchini/summer squash, quartered or sliced figs, red or black seedless grapes (whole if small, halved if large), char-roasted and peeled peppers

Fall

Quartered or sliced figs, red or black grapes (whole if small, halved if large), okra sliced lengthwise, parcooked thinly sliced squash or pumpkin, small broccoli or cauliflower florets, roasted and peeled chestnuts (see page 62), thinly sliced fennel, leeks, or apples

Winter

Thinly sliced fennel or leeks (white and light green parts only), parcooked thinly sliced squash or pumpkin, roasted and peeled chestnuts (see page 62)

Spring

Small broccoli or cauliflower florets, asparagus (whole if skinny, halved lengthwise if thick), peas, whole ramps

Anytime

Frozen corn, frozen peas, oil-preserved tomatoes and red peppers, sliced mushrooms

Focaccia

Makes 16 pieces

For the overnight focaccia dough
5½ cups [715 g] all-purpose flour
2¼ tsp salt
2½ tsp instant yeast
⅓ cup [70 g] extra-virgin olive oil
2 cups [470 g] water, at room temperature
¾ cup [30 g] chopped fresh leafy herbs, or
  2 Tbsp to ¼ cup [10 g] chopped fresh woody
  herbs

For the topping
4 Tbsp [55 g] extra-virgin olive oil
3 garlic cloves, thinly sliced
1 to 2 cups [200 g] prepped seasonal produce
  (see grid on facing page)
¼ to ½ cup [30 to 45 g] flavor boosters
Flaky sea salt (optional)
Fresh herbs, for garnish (optional)

On day one, make the overnight focaccia dough (see Note if you're in a hurry): Combine the flour, salt, yeast, oil, and water in the bowl of a stand mixer fitted with the hook attachment (or large mixing bowl). Mix together on low (or using your hand in the bowl if you don't have a stand mixer) until it forms a lumpy dough and then increase the speed to medium. Knead with the hook for about 3 minutes, just until it smooths out quite a lot and starts to look stringy instead of lumpy (about 5 minutes mixing by hand). The dough should be very wet and sticky but not soupy. For the last 30 seconds or so of mixing, add the chopped herbs and continue mixing until evenly distributed.

Generously coat another mixing bowl with a layer of olive oil and scrape the dough into the oiled bowl. Stretch and fold the edges of the dough in toward the center several times until the opposite side forms a smooth dome. Flip over so the seam side is facedown, cover the bowl with plastic wrap or a large plate, and let sit at room temperature for 15 minutes. After this short rise, leave it in the fridge to finish proofing overnight (up to 36 hours).

On day two, prepare the topping: Spread out about 1 Tbsp of the olive oil on an 18 by 13 in [46 by 33 cm] rimmed baking sheet. Move the dough right from the fridge to the pan, bottom-side up, and drizzle on 1 Tbsp of the oil. Use the pads of your fingers to work the dough out into a flat rectangle. Leave little dimples as you go, digging your fingers almost all the way to the baking sheet below, but try not to pop any big visible bubbles. Then fold into thirds like a trifold pamphlet and flip it so the overlapping flaps are on the bottom.

Let rest at room temperature for about 5 minutes. Once it's rested, top with another 1 Tbsp of the oil and use the pads of your fingers to work it out into a larger rectangle again.

Repeat the folding one more time, let it rest for 5 more minutes, and work the dough out into a larger rectangle again. Add the remaining 1 Tbsp of olive oil as well as the sliced garlic, and this time use the pads of your fingers to work the rectangle all the way out to the edges of the baking sheet.

Top with the seasonal produce and flavor boosters, pushing them down a little to embed

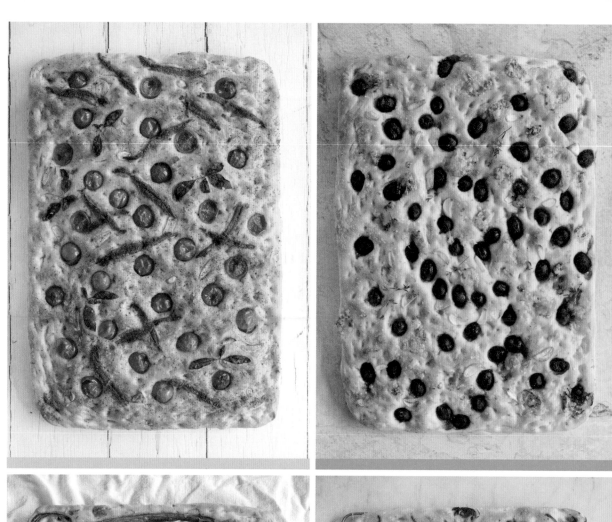

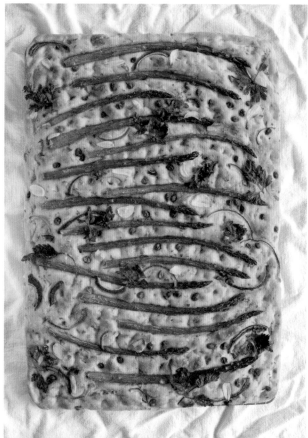

them in the dough, and sprinkle on a little sea salt and extra herbs, if desired.

Let proof, uncovered, at room temperature for 1 hour, until it's got a few big air bubbles and looks noticeably larger.

Preheat the oven to 425°F [220°C] when the dough is almost done proofing.

Bake for about 20 minutes, until the top is golden brown and it's cooked through (200°F [93°C] internal temperature). Let cool for at least 30 minutes before slicing. After completely cooled, store sealed at room temperature for 1 day, and freeze whatever you don't plan to eat right away (bread keeps much better in the freezer than in the refrigerator or at room temperature).

Note: You can do the first rise entirely at room temperature for a total of 45 to 60 minutes, until about doubled in size. It'll have a much more developed flavor and texture after a 12-hour rest in the fridge, but it works well at room temperature too.

Summer Focaccia

Tomatoes, Basil, Anchovies

This focaccia is a classic, featuring a combination of anchovies, tomatoes, and basil. Love it or hate it, anchovy is the real hero of the trio; it's a great way to ground some of the brightness of summer produce with deep umami flavor. If you're not a fan, feel free to omit it.

1 batch Overnight Focaccia Dough (page 129), made with ¾ cup [30 g] chopped fresh basil the day before baking (see Note above for same-day shortcut)
4 Tbsp [55 g] extra-virgin olive oil
3 garlic cloves, thinly sliced

1⅓ cups [200 g] halved small cherry tomatoes
15 to 20 anchovy fillets (optional)
Flaky sea salt (optional)
Pinch of freshly ground black pepper
Whole basil leaves, for garnish (optional)

The day after you've prepared your dough and you're ready to bake, prep, fold, and dimple your dough with the olive oil and garlic, following the directions on page 129.

Top with the cherry tomatoes and anchovies, pushing them down a little to embed them in the dough, and sprinkle on a little sea salt (if using), black pepper, and some fresh basil, if desired.

Let proof, uncovered, at room temperature for 1 hour, until it's got a few big air bubbles and looks noticeably larger.

Preheat the oven to 425°F [220°C] when the dough is almost done proofing.

Bake for about 20 minutes, until the internal temperature of the dough reaches 200°F [93°C] (or until the top is golden brown and it's cooked through). Let cool for at least 30 minutes before slicing. See end of the preceding base recipe for storage.

Fall Focaccia

Grapes, Thyme, Blue Cheese,
Sea Salt

I first learned about Tuscan schiacciata con l'uva from Emiko Davies's lovely recipe. It's a classic for a reason, but I love adding blue cheese and sea salt for an extra-savory twist. Be sure to use black grapes, or another deeply red or purple variety, which are easier to find in early to mid-fall.

1 batch Overnight Focaccia Dough (page 129), made with ¼ cup [10 g] coarsely chopped fresh thyme leaves the day before baking (see Note on page 131 for same-day shortcut)
4 Tbsp [55 g] extra-virgin olive oil
3 garlic cloves, thinly sliced
1¼ cups [200 g] small seedless black grapes, any large ones halved
¼ cup [40 g] crumbled blue cheese
Flaky sea salt (optional)
More fresh thyme, for garnish

The day after you've prepared your dough and you're ready to bake, prep, fold, and dimple your dough with the olive oil and garlic, following the directions on page 129.

Top with the grapes and blue cheese, pushing them down a little to embed them in the dough, and sprinkle on a little sea salt (if using) and some extra thyme.

Let proof, uncovered, at room temperature for 1 hour, until it's got a few big air bubbles and looks noticeably larger.

Preheat the oven to 425°F [220°C] when the dough is almost done proofing.

Bake for about 20 minutes, until the internal temperature of the dough reaches 200°F [93°C] (or until the top is golden brown and it's cooked

through). Let cool for at least 30 minutes before slicing. See page 131 for storage.

Winter Focaccia

Oil-Cured Black Olives,
Jammy Onions, Rosemary

The jammy onions in this recipe are very useful to have on hand—it's never a bad idea to make extra and stash some in the freezer for when a craving hits. If you're a fan of anchovies, feel free to add them to this focaccia for something more similar to French pissaladière.

1 batch Overnight Focaccia Dough (page 129), made with 2 Tbsp (10 g) chopped fresh rosemary the day before baking (see Note on page 131 for same-day shortcut)
1 Tbsp neutral oil, such as avocado or canola
1 large onion, thinly sliced (230 g)
¼ tsp salt
4 Tbsp [55 g] extra-virgin olive oil
3 garlic cloves, thinly sliced
30 pitted and halved oil-cured black olives (75 g)
Flaky sea salt (optional)
Fresh rosemary leaves, for garnish (optional)

The day after you've prepared your dough and you're ready to bake, start by caramelizing the onions. Put the neutral oil in a sauté pan or skillet, followed by the sliced onions, about 2 Tbsp of water, and the salt. Set over medium-high heat, wait for it to start sizzling, cover, and cook for about 5 minutes, until the onions are somewhat softened and a brown film appears on the bottom of the pan. Uncover, stir while scraping the bottom, lower the heat to medium-low or medium, and continue cooking for about 25 minutes. Stir and scrape the bottom of the pan whenever a brown film develops (every few minutes), and deglaze with 1 or 2 Tbsp of water whenever the brown film won't easily scrape up. The onions are done once they're deeply brown all the way through and reduced to a scant ½ cup [95 g].

Once the onions are done caramelizing, prep, fold, and dimple your dough with the olive oil and garlic, following the directions on page 129.

Top with the olives and caramelized onions, pushing them down a little to embed them in the dough, and sprinkle on a little sea salt (if using) and a few small rosemary needles, if desired.

Let proof, uncovered, at room temperature for 1 hour, until it's got a few big air bubbles and looks noticeably larger.

Preheat the oven to 425°F [220°C] when the dough is almost done proofing.

Bake for about 20 minutes, until the internal temperature of the dough reaches 200°F [93°C] (or until the top is golden brown and it's cooked through). Let cool for at least 30 minutes before slicing. See page 131 for storage.

Spring Focaccia

Asparagus, Capers, Red Onions, Parsley

Capers are harvested in the heart of summertime, but we usually experience them preserved in brine, so they're readily available year-round. And that's lucky for us, because capers heighten early spring flavors, especially asparagus. Add a bit extra if you're a big fan, and be sure to push them into the dough so none get left behind at the table. This focaccia is delicious plain but exuberant served with cream cheese and lox.

1 batch Overnight Focaccia Dough (page 129), made with ¾ cup [30 g] chopped fresh parsley the day before baking (see Note on page 131 for same-day shortcut)

4 Tbsp [55 g] extra-virgin olive oil

3 garlic cloves, thinly sliced

15 to 20 small stalks skinny asparagus, trimmed (175 g; see Note)

2 Tbsp rinsed capers

¼ small red onion, thinly sliced (20 g)

Flaky sea salt (optional)

A few fresh parsley leaves, for garnish (optional)

The day after you've prepared your dough and you're ready to bake, prep, fold, and dimple your dough with the olive oil and garlic, following the directions on page 129.

Top with the asparagus, capers, and red onion, pushing them down a little to embed them in the dough, and sprinkle on a little sea salt (if using) and a few parsley leaves, if desired.

Let proof, uncovered, at room temperature for 1 hour, until it's got a few big air bubbles and looks noticeably larger.

Preheat the oven to 425°F [220°C] when the dough is almost done proofing.

Bake for about 20 minutes, until the internal temperature of the dough reaches 200°F [93°C] (or until the top is golden brown and it's cooked through). Let cool for at least 30 minutes before slicing. See page 131 for storage.

Note: Skinny asparagus is easy to find in the spring, but if you can find only thick woody ones, slice them in half lengthwise (or quarter them if they're giant). To trim any asparagus, just hold it from the cut end and the middle, and bend. It'll break naturally above the tough part.

MAINS

Cozy Soups

This section includes some of my favorite traditional hearty soups. You can make most of these just about any time of the year with a few tweaks, and I've included instructions with each to help you cook flexibly with other ingredients, so skim through and feel free to adapt the summer chowder for winter, the spring Vidalia onion soup for fall, and so on. Or if you find yourself wanting to make a soup that uses up pretty much *anything*, try a simple Minestrone (page 138).

The key to an excellent soup is an excellent stock. The winter avgolemono soup in this section has you start out by making a fabulous chicken stock, but the other three are all based around Vegetable Stock (page 139). Make up a batch and stash some away in your freezer for a rainy day, or get right to work making a soup with all the extra produce you've got hanging around the fridge. If you've got extra scraps left over, feel free to use an equivalent amount of those instead of using new ingredients.

Make Your Own Minestrone Grid

SEASONAL PRODUCE

DIRECTIONS

Make a batch of Vegetable Stock (facing page) and set aside. Sauté 1 medium onion, 2 carrots, and 3 stalks of celery in olive oil. Once they soften, add the stock, followed by 2 Tbsp minced or pressed garlic cloves, a pinch of red pepper flakes, and a 14½ oz [410 g] can of diced tomatoes and bring to a boil. Add a 15 oz [420 g] can of cannellini or kidney beans (drained), and 1¼ cups [100 g] of orecchiette or another small pasta, and turn the heat down to medium-low. Set a timer for 2 minutes shy of the time your pasta is supposed to take, so it can coast.

Add your favorite vegetables to your soup in stages, so that they all finish cooking at the same time as the pasta. Use this produce chart to get a sense of how long different vegetables take to simmer (for instance, add corn when there's 1 or 2 minutes left on the timer, and add potatoes with 7 to 10 minutes left). Finish it off with fresh lemon juice, a big handful of chopped parsley, and a generous sprinkling of Parmesan at the table.

SEASONAL COMBINATIONS

In the summer, I like Swiss chard, corn, and zucchini. In the fall and winter, I go with sweet potatoes, kale, and mushrooms. And I love peas, baby spinach, and potatoes for spring. If you're making minestrone in the heart of tomato season, feel free to replace the can of diced tomatoes with an equal amount of chopped very ripe tomatoes (2 cups [400 g]).

SEASONAL PRODUCE

Quick-cooking (1 to 2 minutes)	Longer-cooking (7 to 10 minutes)
Summer	
Raw or grilled corn kernels (see page 139), ½ in [13 mm] diced zucchini or summer squash, chopped Swiss chard leaves	Green bean segments, sliced bell pepper, mini okra, chopped thick Swiss chard stems
Fall	
Small cauliflower or broccoli florets, fresh spinach	Mini okra; thinly sliced fennel; ½ in [13 mm] diced parsnip, winter squash, or sweet potatoes
Winter	
Small cauliflower or broccoli florets, fresh spinach	Chopped kale or collards; thinly sliced fennel; ½ in [13 mm] diced parsnips, winter squash, or sweet potatoes
Spring	
Small cauliflower or broccoli florets, peas, baby spinach	½ in [13 mm] diced parsnips
Anytime	
Frozen corn, frozen peas, frozen carrots	½ in [13 mm] sliced potatoes, thinly sliced mushrooms

Cozy Soups

Anytime Vegetable Stock

Makes about 2 qt [1.9 L]

1 medium onion, unpeeled and cut into big
    chunks (180 g), or scraps
8 to 12 garlic cloves, unpeeled
2 carrots, cut into chunks (130 g), or scraps
3 celery stalks, cut into chunks (150 g), or scraps
1 cup [25 g] whole dried mushrooms
2 Tbsp dried herbs (e.g., 2½ tsp dried basil, 2 tsp
    dried thyme, 1 tsp dried oregano, and ½ tsp
    dried sage)
4 bay leaves
1 tsp whole black peppercorns
1 or 2 Parmesan cheese rinds (optional)
¼ cup [60 g] tomato paste
2½ qt [2.35 L] water
2½ tsp salt, or as needed

In a large stockpot, combine the onion, garlic,
carrot, celery, mushrooms, dried herbs, bay
leaves, peppercorns, Parmesan rinds (if using),
tomato paste, water, and salt. Stir until the
tomato paste mostly dissolves into the water,
then place over high heat to bring up to a simmer. Once simmering, lower the heat to low or
medium-low and simmer, uncovered, for about
1 hour.

Once the stock's flavors have melded and
you're happy with its taste, strain the liquid
through a fine-mesh sieve into a large container,
press the solids against the side of your sieve to
wring out any remaining moisture, and discard
the spent solids. You should end up with about
2 qt [1.9 L]. If not, top it off with a little more
water (either now or when you plan to use it).

Summer Soup

Grilled Corn, Tomato, and Zucchini
Chowder

Makes 6 to 8 servings

Take advantage of nice weather and in-season
corn by grilling whole ears before cutting the
kernels off. Or you can skip the grilling step in the
following recipe; instead, simply add raw kernels
right into the simmering pot. But if you've got the
time, spending just a few minutes developing
that char is like adding a capful of summer.

To make a chowder any time of the year, use
frozen corn kernels in place of fresh (skip the
grilling step), and use your favorite seasonal
produce in place of the tomato and zucchini (see
the chart on the facing page for ideas). I love
sweet potato, corn, and sriracha for the winter
and fall—add 2 tsp of paprika, cut back to 1 tsp of
turmeric, add 2 or 3 Tbsp of sriracha, and serve
with extra at the table.

4 or 5 corn ears (1 kg)
2 Tbsp extra-virgin olive oil
2¼ cups [135 g] chopped green onions
1 red bell pepper, medium diced (125 g)
¼ tsp salt
½ cup [65 g] all-purpose flour

1 tsp freshly ground black pepper

2 tsp ground turmeric

6 cups [1.4 L] Anytime Vegetable Stock or store-bought vegetable or chicken stock

3 garlic cloves, crushed through a press

1½ cups ¼ in [6 mm] unpeeled zucchini slices

1¼ cups [200 g] large-diced tomatoes

1 cup [240 g] half-and-half

1¼ cups [135 g] shredded Cheddar cheese

Heat your grill to high. Place the corn ears directly on the grate and cook for 1 to 2 minutes per side, just until their surface is about 70 percent charred. Once they are cool enough to handle, slice the corn off the cobs (you should end up with 3¾ cups [500 g] kernels; save any extra for garnish).

Heat a large stockpot or Dutch oven over medium heat for a few minutes. Add the olive oil, followed immediately by the onions, bell pepper, and salt. Cook for about 3 minutes, stirring occasionally.

Add the flour, black pepper, and turmeric and stir together for about 30 seconds. Add the stock and garlic and whisk together until smooth. Bring to a simmer over medium-high heat, whisking occasionally. Add the corn, cover, lower the heat to medium-low, and simmer for 8 minutes. Add the zucchini and tomatoes and cook for 2 minutes, just to warm and slightly cook them.

Add the half-and-half, let it come back up to a simmer, and remove from the heat. While it's still hot but no longer bubbling, gradually sprinkle in the Cheddar, whisking constantly until the cheese melts. Taste and season if necessary. Garnish with any reserved corn. Serve right away, store in smaller containers in the refrigerator for 3 or 4 days, or freeze for months.

Fall Soup

Lentil Soup with Carrots, Squash, Lemon, Spices

Makes 6 to 8 servings

Shorbat adas is a lemony, warmly spiced red lentil soup with lots of turmeric, perfect for chilly weather. This version includes roasted squash for some extra body and autumnal flavor. If you'd like to make a more traditional shorbat adas outside of squash season, leave out the squash and add a little extra lemon juice.

7 cups [750 g] ½ in [13 mm] squash slices

Extra-virgin olive oil

Salt

1 medium onion, thinly sliced (180 g)

2 carrots, thinly sliced (130 g)

1 Tbsp minced or pressed garlic

2 tsp turmeric

2 tsp ground coriander

1½ tsp ground cumin

1½ tsp ground fenugreek (see Note)

½ tsp freshly ground black pepper

¼ tsp chili powder

Pinch of cinnamon

2 qt [1.9 L] Vegetable Stock (page 139) or store-bought vegetable or chicken stock

1½ cups [280 g] red lentils, sorted and rinsed

2 Tbsp fresh lemon juice

Preheat the oven to 430°F [220°C].

Place the squash on a baking sheet and coat in about 1 tsp of oil. Sprinkle with about ¼ tsp of salt. Spread out into an even layer and roast for 40 to 45 minutes. They will soften completely after the first 15 to 20 minutes, but you should wait until they caramelize and shrink down before you remove them.

While the squash roasts, place a large stock-pot over medium heat. Once hot, add about 2 Tbsp of oil, the onion, and carrot and season with salt. Cook, stirring occasionally, for about 8 minutes, just until they soften. Add the garlic, turmeric, coriander, cumin, fenugreek, black pepper, chili powder, and cinnamon and stir everything constantly for just about 30 seconds. Add the stock and red lentils and stir. Bring to a simmer over high heat, then cover and lower the heat to low. Let simmer for about 15 minutes, until the red lentils are just starting to fall apart.

Remove the soup from the heat if your squash needs a little longer in the oven. Once your squash is ready, scrape it off the pan into the pot and add the lemon juice. Give everything a stir. At this point, you can purée the soup completely, partially, or not at all (use an immersion blender if you have one). Taste and adjust the seasoning if needed.

Note: If you don't have fenugreek (or another one of these spices), replace the turmeric, cumin, coriander, fenugreek, black pepper, chili powder, and cinnamon with a total of 2½ Tbsp of yellow curry powder.

Winter Soup

Avgolemono Soup:
Lemon, Eggs, Chicken, Rice

Makes 6 to 8 servings

I lived in Chicago over the summers while I was in college. The summer before my senior year, I would often loiter in the Greek diner around the corner from my apartment to write my thesis. I'd order a bowl of avgolemono soup and a sandwich and read my crackly library books. To this day, I still associate the old book smell with diners. And strangely, I still associate this soup with summer.

While you too can enjoy it just about any time of the year, this hearty citrusy winter soup more squarely belongs in the heart of winter, when lemons are plentiful and a good chicken soup recipe is essential.

I learned the following technique from my friend Eleni (author of the blog *My Family's Food Diary*): By whipping the lemon and eggs, you increase the amount of froth and creaminess, and curdling becomes much less likely.

For the chicken stock
1 Tbsp extra-virgin olive oil
3 to 4 lb [1.4 to 1.8 kg] whole chicken, patted dry
1 medium onion, thinly sliced (180 g)
2 celery stalks, thinly sliced (100 g)
10 sprigs fresh thyme, or 2 tsp dried thyme
8 to 12 garlic cloves
2½ qt [2.35 L] water
1 Tbsp salt, or as needed

For the soup
1 Tbsp extra-virgin olive oil
1 medium onion, thinly sliced (180 g)

2 celery stalks, thinly sliced (100 g)
Pinch of salt
1 cup [200 g] medium-grain rice
3 large eggs
¾ cup [175 g] fresh lemon juice

To make the stock: Set a stockpot over medium heat. Once hot, add the olive oil, swirl to coat, and add the chicken, breast-side down. Let sear for about 5 minutes undisturbed, just until it's golden brown. Once browned, flip it on its back and let sear for 5 minutes more. Hold it firmly in place with tongs while you pour out and discard all but 1 Tbsp of oil and rendered fat.

Add the onion, celery, thyme, garlic, water, and salt (use less salt for a smaller chicken, or the full amount for a larger chicken). Increase the heat to high and bring up to a simmer. Once simmering, cover with the lid slightly cracked, and lower the heat to low. Let slow-cook at a bare simmer for 2 hours.

Use tongs to remove the cooked chicken from the pot (don't bother washing the pot) and set aside on a plate to let cool slightly. Strain the stock and reserve it (discard the spent vegetable solids). Use two forks to shred the chicken while removing it from the bones. Set the meat aside and discard or save the leftover bones and skin (see Note).

To make the soup: Set the empty stockpot back over medium heat. Add the olive oil, followed by the onion, celery, and salt. Cook, stirring occasionally, for about 10 minutes, just until softened. Add the reserved stock and bring up to a simmer. Taste to adjust the seasoning— if it's too salty from too much water evaporating, then add ¼ cup [60 g] of water at a time. If it's not salty enough, add a little more salt. Add the rice and reserved chicken meat, cover, lower the heat to low, and simmer for about 20 minutes, until the rice becomes very soft (cook more like 15 minutes for al dente rice). Skim any foam that rises to the top.

Meanwhile, mix the eggs and lemon juice together in a blender for about 1 minute at medium speed. Stop once the egg-lemon mixture is smooth and frothy. Leave it in the blender.

Once the rice has cooked through, remove the pot from heat and gradually temper the egg mixture: With your blender running at low speed, gradually dribble one ladleful of hot stock into the egg mixture through the small opening in the blender's lid (avoid big pieces of chicken). Repeat with three or four more ladlefuls.

Once you've added about 2 cups [470 g] of hot stock to the egg mixture, turn off your blender. Remove the lid and slowly pour the blender contents into the stockpot (still off the heat) while stirring constantly. The soup should be heated to at least 160°F [71°C] (see Note), but it should not boil or simmer. If it's not hot enough, place it back over medium-low heat and stir constantly until it comes up to temperature. Serve right away and make sure each bowl gets some froth, or store for 3 to 4 days in smaller containers in the refrigerator. It will lose its froth after storing, but it'll still be delicious.

Notes: Optionally throw the bones and skin immediately into another pot with vegetable scraps, herbs, salt, and water and repeat the simmering process to make extra stock for another project. The stock in this recipe doesn't penetrate to the bone, and the leftover chicken bones still have lots of collagen and flavor.

As long as you didn't take a big break between taking the soup off the heat and adding the egg mixture to it, it should end up 180°F to 185°F [82°C to 85°C]. Don't let it get much hotter, or it might split.

Spring Soup

Vidalia French Onion Lentil Soup

Makes 10 small or 6 large servings

If you ever find that your enthusiasm for Vidalia onions has outmatched your ability to put them to use, it's time to make a pot of French onion soup. Vidalias are naturally sweet, so they caramelize beautifully, which means you'll end up with a super flavorful and nicely sweet soup. And French onion soup requires an absurd amount, so it should put a dent in your stockpile.

Vidalia season starts in early to mid-spring—you can almost always find them in US supermarkets in April and May, but they start to get a little harder to find later on in the summer and usually disappear entirely by late summer or early fall. This recipe will work great with any sweet onion variety (e.g., Vidalias, Australian Rosalees, French Roscoffs), but you can also use year-round red or yellow onions (see Note).

3 Tbsp [45 g] unsalted butter
5 large Vidalia onions, very thinly sliced (1.2 kg; see Note)
¼ tsp salt
1 Tbsp minced or pressed garlic
2 Tbsp all-purpose flour
½ cup [115 g] dry red wine
2 qt [1.9 L] Vegetable Stock (page 139) or store-bought vegetable, chicken, or beef stock
1 cup [185 g] green, black, or brown lentils, sorted and rinsed (see Note)
½ tsp freshly ground black pepper
½ tsp rubbed sage
½ tsp dried thyme
Cheesy Croûtes (recipe follows)

Place the butter in a large Dutch oven over medium-high heat. Once the butter has melted, swirl to coat and add the onions and salt. Give them a stir, cover, and cook for about 7 minutes, until the onions are softened a bit and a brown film appears on the bottom of the pot. Uncover, scrape the bottom, lower the heat to medium, and continue cooking for about 45 minutes. Lower the heat if necessary as you go, so that a brown film develops about every 5 minutes. Stir and scrape the bottom of the pan whenever a brown film develops and deglaze with 1 Tbsp or so of water any time the brown film won't easily scrape up. The onions are not done until they've shrunk down and turned deeply brown.

During the last minute or two of caramelizing, add the garlic and flour and cook, stirring, for about 1 minute.

Pour the wine into the pot and scrape up any stuck bits on the bottom for just 30 seconds or so. It will bubble and start to thicken almost immediately. Stir in the stock in a steady stream. Add the lentils, pepper, sage, and thyme. Increase the heat to high to bring it up to a simmer.

Once it comes to a simmer, cover, lower the heat to low, and cook for about 30 minutes, until the lentils are tender and have lost their mealiness. Taste and adjust the seasoning. Cover and set aside until the croûtes are ready.

As soon as your croûtes come out of the broiler, ladle some soup into a small bowl and top with a piece of cheesy bread.

Notes: If you're using regular yellow or red onions, just be sure to add a couple of pinches of sugar or a little drizzle of honey along with the salt to help them caramelize more deeply. If you can't find 4 large onions, simply use 10 small onions or 6 or 7 medium onions (for a total of 2.65 lb [1.2 kg] sliced onion). Large Vidalias tend to be the easiest to find, but other varieties sometimes run a little smaller.

Omit the lentils to make this more of a classic French onion soup, and serve as a side or appetizer.

Cheesy Croûtes

One 14 oz [400 g] loaf crusty bread, cut into ¾ in [2 cm] thick bowl-width slices
Unsalted butter, at room temperature, for coating the bread
1 garlic clove
10 oz [285 g] sliced or grated melting cheese, such as Jarlsberg or Gruyère
¼ cup [15 g] finely grated Parmesan cheese

Preheat the broiler.

Lightly butter both sides of the bread slices and place them on a baking sheet. Broil until toasted on one side (1 to 5 minutes, depending on your broiler—keep an eye on it!).

Rub the garlic on the toasted sides of the bread as soon as they come out of the oven.

Place the cheese slices (or sprinkle grated cheese) on the untoasted sides, then sprinkle with the Parmesan. Place back under the broiler until the cheese is melted and browned in spots (another 1 to 5 minutes).

Grain Bowls

We start with a few humble ingredients: roasted or steamed veggies, a scoop of chickpeas, maybe some feta, and a perfectly cooked pot of simple grains. On their own, these ingredients aren't particularly exciting, but they come to life once you top them with a super flavorful sauce.

I've included four of my favorite easy sauces in this section (three of which can be made vegan), but you can experiment with others—vinaigrettes even work quite nicely if you're using lots of heavy, starchy ingredients, especially if you add a little extra feta. Sesame miso goes with starchy sweet produce. Avocado lime goes with earthier and fragrant flavors such as cumin and coriander. Lemon tahini goes with cauliflower, especially when you top it with some dried fruit (raisins or chopped dates). And the herby yogurt sauce is lovely with cucumber, red pepper, or beets.

Make Your Own Grain Bowls Grid

Ingredients to swap in for the base recipe on the facing page

GRAINS

+ Buckwheat
+ Freekeh
+ Wheat berries
+ Brown rice
+ Barley
+ Coarse bulgur
+ Wild rice
+ Rye berries
+ White rice
+ Quinoa

EXTRA TOPPINGS

+ Dukkah (page 151)
+ Za'atar
+ Ground pistachios
+ Sesame seeds
+ Slivered almonds
+ Chopped walnuts
+ Raisins
+ Dates
+ Fresh herbs

SAUCES

+ Herby Yogurt Sauce (page 155)
+ Sesame Miso Sauce (page 154)
+ Lemon Tahini Sauce (page 152)
+ Avocado Lime Mint Sauce (page 151)

SEASONAL PRODUCE

Summer

Blanched or grilled corn kernels (1 minute blanched; see page 141 for grilling), blanched or roasted green beans (2 minutes blanched; 10 to 15 minutes roasted), steamed or roasted ½ in [13 mm] chunks of zucchini or summer squash (3 minutes steamed; 5 to 10 minutes roasted), charred and peeled red bell peppers, steamed Swiss chard leaves (1 minute), diced cucumbers, slow-roasted (see page 113) or diced tomatoes

Fall

Roasted okra (see page 21), pomegranate arils (use in moderation), steamed ¼ in [6 mm] sliced squash, pumpkin, parsnips, or carrots (3 minutes) , steamed or roasted small cauliflower or broccoli florets (2 minutes steamed; 12 minutes roasted), steamed chopped kale or collards (5 minutes), roasted peeled chestnuts (see page 62), sautéed chanterelles

Winter

Steamed ¼ in [6 mm] sliced squash, pumpkin, sweet potatoes, carrots or parsnips (3 minutes), steamed small cauliflower or broccoli florets (2 minutes), steamed chopped kale or collards (5 minutes)

Spring

Steamed small broccoli florets (2 minutes), steamed asparagus (2 minutes), blanched and peeled fava beans or peas (1 minute; see page 98), sautéed ramps or prepped fiddlehead ferns (see page 21), sautéed morels, blanched shelled peas/snow peas/snap peas

Anytime

Sautéed mushrooms, thawed frozen corn, thawed frozen peas, oil-preserved red peppers

Grain Bowls

Makes 4 servings

1⅓ cups [240 g] uncooked grain
4 to 5 cups [500 g] prepared produce (try to use at least two different complementary vegetables from the grid on the facing page)
One 15 oz [425 g] can chickpeas, strained and rinsed (see Note)
1 batch grain bowl sauce
½ cup [70 g] crumbled feta (optional)
Extra toppings

If you're making quinoa or white rice, cook according to the instructions on page 154. If you're making buckwheat, follow the instructions on page 152. Otherwise, place your grains in a small to medium saucepan, cover with 2 in [5 cm] of water, and simmer until tender (top up the water as time goes on if you are cooking something that takes a long time). Certain whole grains such as wheat berries and brown rice will take longer to cook, 30 to 45 minutes. Others such as coarse bulgur and cracked freekeh will take more like 15 minutes. Even with the same kind of grain, cook times will sometimes vary from one brand to another, so always read the package and taste as you go.

Prepare your produce according to the Grain Bowl Seasonal Produce chart on the facing page. Roasting times are for a 440°F [225°C] oven with the vegetables coated in a light layer of oil first.

While everything is roasting or steaming, prep your chickpeas, sauce, and any additional toppings.

To assemble in each bowl, add a scoop of cooked grains and top with a scoop of steamed or roasted produce, a scoop of chickpeas, a drizzle of your sauce of choice, a small scoop of feta, and any extra toppings. Serve with any leftover sauce at the table.

Note: Chickpeas are super versatile and will work with just about anything here, but you can sub in your favorite bean or legume, using whatever you've got on hand.

Summer Grain Bowl

Slow-Roasted Tomatoes, Chard, Yellow Squash, Dukkah, Mint, Freekeh, Avocado Lime Mint Sauce

This grain bowl is full of bright summer flavor, so top it with plenty of dukkah to bring it down to earth. The roasted nuts and earthy spices perfectly balance the tomatoes, mint, and tangy avocado sauce.

2 pt [600 g] cherry tomatoes, halved
Neutral oil, such as avocado or canola, for coating the tomatoes
Salt
¼ tsp freshly ground black pepper
1⅓ cups [240 g] whole freekeh
6 baby or 2 medium [200 g] pattypan squash, cut into ½ in [13 mm] pieces

3 cups [100 g] packed coarsely chopped Swiss chard

½ cup [70 g] crumbled feta

15 oz [425 g] can chickpeas, drained and rinsed

Avocado Lime Mint Sauce (recipe follows)

Fresh mint leaves, for garnish

Dukkah, for sprinkling (recipe follows)

Preheat the oven to 350°F [180°C].

Coat the tomato halves in a light layer of the oil, place on a rimmed baking sheet cut-side up, and sprinkle with salt and pepper (about ¼ tsp salt and ¼ tsp pepper).

Roast for about 50 minutes, opening the door once or twice to allow the steam to escape, until they've shrunk down and become syrupy but are still quite soft.

Rinse the freekeh under cold water for about 30 seconds. Place the rinsed freekeh in a medium saucepan and cover with at least 3 in [7.5 cm] of water. Add about 1 tsp of salt.

Raise the heat to high, bring to a simmer, and then lower the heat to medium-low to maintain a simmer. Continue cooking for 15 to 45 minutes (cracked freekeh takes less time; whole freekeh takes more time) until al dente. Drain the freekeh, return it to the saucepan, and season with a bit more salt, if needed. Cover so it stays warm and set aside off the heat.

Set up a steamer basket over a pot of boiling water and place the squash inside. Season with salt and let it steam for about 3 minutes, just until softened. Remove from the steamer and set aside. Place the Swiss chard in the steamer basket, season with salt, and steam for about 1 minute, just until it shrinks down. Set aside.

To assemble, in each bowl, place a scoop of freekeh and top with some squash, tomatoes, Swiss chard, feta, a scoop of chickpeas, a dollop of avocado sauce, a few mint leaves, and a generous sprinkling of dukkah.

Avocado Lime Mint Sauce

1 garlic clove

1 avocado, peeled and pitted (150 g flesh)

2 Tbsp Greek yogurt (see Note)

3 Tbsp [45 g] fresh lime juice

1 bunch mint, stemmed (25 g leaves)

¼ tsp salt

2 to 3 Tbsp water

Put the garlic in a food processor or blender and pulse until minced. Add the avocado, yogurt, lime juice, mint, and salt and blend. Add water 1 Tbsp at a time until it smooths out into a thick sauce.

Note: To make this vegan, use a larger avocado and omit the yogurt.

Dukkah

⅓ cup [35 g] ground pistachios

2 Tbsp ground cumin seeds

1 Tbsp ground fennel seeds

1 Tbsp ground coriander seeds

1 tsp freshly ground black pepper

Pinch of allspice

Combine the pistachios, cumin, fennel, coriander, black pepper, and allspice in a skillet over medium heat. Stir constantly while it toasts, and remove from the pan once it smells a little toasty (2 to 3 minutes).

Fall Grain Bowl

Cauliflower, Za'atar, Pomegranate Arils, Pistachios, Raisins, Buckwheat, Lemon Tahini Sauce

Za'atar is a wild herb that grows in the Eastern Mediterranean and throughout much of the Middle East; it is frequently blended with sesame seeds and sumac. It's often translated into English as "wild thyme," but that description doesn't do it justice. My eyes were first opened to the difference when I had the chance to try freshly grown za'atar from my friend Mai's garden (author of the blog *Almond and Fig*); oregano is the closest point of comparison, even more so than thyme, but za'atar has a flavor all its own that defies analogy. So while we recipe writers normally encourage you to blend your own spices, za'atar is one of those that's much better store-bought. Blending dried French thyme with sumac and sesame is delicious, but it won't always bring the right flavor to recipes that call for za'atar. Buy a big bag of the real deal at your local Middle Eastern market and be prepared to sprinkle it on absolutely everything.

1⅓ cups [240 g] buckwheat groats
Salt
Extra-virgin olive oil
⅓ cup [40 g] za'atar, plus more for sprinkling
1 small cauliflower, cut into small florets (500 g)
½ cup [70 g] raisins
One 15 oz [425 g] can chickpeas, drained and rinsed
Lemon Tahini Sauce (recipe follows)
½ cup [70 g] crumbled feta
½ cup [65 g] pomegranate arils
¼ cup [30 g] coarsely ground pistachios

Preheat the oven to 440°F [225°C].

Place the buckwheat groats in a medium saucepan over medium-high heat and stir constantly until the groats are lightly golden brown and smell toasty, about 4 minutes (about 1 minute after they start crackling). Immediately pour water over them so they're covered by at least 3 in [7.5 cm]. Season with salt.

Raise the heat to high, bring to a simmer, then lower the heat to medium-low to maintain a simmer. Continue cooking for about 6 minutes more, until they're no longer crunchy but still nicely al dente. Drain the buckwheat groats, return them to the saucepan, and stir in 1 Tbsp of oil. Cover so it stays warm, and set aside off the heat.

In a small mixing bowl, combine the za'atar, 3 Tbsp [40 g] of oil, and ¼ tsp of salt. Place the cauliflower on a rimmed baking sheet, drizzle with the za'atar mixture, and toss together with your hands to evenly coat. Spread into an even layer and roast for about 12 minutes, just until tender and lightly browned.

During the last 2 minutes of roasting, add the raisins and let them roast until they puff up slightly and caramelize.

To assemble, in each bowl, place a scoop of buckwheat and top with a scoop of cauliflower/raisins, a scoop of chickpeas, a drizzle of tahini sauce, a scoop of crumbled feta, and a sprinkling of pomegranate and pistachio. Top with a little extra za'atar.

Lemon Tahini Sauce

⅓ cup [80 g] tahini
¼ cup [60 g] fresh lemon juice
⅓ cup [80 g] water
1 garlic clove, crushed through a press
¼ tsp salt

Combine the tahini, lemon juice, water, garlic, and salt in a small mixing bowl, whisk together until completely smooth, and set aside. It will start out watery and broken, but it will smooth out and thicken as you whisk it, and it will continue to thicken more after sitting for about 2 minutes.

Winter Grain Bowl

Sweet Potatoes, Mushrooms, Sesame Seeds, Sesame Miso Sauce, Brown Rice

Back when my husband was studying philosophy and I was studying medieval poetry in grad school, we used to throw big parties in our modest two-bedroom apartment, occasionally even for both our departments combined. There was barely enough room for people to walk around, let alone sit down, so we always made sure there were plenty of passed appetizers to go with the cocktails.

I always kept a running list of my favorite easy, pretty, and inexpensive one-bite recipes, and my hands-down favorites were Emily Han's miso sweet potato bites. You simply roast round sweet potato slices, top them with a dab of sesame miso sauce, sprinkle with green onion slivers and black sesame seeds, and watch them disappear as you pass them around the room.

This grain bowl recipe is inspired by those bites, and it certainly would've come in handy once those parties started to die down as I began studying for my oral exams all winter long. So whether you're in a passed hors d'oeuvre or Sunday meal prep season right now, you can't go wrong with these flavors.

1⅓ cups [240 g] brown rice
Salt
1 Tbsp neutral oil, such as avocado or canola
1 very large sweet potato, unpeeled and cut into ½ in [13 mm] wedges (300 g)
12 oz [340 g] cremini mushrooms, sliced
One 15 oz [425 g] can chickpeas, strained and rinsed
Sesame Miso Sauce (recipe follows)
2 Tbsp sesame seeds

Put the brown rice in a medium saucepan, season with salt, cover with 3 in [7.5 cm] of water, and bring to a boil over high heat. Once it starts to simmer, lower the heat to low, cover, and simmer for about 30 minutes (this will vary, depending on the variety, so check on it every once in a while). Once the rice is chewy and soft (before it becomes soggy and mushy), drain well, cover, and set aside to stay warm off the heat.

Place a large nonstick or cast-iron sauté pan or skillet over medium heat, and let it preheat for a few minutes. Once hot, add the oil and swirl to coat. Add the sweet potato wedges, season with salt, and let cook for about 7 minutes on each side. After about 14 minutes total, they should be soft on the inside and nicely browned on the outside. Transfer to a bowl.

In the same pan over medium heat, add the sliced mushrooms and season with salt. Let cook for about 10 minutes. They will first give off some juices, then those juices will evaporate, then they will nicely brown.

To assemble, in each bowl, place a scoop of rice; top with a scoop each of sweet potatoes, mushrooms, and chickpeas; drizzle on the sesame miso sauce; and sprinkle with sesame seeds.

Sesame Miso Sauce

⅓ cup [80 g] tahini
⅓ cup [80 g] water
2 Tbsp rice vinegar
2½ Tbsp miso paste
2 tsp brown sugar, or 1 tsp honey
1½ tsp sesame oil
1 Tbsp minced ginger
1 garlic clove, crushed through a press

Combine the tahini, water, vinegar, miso, brown sugar, sesame oil, ginger, and garlic in a small mixing bowl. Whisk until completely smooth, and set aside. It will start out watery and will thicken after sitting for about 2 minutes.

Spring Grain Bowl

Roasted Carrots, Beets, Sugar Snap Peas, Quinoa, Herby Yogurt Sauce

Beets and yogurt are a tried-and-true pairing of earthy and tangy. I love combining them in a grain bowl—since they are mixed together at the table, everyone gets to experience that magical surprise when you give it a stir and everything turns bright magenta.

This recipe also yields a perfect batch of quinoa, a good trick to have up your sleeve. Just like excellent rice, the key to fluffy quinoa is to cook it covered without peeking and then let it steam the rest of the way off the heat once it's absorbed nearly all its liquid. For this technique to work, you've got to use the right amount of liquid to start with, which I've detailed here. For a simple pot of white rice, use the same technique and quantities, substituting rice in place of quinoa, using water in place of stock, and using about ¾ tsp of salt.

1⅓ cups [240 g] tricolored quinoa
1¾ cups [410 g] stock
1 large beet, peeled and cut into ½ in [13 mm] thick wedges (250 g)
3 carrots (210 g), cut ½ in [13 mm] sticks
Olive oil
Salt
1½ cups [150 g] sugar snap peas, strings removed
One 15 oz [425 g] can chickpeas, drained and rinsed
Herby Yogurt Sauce (recipe follows)
½ cup [70 g] crumbled feta
Chopped fresh dill, parsley, and/or cilantro, for garnish

Preheat the oven to 440°F [225°C].

Rinse your quinoa well under cool water. Place the rinsed quinoa in a small saucepan and add the stock. Bring to a simmer over medium-high heat. Once rapidly simmering, cover and lower the heat to low. Let cook on low for 15 minutes undisturbed (without stirring or peeking), then keep covered and remove from the heat once 15 minutes have passed. Do not lift the lid, and let it steam, covered, for at least 15 minutes and up to 30 minutes off the heat.

While the quinoa is cooking, place the beets and carrots on a baking sheet, coat with a light layer of oil, spread out into an even layer, and sprinkle with salt. Roast for about 25 minutes, just until they are fork-tender and lightly charred. Once the carrots and beets are just about done, sprinkle on the snow peas and return to the oven for the last 2 minutes. They're done once they're bright green.

To assemble, in each bowl, place a scoop of quinoa, and top with a scoop of veggies, a scoop of chickpeas, a drizzle of yogurt sauce, a scoop of crumbled feta, and a pinch of chopped fresh herbs.

Herby Yogurt Sauce

This is my favorite version of several related yogurt sauces (Iraqi jajik, Indian raita, Greek tzatziki, etc.). If you're making this sauce in the middle of the summer and you have a ton of cucumber, you can grate some into the sauce. If you're making it in the middle of winter or don't have fresh herbs on hand, substitute 1 tsp dried mint and 1 tsp dried dill in place of the herbs.

¾ cup [180 g] Greek yogurt
2 Tbsp fresh lemon juice
2 Tbsp extra-virgin olive oil
¼ cup [10 g] chopped fresh dill
¼ cup [10 g] chopped fresh parsley or cilantro
1 garlic clove, crushed through a press
¼ tsp freshly ground black pepper
¼ tsp salt

Combine the yogurt, lemon juice, olive oil, dill, parsley or cilantro, garlic, pepper, and salt in a small mixing bowl and whisk until completely smooth.

Quesadillas

My husband and his dad once went on a backpacking trip in the Rocky Mountains, and on the last day they ended up at a restaurant where they had the best Southwestern quesadillas of all time. I've never had the original *best quesadillas of all time*, but I've had my father-in-law's adaptation, and it doesn't get much better.

This section takes inspiration from those fabled quesadillas, mixing things up depending on the season. While I normally love roasting and sautéeing produce, I usually like to stuff quesadillas with steamed or blanched veggies; that way, you get a lovely golden brown and delicious contrast from the toasted flour tortilla, and the vegetables' flavors are allowed to shine.

Make Your Own Quesadilla Grid

Ingredients to swap in for the base recipe on the facing page

MEATS

+ Seared and then ⅛ in [3 mm] sliced steak (see page 164)
+ Cumin shrimp or chicken (see page 163)

SALSAS

+ Salsa verde (see page 21)
+ Salsa Roja (page 165)
+ Pineapple Salsa (page 164)
+ Drained Pico de Gallo (page 161)

TO ESTIMATE

Be careful not to overstuff the quesadillas. A lot of extra produce and salsa will make them soggy and heavy; it's better to serve them with extra salsa and veggie sides at the table.

SEASONAL PRODUCE

Summer

Grilled or blanched corn kernels (see page 141 for grilling; 1 minute blanched), drained Pico de Gallo (page 161), blanched or steamed green beans (2 minutes blanched; 3 to 4 minutes steamed), steamed ¼ in [6 mm] sliced zucchini/summer squash (1 to 2 minutes), chopped fresh cilantro, charred and peeled red bell peppers

Fall

Roasted okra (see page 21), steamed ¼ in [6 mm] sliced squash, pumpkin, parsnips, or carrots (3 minutes), steamed small cauliflower or broccoli florets (2 minutes), steamed chopped kale (5 minutes)

Winter

Steamed ¼ in [6 mm] sliced squash, pumpkin, sweet potatoes, carrots, or parsnips (3 minutes); steamed small cauliflower or broccoli florets (2 minutes); steamed chopped kale (5 minutes)

Spring

Steamed small broccoli florets (2 minutes), steamed asparagus (2 minutes), blanched and peeled fava beans or peas (1 minute; see page 98), chopped fresh cilantro or chives, sautéed ramps or prepped fiddlehead ferns (see page 21)

Anytime

Sautéed mushrooms, thawed frozen corn, thawed frozen peas, oil-preserved red peppers

Quesadillas

Makes 10 quesadillas

3½ to 4½ cups [460 to 690 g] prepared produce (see grid on facing page), less if you're including meat

14 oz [395 g] seared meat (optional)

Salt

One 16 oz [455 g] can refried beans

1 Tbsp fresh lime juice

1½ tsp ground cumin

1½ tsp ground coriander

Ten 8 in [20 cm] flour tortillas

16 oz [455 g] salsa

2½ cups [275 g] grated Monterey Jack cheese

Neutral oil, such as avocado or canola, for frying

Lime wedges and sour cream

Prep your produce according to the Quesadilla Seasonal Produce chart on the facing page and decide how much produce and meat (if any) you'll use. If you're including meat, choose very dense and flavorful produce to accompany it (kale, fava beans, sweet potatoes, corn, drained pico de gallo) and cut back the amount of produce to 1¼ to 2½ cups [170 to 350 g]. Don't overstuff.

Combine the refried beans with the lime juice, cumin, and coriander in a small mixing bowl. Spread about 3 Tbsp of the refried bean mixture into a semicircle on half of one tortilla, leaving a border of about ½ in [13 mm].

Top the refried beans with some of the veggies, about 1 Tbsp salsa (don't use the whole amount—some is for serving), and ¼ cup cheese, and then fold the other side of the

tortilla over. Repeat with the remaining tortillas, refried bean mixture, veggies, salsa, and cheese.

Preheat a large sauté pan or skillet on the stove over medium heat. Once it's hot, add about 1 tsp oil and swirl to coat. Place a quesadilla on the skillet (or two at a time, if your skillet is large, but don't crowd the pan). Let cook for 2 to 3 minutes per side, until golden brown, blistered, and crispy on the outside and the cheese has melted on the inside. Work in batches, and use two pans if you're cooking for a crowd and don't mind multitasking.

Serve with the lime wedges, sour cream, and remaining salsa at the table.

To make ahead: Fried leftovers keep pretty well in the fridge for a couple of days, but they won't be as crispy as the first day. It's best to freeze before frying: Assemble the quesadillas, freeze them solid in a single layer on a parchment-lined baking sheet, move them to a tightly sealed bag, and store in the freezer. To cook, microwave them for 30 seconds to 1 minute, just until their shells are flexible. Then fry with 1 tsp of oil over medium-low heat, covered, for about 4 minutes per side. Once they're warmed all the way through, if they're not yet brown and crispy enough, increase the heat to medium and cook them again for about 1 minute per side.

Summer Quesadillas

Corn, Pico de Gallo

While most of the quesadilla recipes in this section use both fresh produce and salsa, pico de gallo is the best of both worlds, and it shines brightly as the star of this dish. If you've got a ton of summer tomatoes, homemade pico de gallo is a wonderful treat, but store-bought works great here too.

2 lb [905 g] Pico de Gallo (recipe follows)
Salt
2 cups [270 g] fresh corn kernels
One 16 oz [455 g] can refried beans
1 Tbsp fresh lime juice
1½ tsp ground cumin
1½ tsp ground coriander
Ten 8 in [20 cm] flour tortillas
2½ cups [275 g] grated Monterey Jack cheese
Neutral oil, such as avocado or canola
Lime wedges and sour cream, for serving

Let your pico de gallo sit for about 30 minutes. Scoop slightly more than half of it into a fine-mesh sieve. Reserve the drained pico de gallo to stuff the quesadillas (you should end up with about 1½ cups [310 g]) and discard the drained liquid. Save the remaining pico de gallo for serving.

Bring a pot of water to a boil, season liberally with salt, and add the corn. Drain after 2 minutes and rinse with cold water. Drain them well and set aside.

Combine the refried beans with the lime juice, cumin, and coriander in a small mixing bowl. Spread about 3 Tbsp of the refried bean mixture into a semicircle on half of one tortilla, leaving a border of about ½ in [13 mm].

Top the refried beans with about 3 Tbsp corn, 2 Tbsp drained pico, and about ¼ cup cheese, and then fold the other side of the tortilla over. Repeat with the remaining tortillas, refried bean mixture, corn, drained pico, and cheese.

Preheat a large sauté pan or skillet on the stove over medium heat. Once it's hot, add about 1 tsp of oil and swirl to coat. Place a quesadilla on the skillet (or two at a time, if your skillet is large, but don't crowd the pan). Let cook for 2 to 3 minutes per side, until golden brown, blistered, and crispy on the outside and the cheese has melted on the inside. Work in batches, and use two pans if you're cooking for a crowd and don't mind multitasking.

Serve with the reserved pico de gallo, lime wedges, and sour cream at the table.

Pico de Gallo

4 vine-ripened tomatoes, finely diced (630 g)
1 small red or white onion, minced (130 g)
1 cup [40 g] chopped fresh cilantro
1 Tbsp minced or pressed garlic
1 jalapeño, seeded, deribbed, and minced (30 g)
3 Tbsp fresh lime juice
Pinch of lime zest
½ tsp salt

Combine the tomatoes, onion, cilantro, garlic, jalapeño, lime juice, and lime zest in a bowl. Season with the salt and stir everything together.

Fall Quesadillas

Broccolini, Pesto, Acorn Squash

When I went to college in Bloomington, Indiana, I lived a few blocks away from the original Laughing Planet Cafe, which has since become a popular chain in Portland. I always got the "pestato," which was loaded with melted cheese, fresh local veggies, and basil pesto. These quesadillas are inspired by those salad days (with squash in place of the potato), but I think you're gonna love them even if you don't have the same nostalgia for my old college town. Use store-bought pesto here, or make and freeze your own in the late summer and early fall so you've got plenty for the colder months ahead.

9 stalks [220 g] broccolini, halved lengthwise
½ acorn squash, peeled and cut into ¼ in [6 mm] slices (220 g; see Note)
¼ tsp salt
One 16 oz [455 g] can refried beans
1 Tbsp fresh lime juice
1½ tsp ground cumin
1½ tsp ground coriander
Ten 8 in [20 cm] flour tortillas
8 oz [225 g] basil Pesto (page 227)
2½ cups [275 g] grated Monterey Jack cheese
Neutral oil, such as avocado or canola
Lime wedges, sour cream, and Salsa Roja (page 165) for serving

Steam the broccolini and squash, either by microwaving (times vary) or placing in a tight-lidded stove-top steamer set over boiling water. The broccolini and squash will each take about 2 minutes on the stove. Steam each vegetable separately for maximum control over doneness, and check on them promptly. The broccolini is done once it turns bright green and softens a bit yet retains some bite. The squash is done once it's soft and slightly custardy on the inside but not yet mushy. Remove from the heat, season with the salt, and set aside to cool slightly.

Combine the refried beans with the lime juice, cumin, and coriander in a small mixing bowl. Spread about 3 Tbsp of the refried bean mixture into a semicircle on half of one tortilla, leaving a border of about ½ in [13 mm].

Top the refried beans with about 2 broccolini halves, a few pieces of squash, 1½ Tbsp pesto, and ¼ cup cheese, and then fold the other side of the tortilla over. Repeat with the remaining tortillas, refried bean mixture, broccolini, squash, pesto, and cheese.

Preheat a large sauté pan or skillet on the stove over medium heat. Once it's hot, add about 1 tsp oil and swirl to coat. Place a quesadilla on the skillet (or two at a time, if your skillet is large, but don't crowd the pan). Let cook for 2 to 3 minutes per side, until golden brown, blistered, and crispy on the outside and the cheese has melted on the inside. Work in batches, and use two pans if you're cooking for a crowd and don't mind multitasking.

Serve with lime wedges, sour cream, and salsa roja at the table.

Note: If your acorn squash's skin is thin and delicate, don't bother peeling it. If the skin is on the tough and thick side, peel it by first slicing between the ridges into wedges, then peel the wedges with a Y-peeler. Be careful and always cut away from your hand. Also feel free to use a peeled Kent pumpkin, butternut squash, or another firm-fleshed winter squash.

Winter Quesadillas

Kale, Cumin Shrimp, Pineapple Salsa

When I'm making salsa in the colder months, I tend to turn to pantry ingredients. Sometimes I use canned tomatoes (see page 165), but canned pineapple is another delicious option, and it goes great with most hearty winter ingredients (in this case, steamed kale). While this particular salsa is also delicious made with fresh jalapeños and cilantro, here I've made it entirely with pantry ingredients, opting for chipotle peppers and dried cilantro. The rest of the ingredients are similarly pantry-friendly, so you might not even need to bundle up and venture out to the grocery store to enjoy this one.

5½ cups [550 g] frozen raw peeled shrimp, thawed
Neutral oil, such as avocado or canola
Salt
1 Tbsp ground cumin
7 cups [175 g] packed chopped kale leaves, from about 1 big bunch
One 16 oz [455 g] can refried beans
1 Tbsp fresh lime juice
1½ tsp ground coriander
Ten 8 in [20 cm] flour tortillas
Pineapple Salsa (recipe follows)
2½ cups [275 g] grated Monterey Jack cheese
Lime wedges, for serving

Drain your thawed shrimp of any excess moisture. After thawing and draining, you should have 2⅔ cups [460 g].

Preheat a large skillet on the stove over medium-high heat. Once it's hot, add about 1 tsp of oil, swirl to coat, and add the shrimp. Stir frequently and season with salt. Once the shrimp are mostly pink and opaque (about 2 minutes, or longer if you're using larger shrimp), sprinkle on half of the cumin and cook for about 1 minute more, until they're completely pink and opaque. Remove from the heat and set aside.

Place the kale in a steamer basket over simmering water, cover, and steam for about 5 minutes, just until tender and brighter green (the kale will shrink down to about one-third its original volume). Season with salt.

Combine the refried beans with the lime juice, coriander, and remaining half of the cumin in a small mixing bowl. Spread about 3 Tbsp of the refried bean mixture into a semicircle on half of one tortilla, leaving a border of about ½ in [13 mm].

Top the refried beans with a few pieces of shrimp, 1 Tbsp salsa (don't use the whole batch—some is for serving), a small handful of steamed kale, and ¼ cup cheese and then fold the other side of the tortilla over. Repeat with the remaining tortillas, refried bean mixture, shrimp, salsa, kale, and cheese.

Preheat a large sauté pan or skillet on the stove over medium heat. Once it's hot, add about 1 tsp oil and swirl to coat. Place a quesadilla on the skillet (or two at a time, if your skillet is large, but don't crowd the pan). Let cook for 2 to 3 minutes per side, until golden brown, blistered, and crispy on the outside and the cheese has melted on the inside. Work in batches, and use two pans if you're cooking for a crowd and don't mind multitasking.

Serve with the remaining salsa and lime wedges at the table.

Note: You can substitute chicken cutlets that have been cut into bite-size pieces. Like shrimp, they are done once they are opaque all the way through, but they will take a few minutes longer. Season the chicken with salt at least 10 minutes before you plan to cook it.

Pineapple Salsa

One 20 oz [565 g] can crushed pineapple (in juice)
½ small onion, minced (60 g)
1½ Tbsp minced chipotle in adobo sauce
2 tsp dried cilantro, or 2 Tbsp chopped fresh cilantro
1 to 3 garlic cloves, crushed through a press
1½ Tbsp fresh lime juice
¼ tsp salt

Let the crushed pineapple drain in a fine-mesh sieve until it slows to a slow trickle, and set the juice aside for another project. You should end up with about 1⅔ cups [380 g] pineapple.

Combine the drained pineapple with the onion, chipotle, dried cilantro, garlic, lime juice, and salt in a bowl and stir everything together.

Spring Quesadillas

Favas, Steak, Salsa Roja

Spring produce tends to be a little on the bright side, so it's usually a natural fit with anything strongly umami, such as seared steak. Take fresh fava beans—they're a little funky and zesty, so they go great with heartier flavors. After you sear your steak, make sure you slice it very thinly, so that you end up with a little bit of steak with each bite of quesadilla.

One 14 oz [395 g] rib-eye or strip steak, trimmed of fat
¼ tsp salt
Neutral oil, such as avocado or canola
One 16 oz [455 g] can refried beans
1 Tbsp fresh lime juice
1½ tsp ground cumin

1½ tsp ground coriander
Ten 8 in [20 cm] flour tortillas
1⅓ cups [200 g] shelled, blanched, and peeled
    fava beans (see page 98)
Salsa Roja (recipe follows)
2½ cups [275 g] grated Monterey Jack cheese
Lime wedges and sour cream, for serving

Season the steak with the salt and coat in a light layer of oil. Let sit while you preheat a sauté pan or skillet on the stove over high heat. Turn on your exhaust and/or open a window. Once the skillet is very hot, add the steak and leave it alone for 3 to 4 minutes. Turn and let the other side sear for about another 3 to 4 minutes. Remove from the skillet once it's medium-rare (135°F [57°C] internal). Let rest for at least 5 minutes, and then slice into about 30 very thin pieces (about ⅛ in [3 mm] thick).

Combine the refried beans with the lime juice, cumin, and coriander in a small mixing bowl. Spread about 3 Tbsp of the refried bean mixture into a semicircle on half of one tortilla, leaving a border of about ½ in [13 mm].

Top the refried beans with about four slices of steak, 2 Tbsp fava beans, about 1 Tbsp salsa (don't use the whole amount—some is for serving), and ¼ cup cheese and then fold the other side of the tortilla over. Repeat with the remaining tortillas, refried bean mixture, steak, fava beans, salsa, and cheese.

Preheat a large sauté pan or skillet on the stove over medium heat. Once it's hot, add about 1 tsp of oil and swirl to coat. Place a quesadilla on the skillet (or two at a time, if your skillet is large, but don't crowd the pan). Let cook for 2 to 3 minutes per side, until golden brown, blistered, and crispy on the outside and the cheese has melted on the inside. Work in batches, and use two pans if you're cooking for a crowd and don't mind multitasking.

Serve with the lime wedges, sour cream, and remaining salsa at the table.

Salsa Roja

One 14½ oz [410 g] can diced tomatoes
½ medium onion (90 g)
1 jalapeño, seeded and deribbed (30 g)
½ cup [20 g] packed fresh cilantro leaves
3 garlic cloves, crushed through a press
2 Tbsp fresh lime juice
Salt

Place the diced tomatoes in a sauté pan or skillet over medium-high heat. Once they come to a simmer, lower the heat to medium and let them bubble away for about 5 minutes, just until they've reduced down to about two-thirds their original volume.

Place the onion, jalapeño, cilantro, and garlic in a food processor and pulse until very finely chopped. Add the reduced tomato and the lime juice and pulse a few more times until it becomes a chunky salsa. Taste and season with salt.

Veggie Burgers

Veggie burger recipes tend to accumulate ingredients over time—they get passed from friend to friend, and before you know it, they're held together by three different binders, they've got four or five different vegetables, and they're flavored with a dozen spices and pastes.

I keep mine minimalist, relying on a few key building blocks to hold everything together, which allows the important flavors to shine—but that doesn't mean you can't get creative. Just stick to the essential components and have fun with flavor and texture to come up with your own unique creation. While most vegetables *can* be incorporated into a veggie burger, it's best to use only super-flavorful and/or highly textural ingredients, because subtler vegetables will not shine through.

The trick to shaping your burgers is to make them thicker than you want them to end up. Veggie burgers start out a bit on the soft side and set more firmly as they cook through, so it's important to start them out thicker, flip them only once, and handle them gently before they finish cooking. For this reason, I much prefer cooking them on the stove instead of the outdoor grill. Veggie burgers that are solid enough for easy grilling don't have the best texture once cooked.

Make Your Own Veggie Burgers Grid

Ingredients to swap in for the base recipe on the facing page

BEANS

+ Black
+ Kidney
+ Pinto
+ Butter
+ Cannellini
+ Navy

FLAVORINGS

+ Minced fresh hot peppers (1 jalapeño)
+ Leafy herbs (up to 2 cups [40 g] chopped fresh parsley, cilantro, chives, or basil)
+ Woody herbs (1 Tbsp fresh rosemary, 2 Tbsp thyme, 1 Tbsp sage, or 1 Tbsp oregano)
+ Minced chipotle (3 Tbsp)
+ Miso paste (1 Tbsp, and cut back on the salt in the recipe)
+ Citrus zest (1 tsp)
+ Capers (¼ cup [40 g], rinsed)
+ Deeply caramelized onions (⅓ cup [60 g], see page 132)
+ Spices (1 to 3 tsp, e.g., za'atar, paprika, black pepper, cumin, coriander)
+ Large-diced Castelvetrano olives (¼ cup [35 g])
+ Sriracha (2 Tbsp)
+ Minced anchovy
+ Tomato paste (3 Tbsp [45 g])

TO ESTIMATE

Keep the two categories of vegetables in balance. If your veggies give off too much liquid, you'll have to add even more oats to help them hold together, which dilutes the flavor. Likewise, if your veggies are all super dry, your burgers will be too. Be careful not to add so much moisture that you end up having to overcompensate with too much oatmeal.

SEASONAL PRODUCE

Ingredients for texture (choose 1 or 2 and measure ⅔ to 1 cup [130 to 200 g] total after prepping/cooking your ingredients)	Ingredients for moisture (choose 1)
Summer	
Sautéed chopped bell peppers, fresh corn kernels	1 medium zucchini/summer squash grated and wrung out, 2 chopped tomatoes run through a sieve until there's ½ cup [120 g] left (see page 171)
Fall	
Sautéed sliced fennel; sautéed kale or collards; chopped broccoli (steamed or microwaved for just 1 minute); shredded raw beets, parsnips, or carrots	½ cup [120 g] mashed microwaved/steamed pumpkin or squash (choose a flavorful variety, such as kabocha or hubbard)
Winter	
Sautéed sliced fennel; sautéed kale or collards; chopped broccoli (steamed or microwaved for just 1 minute); shredded raw beets, parsnips, or carrots	½ cup [120 g] mashed microwaved/steamed pumpkin or squash (choose a flavorful variety, such as kabocha or hubbard)
Spring	
Shredded raw beets, parsnips, or carrots; fresh peas; chopped raw asparagus	Choose from the "anytime" veggies (below)
Anytime	
Chopped drained kimchi, frozen corn, frozen peas, thawed and wrung-out frozen spinach	One 12 oz [340 g] container mushrooms chopped and sautéed (see page 173), ½ cup [120 g] strained and diced tomatoes (see page 172), ¾ cup [180 g] ricotta plus 1 large egg

Veggie Burgers

Makes 10 patties

Ingredients for texture (see grid on facing page)
Ingredients for moisture (see grid on facing page)
1 medium onion, quartered (180 g)
Neutral oil, such as avocado or canola
Salt
6 to 10 medium garlic cloves
¾ cup [75 g] rolled oats
Two 15 oz [425 g] cans beans, drained and rinsed
1 or 2 additional flavorings (see grid on facing page)
1 large egg
Buns and your favorite condiments and toppings, for serving

Prepare all your ingredients according to the this section's chart and feel free to use a food processor whenever possible (use the grater attachment to shred and the blade attachment to chop). Don't wash the food processor between ingredients—you'll be using it again and again.

Use your food processor with its blade attachment to chop the onion by pulsing several times. Don't purée it, and stop once it's just finely chopped.

Place a small nonstick or cast-iron sauté pan or skillet over medium heat and let it heat up for a few minutes. Add about 2 Tbsp of oil, the onions, and a pinch of salt. Cook for 7 to 10 minutes, stirring occasionally, until softened and lightly golden brown. Transfer to a medium mixing bowl.

Sauté any other vegetables that need to be sautéed (see the chart). Give the pan a quick rinse so you can use it to cook the burgers.

Add the garlic to the food processor and pulse a few times until minced. Add the rolled oats and process until they break down into a coarse meal. Add the beans and pulse several more times until mashed, almost puréed. Transfer the mixture to the mixing bowl.

Add the prepared ingredients for texture, prepared ingredients for smoothness, any additional flavorings, the egg, and about ½ tsp of salt to the mixing bowl (use more or less, depending on the sodium content of your beans). Mix everything together with your hands or a wooden spoon. Refrigerate the mixture for about 30 minutes to firm up.

Return the pan to medium heat and let it preheat for a couple of minutes. Add about 1 tsp of oil to the pan, swirl to coat, and form half of the mixture into about five 1 in [2.5 cm] thick patties, adding them to the pan as you shape them. Err on the side of a little too thick—they will thin slightly after you flip them.

Season to taste with a pinch or two of salt. Control the heat while they cook to make sure they're not burning and let cook for about 8 minutes on each side, until cooked through and nicely browned. Handle them gently and try not to flip them more than once. Repeat with the other half of the mixture and don't crowd the pan.

Serve on toasted buns with your favorite condiments and toppings.

Summer Burgers

Black Beans, Jalapeños, Tomatoes, Cilantro

These veggie burgers are so light and refreshing—serve them with a healthy scoop of pico de gallo and a little squeeze of fresh lime juice. You can make your own pico de gallo with my recipe on page 161, or use store-bought for a shortcut.

1 medium onion (180 g), quartered
Neutral oil, such as avocado or canola
Salt
¾ cup [75 g] rolled oats
6 to 10 medium garlic cloves
2 jalapeños, seeded and deribbed (60 g)
2 cups [80 g] packed fresh cilantro leaves
Two 15 oz [425 g] cans black beans, drained and
    rinsed
2 tomatoes, diced (220 g)
1¼ cups [170 g] fresh corn kernels
1 large egg
½ tsp freshly ground black pepper
Buns, limes, and Pico de Gallo (page 161), for
    serving

Use your food processor to chop the onion (do not wash the food processor until the very end).

Place a small nonstick or cast-iron sauté pan or skillet over medium heat and let it heat up for a few minutes. Add about 2 Tbsp of oil, the onions, and a pinch of salt. Cook for 7 to 10 minutes, stirring occasionally, until softened and lightly golden brown. Transfer to a medium mixing bowl (give the pan a quick rinse so you can use it to cook the burgers).

Add the rolled oats to the food processor and process until they break down into a coarse meal. Add the garlic, jalapeños, and cilantro and pulse a few times until minced. Add the

black beans and pulse several more times until mashed, almost puréed. Transfer the mixture to the mixing bowl.

Set a fine-mesh sieve over your sink or a bowl. Place the diced tomatoes in the sieve and press them against the side of the sieve with the back of a spoon. Once the majority of the runny tomato juice has drained away, add ½ cup [120 g] of the drained tomatoes to the bean mixture. (Save any leftovers and the tomato juice for Minestrone, page 138.)

Add the corn, egg, black pepper, and about ½ tsp of salt to the mixing bowl. Mix everything together. Refrigerate the mixture for about 30 minutes to firm up.

Return the pan to medium heat and let it preheat for a couple of minutes. Add about 1 tsp of oil to the pan, swirl to coat, and form half of the mixture into about five 1 in [2.5 cm] thick patties, adding them to the pan as you shape them. Err on the side of a little too thick—they will thin slightly after you flip them.

Season to taste with a pinch or two of salt. Control the heat while they cook to make sure they're not burning and let cook for about 8 minutes on each side, until cooked through and nicely browned. Handle them gently and try not to flip them more than once. Repeat with the other half of the mixture and don't crowd the pan.

Serve on toasted buns with pico de gallo, and lime wedges on the side.

Fall Burgers

Red Kidney Beans, Beets,
Chipotle, Diced Tomatoes

If you're kind of on the fence about beets but
want to find some delicious ways to incorporate them into your diet, you should start with a
veggie burger. They add such a lovely texture
and color, and the bold and smoky chipotle in
this recipe highlights the beets' earthiness in the
best way possible. If you're already a total beet
lover, serve it with an additional little heap of
shredded raw beets on top.

1 medium onion, quartered (180 g)
Neutral oil, such as avocado or canola
Salt
1 large beet, peeled and cut into smaller chunks
    (170 g), plus extra shredded raw beets for
    topping
6 to 10 medium garlic cloves
3 Tbsp [45 g] chipotle in adobo
¾ cup [75 g] rolled oats
Two 15 oz [225 g] cans red kidney beans,
    drained and rinsed
One 14½ oz [410 g] can diced tomatoes
1 large egg
Buns and your favorite condiments, for serving
Cheese slices (optional), for serving

Use your food processor with its blade attachment to chop the onion by pulsing several
times (do not wash the food processor until the
very end).

Place a small nonstick or cast-iron sauté pan
or skillet over medium heat and let it heat up
for a few minutes. Add about 2 Tbsp of oil,
the onions, and a pinch of salt. Cook for 7 to
10 minutes, stirring occasionally, until softened
and lightly golden brown. Transfer to a medium

mixing bowl (give the pan a quick rinse so you
can use it to cook the burgers).

Shred the beet using the shredder attachment
of your food processor, carefully feeding the
beet chunks through the tube with the fitted
plastic tamper. Once they're shredded, transfer
to the mixing bowl.

Replace the shredder attachment with a blade
attachment, add the garlic and chipotle, and
pulse a few times until minced. Add the rolled
oats and process until they break down into a
coarse meal. Add the beans and pulse several
more times until mashed, almost puréed. Transfer to the mixing bowl.

Set a fine-mesh sieve over your sink or a
bowl. Place the diced tomatoes in the sieve
and let it drain for 3 minutes while folding and
pressing the tomatoes to help them drain. Add
½ cup [120 g] of the drained tomato pulp to the
bowl. (Save any leftovers and the tomato juice
for Minestrone, page 138.)

Add the egg and about ½ tsp of salt to the
mixing bowl. Mix everything together. Refrigerate the mixture for about 30 minutes to
firm up.

Return the pan to medium heat and let it
preheat for a couple of minutes. Add about 1 tsp
of oil to the pan, swirl to coat, and form half of
the mixture into about five 1 in [2.5 cm] thick
patties, adding them to the pan as you shape
them. Err on the side of a little too thick—they
will thin slightly after you flip them.

Season to taste with a pinch or two of salt.
Control the heat while they cook to make sure
they're not burning and let cook for about
8 minutes on each side, until cooked through
and nicely browned. Handle them gently and
try not to flip them more than once. Repeat
with the other half of the mixture and don't
crowd the pan.

Serve on toasted buns with extra shredded
raw beets, your favorite condiments, and sliced
cheese, if desired.

Winter Burgers

Red Kidney Beans, Kimchi, Mushrooms

Late fall/early winter is the season for making kimchi, and it just gets better and better all winter long as it ferments. I'm not a total stranger to lacto-fermenting, but Middle Eastern pickles are more in my wheelhouse, so I usually tend to rely on the offerings at Korean markets whenever I'm craving kimchi.

1 medium onion (180 g), quartered

Neutral oil, such as avocado or canola

Salt

12 oz [340 g] cremini mushrooms

⅔ cup [130 g] kimchi, plus more for topping

6 to 10 medium garlic cloves

¾ cup [75 g] rolled oats

Two 15 oz [425 g] cans red kidney beans, drained and rinsed

1 large egg

Buns and your favorite condiments, for serving

Use your food processor with its blade attachment to chop the onion by pulsing several times (do not wash the food processor until the very end).

Place a small nonstick or cast-iron sauté pan or skillet over medium heat and let it heat up for a few minutes. Add about 2 Tbsp of oil, the onions, and a pinch of salt. Cook for about 5 minutes, stirring occasionally, until softened.

While the onions are cooking, use the food processor to chop the mushrooms as you did with the onions. Once the onions have softened, add the mushrooms to the onions, season with a pinch of salt, raise the heat to medium-high, and continue cooking for about 7 minutes, until their juices accumulate and evaporate and they shrink down. Transfer the mushrooms and onions to a medium mixing bowl (give the

pan a quick rinse so you can use it to cook the burgers).

Add the kimchi to the food processor and coarsely chop it (just pulse a couple of times). Transfer it to the mixing bowl.

Add the garlic to the food processor and pulse a few times until minced. Add the rolled oats to the garlic and process until they break down into a coarse meal. Add the beans to the oat flour and pulse several more times until mashed, almost puréed. Transfer the mixture to the mixing bowl.

Add the egg and about ½ tsp of salt to the mixing bowl. Mix everything together. Refrigerate the mixture for about 30 minutes to firm up.

Return the pan to medium heat and let it preheat for a couple of minutes. Add about 1 tsp of oil to the pan, swirl to coat, and form half of the mixture into about five 1 in [2.5 cm] thick patties, adding them to the pan as you shape them. Err on the side of a little too thick—they will thin slightly after you flip them.

Season to taste with a pinch or two of salt. Control the heat while they cook to make sure they're not burning and let cook for about 8 minutes on each side, until cooked through and nicely browned. Handle them gently and try not to flip them more than once. Repeat with the other half of the mixture and don't crowd the pan.

Serve on toasted buns with extra kimchi and your favorite condiments.

Spring Burgers

White Beans, Parsnips, Chives, Ricotta

I love cooking in-season root vegetables in cooler months, but I tend to go a little crazy for parsnips in the springtime because their slightly spicy, almost radish-like flavor goes so nicely with other spring flavors, such as chives.

1 medium onion (180 g), quartered

Neutral oil, such as avocado or canola

Salt

2 parsnips, peeled and cut into smaller chunks (170 g)

3 oz [80 g] chives, plus more for serving

6 to 10 medium garlic cloves

¾ cup [75 g] rolled oats

Two 15 oz [425 g] cans cannellini beans, drained and rinsed

¾ cup [180 g] ricotta

2 large eggs

½ tsp freshly ground black pepper

Buns and your favorite greens and condiments, for serving

Use your food processor with its blade attachment to chop the onion by pulsing several times (do not wash the food processor until the very end).

Place a small nonstick or cast-iron sauté pan or skillet over medium heat and let it heat up for a few minutes. Add about 2 Tbsp of oil, the onions, and a pinch of salt. Cook for 7 to 10 minutes, stirring occasionally, until softened and lightly golden brown. Transfer to a medium mixing bowl (give the pan a quick rinse so you can use it to cook the burgers).

Shred the parsnips using the shredder attachment of your food processor, carefully feeding the parnsnip chunks through the tube with the fitted plastic tamper. Once it's shredded, transfer it to the mixing bowl.

Replace the shredder attachment with a blade attachment, add the chives and garlic, and pulse a few times until minced. Add the rolled oats and process until they break down into a coarse meal. Add the beans and pulse several more times until mashed, almost puréed. Transfer the mixture to the mixing bowl.

Add the ricotta, eggs, black pepper, and about ½ tsp of salt to the mixing bowl. Mix everything together. Refrigerate the mixture for about 30 minutes to firm up.

Return the pan to medium heat and let it preheat for a couple of minutes. Add about 1 tsp of oil to the pan, swirl to coat, and form half of the mixture into about five 1 in [2.5 cm] thick patties, adding them to the pan as you shape them. Err on the side of a little too thick—they will thin slightly after you flip them.

Season to taste with a pinch or two of salt. Control the heat while they cook to make sure they're not burning and let cook for about 8 minutes on each side, until the parsnips are sligthly softened and the patties are nicely browned. Handle them gently and try not to flip them more than once. Repeat with the other half of the mixture and don't crowd the pan.

Serve on toasted buns with extra chives, greens, and your favorite condiments.

Fish Tacos

While my hometown, Chicago, isn't exactly known for its seafood, we've got some of the best Baja tacos around. We Chicagoans can be found huddled together in taquerias all through the long winter. Every time the door opens to let in a little subzero wind, the juices dripping down our arms nearly freeze, but we're all too happy to care.

A delicious cabbage slaw tops my favorite classic fish tacos, and that's exactly what you'll find in my Spring Fish Taco variation (page 183). These springy ingredients are readily available just about all year, so the classic is always in season. For some fun ways to change things up, skim through the seasonal variations or create your own.

When it comes to the fish itself, any kind of white fish will work well—if you've got the time, it's a good idea to check the Monterey Bay Aquarium website to see what's not currently in danger of overfishing. Luckily, thawed previously frozen fish works best for battering and frying, which means you can keep the ingredients for these tacos on hand in the freezer. Whether you're using fresh or frozen, you're going to need to pat those fillets as dry as possible before dredging and dipping.

Choose one or two vegetables from the list. When combining vegetables, it's usually a good idea to aim for one or two complementary flavors and textures (sweet and savory, creamy and crunchy, or rich and acidic). If you're going with a plain vegetable, it's always nice to top it with a little fresh lime juice.

Store leftover prepared components in separate containers in the fridge for a day or two—simply pop the fried fish pieces in a toaster oven until warmed through and crisped up, and prepare as usual.

Make Your Own Fish Taco Grid

Ingredients to swap in for the base recipe on the facing page

TO ESTIMATE

If you're winging it, just make sure you don't overload your tacos with too many ingredients. You should be able to close one side to the other.

SEASONAL PRODUCE

Summer

Grilled corn kernels (see page 141), drained Pico de Gallo (page 161), grilled blistered poblano peppers, grilled eggplant with charred skin peeled away, Peach Cucumber Salsa (page 181), sautéed zucchini/summer squash (or roast as on page 111)

Fall

Roasted okra (see page 21), pomegranate arils (use sparingly), fennel or cabbage slaw (see page 183), cumin-roasted squash or pumpkin (see page 182), southern-style greens (see page 183), sautéed chanterelles

Winter

Fennel or cabbage slaw (see page 183), cumin-roasted squash or pumpkin (see page 182), southern-style greens (see page 183), butter-sautéed leeks, roasted sweet potatoes

Spring

Sliced radishes, garlicky fava beans (see page 98), sautéed asparagus, sautéed morels

Anytime

Drained store-bought pico de gallo, Pineapple Salsa (page 164), sliced mango (use in moderation), spicy cabbage coleslaw (see page 183; if using cabbage slaw, don't include the chipotle mayo), steamed frozen corn with minced chipotle, pepitas (use sparingly), extra cilantro leaves

Fish Tacos

Makes 15 tacos

15 small corn tortillas, warmed for a
    few seconds in the microwave or on the stove
1 batch Beer-Battered Fish (recipe follows)
3 to 5 cups [600 g] prepared fruits/vegetables
    from the grid on the facing page, seasoned
1 large or 2 small ripe avocados, thinly sliced
    (230 g) and tossed with 1 tsp lime juice and a
    pinch of salt
½ cup [115 g] mayonnaise mixed with 1 to 2 Tbsp
    minced chipotle in adobo
Lime wedges, for serving

Build the tacos at the very last second before
eating (or set up a taco bar/taco table if you're
cooking for a group). Each tortilla should
be topped with a piece of fried fish, prepared
produce, avocado, and chipotle mayo, with lime
wedges on the side. Serve immediately.

Beer-Battered Fish

1 to 2 cups [210 to 420 g] neutral high-smoke-
    point oil, such as canola, sunflower, or peanut
¾ cup [100 g] all-purpose flour for batter, plus
    ⅓ cup [45 g] all-purpose flour for dredging
¼ tsp freshly ground black pepper
Additional spices (e.g., cumin, coriander, or
    paprika)
Salt
¾ cup [175 g] Mexican-style lager (half of a 12 oz
    [340 g] bottle; see Note)
19 oz [540 g] frozen tilapia, thawed and cut into
    15 pieces

Let about ¾ in [2 cm] of oil heat in a 10 in
[25 cm] nonstick or cast-iron sauté pan or skillet
set over medium to medium-high heat. The
oil is ready when you dip the end of the fish in
it and it immediately sizzles. Line a plate with
paper towels.

While the oil heats, in a small mixing bowl,
combine ¾ cup [100 g] of the flour, the black
pepper, additional spices, and ¼ tsp of salt, then
pour in the half bottle of beer and mix everything together (don't overmix). On a plate,
place the remaining ⅓ cup [45 g] of flour. Set
both aside.

Pat the fish dry with paper towels and season
with salt. It should lose quite a bit of water (it
will weigh 1 lb [455 g] after thawing and patting
dry). Once the oil is hot, dredge the fish in the
flour, shake off all the excess, and dip in the
batter. Remove the fish from the batter and flap
the fish on the side of the bowl once or twice to
let the excess batter drip off.

Gently lower the fish into the hot oil and then
repeat with about four more pieces. Let cook
for about 3 minutes per side (carefully flip them
once they've turned golden brown on one side,
and cook thick pieces for 1 minute longer).
Lower the heat if they brown too quickly and
keep an eye on them.

Remove the fried fish to the paper towel–
lined plate and work in batches until all the
pieces are fried.

Note: To make without beer: Simply add ½ tsp
of baking powder to the flour and replace the
beer with ¾ cup [175 g] of water and 1 tsp of
apple cider vinegar.

Summer Fish Tacos

Peach Cucumber Salsa,
Coriander Seed and Leaf

My dad has never been much of a cook; whenever it was his turn to make us lunch, he'd place slices of American cheese between slices of Wonder Bread, shred up the outside of the bread with cold butter, and pan-sear them on high until completely charred on the outside and ice cold on the inside. But he also introduced me to many of my favorites, such as buttered Pop-Tarts, rice with cinnamon sugar, deep-fried wild mushrooms we'd hunt with my grandpa, and of course, his famous peach pie.

Once every summer, our next-door neighbors would bring us a basket of peaches from their tree, and my dad would, apropos of nothing, bake the most incredible pie. Perhaps part of his momentary metamorphosis into an amazing baker had something to do with the quality of ingredients—there's nothing better than in-season peaches. That brings me to this salsa, which I'm pretty sure even my dad could do justice to. Make sure you use in-season peaches for the best flavor.

1 batch Peach Cucumber Salsa (recipe follows)
15 small corn tortillas
1 batch Beer-Battered Fish (page 179), made
    with ½ tsp ground coriander in the batter
Sliced avocado sprinkled with fresh lime juice
    and a pinch of salt, for serving
½ cup [115 g] mayonnaise mixed with 1 to 2 Tbsp
    minced chipotle in adobo
Lime wedges, for serving
Whole cilantro leaves, for serving

To assemble, top each tortilla with a piece of fried fish, peach cucumber salsa, avocado, chipotle mayo, and a few cilantro leaves and serve with lime wedges on the side.

Peach Cucumber Salsa

3 Persian cucumbers, cut into ¼ in [6 mm] dice
    (360 g)
2 ripe peaches, pitted and cut into ¼ in [6 mm]
    dice (230 g)
1 jalapeño, seeded, deribbed, and minced (20 g)
½ medium red onion, minced (90 g)
½ cup [20 g] chopped fresh cilantro
2 Tbsp fresh lime juice
1 Tbsp peach or apricot preserves
½ tsp lime zest
1 garlic clove, crushed through a press
½ tsp ground coriander seed
½ tsp salt

Combine the cucumbers, peaches, jalapeño, red onion, cilantro, lime juice, preserves, lime zest, garlic, coriander seed, and salt in a bowl and stir to combine.

Fall Fish Tacos

Cumin-Lime Pumpkin,
Pepitas, Pomegranate Arils

This cumin-lime roasting method works wonders on summer squash and zucchini as well as winter squash and pumpkin. Feel free to use just about any squash under the sun (if you're going with spaghetti squash, roast it whole, then break up and top with cumin and lime juice instead). Summer squashes will take less time to roast than winter ones. Your squash are done once they're tender but still firm, but even batches that you accidentally overcook can still be super delicious. If they go a little past the point of no return, let them go a bit longer until they're crispy on the outside and develop some golden-brown character.

6 cups [600 g] peeled ¼ in [6 mm] pumpkin wedges

1 Tbsp ground cumin

1 Tbsp fresh lime juice

2 tsp neutral oil, such as avocado or canola

2 tsp lime zest

½ tsp salt

15 small corn tortillas

1 batch Beer-Battered Fish (page 179), made with 1 tsp ground cumin and 1 tsp lime zest in the batter

Sliced avocado sprinkled with fresh lime juice and a pinch of salt, for serving

½ cup [115 g] mayonnaise mixed with 1 to 2 Tbsp minced chipotle in adobo

⅔ cup [85 g] pomegranate arils

¼ cup [35 g] raw pepitas

Lime wedges, for serving

Preheat the oven to 400°F [205°C].

Place the pumpkin on a baking sheet. In a small mixing bowl, combine the cumin, lime juice, oil, half of the lime zest, and the salt. Drizzle over the pumpkin, use your hands to evenly coat everything with the spice oil, distribute in an even layer, and roast for about 15 minutes, until lightly browned in spots and softened. Once it comes out of the oven, top evenly with the remaining half of lime zest. Set aside.

To assemble, top each tortilla with a piece of fried fish, a scoop of cumin-lime pumpkin, avocado, chipotle mayo, pomegranate arils, and pepitas and serve with lime wedges on the side.

Winter Fish Tacos

Southern-Style Greens, Corn

While traditional cabbage slaw is in season in the wintertime, I love changing things up and occasionally substituting slow-cooked greens for a warm and comforting take on a typically light and refreshing taco. I learned so much about southern greens from the Kitchenista Angela Davis's recipe. Angela says, "When I see a bowl of southern collards, I see the time somebody spent." Indeed, I can think of no better way to bring some love and warmth into the colder months. You can use any hearty greens you've got—just taste them as you cook and stop once they are done to your liking.

4 slices bacon, chopped (100 g; see Notes)

1 small onion, chopped (120 g)

3 cups [705 g] chicken, beef, or vegetable stock

1 Tbsp minced or pressed garlic

5 sprigs fresh thyme leaves, or ½ tsp dried

5 fresh sage leaves, torn, or ¼ tsp rubbed

1 Tbsp apple cider vinegar

1 Tbsp brown sugar

1 to 2 tsp Louisiana-style hot sauce

2 bunches collards or lacinato kale, stemmed and chopped (260 g leaves)

¾ cup [100 g] frozen corn

Salt (optional)

15 small corn tortillas

1 batch Beer-Battered Fish (page 179), made with 1½ tsp paprika in the batter

Sliced avocado sprinkled with fresh lime juice, for serving

½ cup [115 g] mayonnaise mixed with 1 to 2 Tbsp minced chipotle in adobo

Lime wedges, for serving

Spread the bacon in an even layer on the bottom of a large stockpot. Set over medium heat. Once the bacon starts sizzling, let cook for about 10 minutes, stirring occasionally. Once it's browned and crisp-chewy, add the onion. Let cook for about 5 minutes more, stirring occasionally, until softened and lightly browned. Add the stock, followed by the garlic, thyme, sage, apple cider vinegar, brown sugar, and hot sauce. Bring up to a simmer over high heat.

As soon as the stock simmers, add the collards and frozen corn. Fold together for about 1 minute, just until the collards shrink down and are halfway submerged. Season with salt if necessary (if your stock is salty, you may not need more).

Cover the pot, lower the heat to low, and simmer until the collards are very dark green and tender, about 30 minutes. Give it a stir once or twice while it cooks, and re-cover each time.

To assemble, top each tortilla with a piece of fried fish, collards and corn (see Notes), avocado slices, and chipotle mayo and serve with lime wedges on the side.

Notes: You can also use smoked turkey necks or ham hocks.

To serve the collards and corn, lift it out of the liquid with a slotted spoon before placing on a taco (some will cling to it, which is lovely).

Spring Fish Tacos

Radishes, Spicy Coleslaw

Whenever I visit family in Chicago and Phoenix, a typical day consists of visiting one of my favorite local taqerias and ordering a bunch of tacos de pescado and then heading home and making a big batch of tacos for friends and family. This recipe is perfect for one of those back-to-back taco days when you want to re-create the magic of that slaw and beer-battered crunch

you enjoyed at lunch. Coleslaw and radishes are abundant in early spring but also a classic way to serve Baja tacos, and luckily you can find quality ingredients for these just about any time of the year.

6½ cups [420 g] thinly shaved green cabbage
⅓ cup [70 g] mayonnaise
½ cup [20 g] chopped fresh cilantro
2 Tbsp fresh lime juice
1½ Tbsp minced chipotle in adobo sauce
½ tsp salt
15 small corn tortillas
1 batch Beer-Battered Fish (page 179)
Sliced avocado sprinkled with fresh lime juice, for serving
3 or 4 radishes, thinly sliced (65 g)
Lime wedges, for serving

Place the cabbage in a medium mixing bowl. Top with the mayonnaise, cilantro, lime juice, chipotle, and salt. Toss together until very evenly coated. Set aside (you can make the slaw and refrigerate it a few hours ahead of serving).

To assemble, top each tortilla with a piece of fried fish, a generous scoop of slaw, a few pieces of avocado, and a few slices of radish and serve with lime wedges on the side.

Sandwiches

I could write a whole book about sandwiches, one of the most varied foods of all time. Deli sandwiches are easy to mess up, but fortunately they're just as easy to get right. Simply look to your favorite salads and cheese board pairings for inspiration, never skip the condiments, and layer your ingredients together thoughtfully.

For this section's base recipe, I've put together some tips for crafting the perfect deli sandwich, and each seasonal variation features an entirely different kind of sandwich (everything from falafel to bánh mì), with extra instructions for easily adapting each to suit the season. So no matter the time of year, give the variations a browse, because they're all super flexible.

Make Your Own Deli Sandwich Grid

Incorporate some seasonal produce into the deli sandwich guide on the facing page.

SEASONAL COMBINATIONS

SUMMER

Thin tomato slices, thin nectarine slices, whole basil leaves, mozzarella, balsamic reduction, on lightly toasted ciabatta

FALL

Very thin fig slices, fresh goat cheese, prosciutto, arugula lightly dressed in a vinaigrette, on toasted multigrain (later in the fall or another time of the year, once figs are out of season, you can use a very moderate amount of chopped dried figs)

WINTER

Garlicky kale, sliced turkey, soft roasted squash, pepitas on rye

SPRING

Grated carrots, grated beets, lightly dressed spring greens, hummus, avocado, za'atar on multigrain

SEASONAL PRODUCE

Summer

Sautéed corn kernels, sliced tomatoes, cucumbers, peaches, or nectarine, sautéed zucchini or summer squash, very thinly sliced figs

Fall

Thinly sliced apples or fennel, grated raw carrots, beets, or parsnips, garlicky massaged kale (see the salad on page 61), roasted squash or pumpkin (see page 111), very thinly sliced figs, very thinly sliced persimmons later in the fall

Winter

Thinly sliced fennel, Caramelized Fennel (page 194), grated raw carrots, beets, or parsnips, garlicky massaged kale (see the salad on page 61), roasted squash or pumpkin (see page 111), very thinly sliced persimmon

Spring

Grated raw carrots, beets, or parsnips, thinly sliced radishes, blanched fava beans (see page 98), prepped fiddlehead ferns (see page 21), blanched peas/snap peas/snow peas, spring greens, greens from green onions

Anytime

Fresh herbs (especially in the summer), sautéed mushrooms, frozen corn, avocado with lime, garlic powder, and salt, alfalfa sprouts, shredded lettuce

A Perfect Deli Sandwich

A good deli sandwich should have the following features:

○ Something crunchy (e.g., crisp lettuce, crunchy bacon, potato chips, grated carrots, nuts, toasted bread)

○ Something rich or creamy (e.g., cheese, sardines, boiled eggs, pâté, hummus, mayo, avocado)

○ A bold flavor (e.g., fresh herbs, sriracha mayo, mustard, pesto, other bold condiments)

○ Something refreshing (e.g., lettuce, cucumbers, tomatoes, just about any high-moisture vegetable)

○ Something tangy (e.g., pickles, Lemon Tahini Sauce (page 152), lightly vinaigrette-dressed vegetables, balsamic reduction, fruit slices used sparingly)

○ Protein (e.g., lunchmeat, charcuterie, any thinly sliced meat, fried tofu, falafel, cheese

○ Something sweet (optional) (e.g., quince butter [see page 51], fruit, jam [see page 50])

○ Salt, if your ingredients aren't already salty

These categories aren't mutually exclusive, so if you're trying to keep things simple, you can always knock out two or three components with a single ingredient (e.g., a classic BLT checks almost every box with just three ingredients. Bacon is rich, crunchy, and boldly flavored, romaine is crunchy and refreshing, mayo is creamy and tangy, and the tomatoes just send it over the top to be one of the best sandwiches of all time).

Once you've chosen your ingredients, here are a few simple guidelines for successful layering:

○ Avoid piling a bunch of slippery ingredients together, lest the sandwich fall apart. Slippery ingredients such as sliced tomatoes and sliced cucumbers should be separated as much as possible by sturdy/grippy ingredients such as cheese slices and dry-spun lettuce leaves.

○ If you've slathered the bread with condiments or a spread such as hummus or pâté, follow that layer up with any super-loose ingredients that will stick to it (e.g., shredded carrots, sprouts, peas). This keeps loose ingredients from falling out of the sides and also keeps spreads and condiments from escaping by forming a sort of mortar.

○ When possible, wet ingredients such as tomatoes should never go right next to bread. Add a layer of something oily such as mayo or pesto to stave off the sogginess or use a lettuce leaf as a barrier.

○ Never put hot ingredients right next to ingredients that wilt easily.

○ Don't overstuff your sandwich, and try to keep it manageable in size. Go open-face if you're trying to cut back on carbs.

Summer Sandwiches

Shrimp Rolls, Boiled Corn, and Potatoes

Makes 6 rolls

Lobster rolls are my favorite summertime treat, but only when someone else is making them. When I very occasionally go to the trouble and expense of cooking whole lobsters, I serve them simply with clarified butter and think to myself, *I'll use the leftovers to make lobster rolls for lunch tomorrow*, but of course we never have any left.

But frankly, ever since I developed this shrimp roll recipe, lobster rolls haven't crossed my mind. You can absolutely adapt it to include lobster if you don't mind going to the trouble and expense, or you can easily sub in shredded or diced chicken breast or shredded salmon. Use about 2 medium chicken breasts, 2 large salmon fillets, or 3 to 4 lobster tails. You can also substitute celery, carrot, radish, apple, celeriac, fennel, or anything crunchy and flavorful in place of the bell pepper. If you're changing things around, you can also sub in your favorite spice blend, and/or replace the parsley with an equal amount of basil or cilantro, or 1 Tbsp dill.

1 tsp neutral oil, such as avocado or canola
6 cups [600 g] frozen raw peeled shrimp, thawed and drained, or 3 cups [500 g] thawed shrimp
Salt
¼ cup [60 g] mayonnaise
1 Tbsp fresh lemon juice
1 tsp Dijon mustard
1 tsp Seafood/Chicken Seasoning (recipe follows), plus more for serving
1 red bell pepper, thinly sliced (110 g)
2 Tbsp chopped fresh parsley or cilantro
8 small new potatoes, or 2 medium waxy potatoes cut into 8 pieces (300 g)
3 ears corn (775 g), broken into 3 pieces each
Butter, for the potatoes and corn sides
6 hot dog buns (preferably split-top or unsliced, optionally toasted)

Place a large sauté pan or skillet over medium-high heat. Once it's moderately hot, add the oil and swirl to coat. Add the shrimp and season with a pinch of salt. Sauté for about 3 minutes (longer if you're using larger shrimp), just until they're completely pink and opaque. Remove from the heat and set aside to cool for a few minutes.

While the shrimp is cooling, in a small mixing bowl, whisk together the mayonnaise, lemon juice, mustard, and the 1 tsp seafood seasoning and season with salt (if you're using homemade seasoning, use about ¼ tsp; if your store-bought seasoning has salt already, you may want to dial it back quite a lot).

Chop the cooled shrimp into ½ in [13 mm] pieces. Add to a medium mixing bowl, top with the dressing, bell pepper, and parsley, and toss together.

Chill the shrimp salad in the refrigerator for at least 1 to 2 hours.

When it's just about done chilling, bring a big stockpot of salted water to a boil over high heat. Add the potatoes and let them boil for 12 to 15 minutes, just until you can easily pierce them to their center with a knife. Boil the corn during the last 2 minutes. Drain everything and transfer to a plate. Top the hot corn and potatoes with butter.

If the rolls are not split already, use a serrated knife to slice through just the top without going through more than halfway, and then pull them open a bit more using your hands. Stuff the rolls with the shrimp salad, sprinkle the potatoes and corn with extra seafood seasoning and salt, and enjoy.

Seafood / Chicken Seasoning

2 tsp paprika
1 tsp celery seed
1 tsp powdered bay leaf
¼ tsp ground mustard
¼ tsp black pepper
Pinch of cinnamon

Combine the paprika, celery seed, powdered bay leaf, mustard, black pepper, and cinnamon in a small mixing bowl or jar and stir together.

Fall Sandwiches

Falafel with Lemon Tahini Sauce
and Lacto-Fermented Torshi

Makes 30 to 35 falafel

In Iraq, where my mom spent the early part of her childhood, you'll often find falafel with amba, a pickled mango influenced by South Asian cuisine and introduced to the country by Iraqi Jews. Throughout the Levant and Middle East, pink Pickled Turnips (page 81) and Jerusalem salad are ubiquitous toppings. And in my family, we love to eat our falafel with torshi, or pickled fall vegetables.

Perhaps falafel is so ubiquitously served with tangy sauces and pickles because its pH is slightly basic. Falafel can't be made with already-cooked chickpeas (it's like the difference between hash browns and fried mashed potatoes), so the only chance for the raw soaked chickpeas to cook through is in the deep fryer. Raising their pH helps them cook through faster and fluffier as they fry.

For the chickpeas

1½ cups [285 g] dried chickpeas
4 qt [3.8 L] water
4 tsp baking soda

For the falafel

2 qt [1.9 L] neutral oil, such as canola, sunflower, or peanut, for deep-frying
4 to 6 garlic cloves
1 cup [40 g] packed fresh cilantro leaves, plus more for garnish
2 green onions (40 g)
½ tsp paprika
½ tsp freshly ground black pepper
¼ tsp ground coriander
¼ tsp ground cumin
Pinch of cinnamon
1 Tbsp sesame seeds
1 tsp salt
¼ tsp baking soda
2 Tbsp all-purpose flour
1 Tbsp water
Pita, for serving
Torshi (recipe follows), for serving
Lemon Tahini Sauce (page 152), for serving

To soak the chickpeas: Place the chickpeas in a medium mixing bowl and cover with 2 qt [1.9 L] of water. Add half of the baking soda and stir until it dissolves. Cover and set aside at room temperature for a total of about 24 hours. About halfway through soaking, drain and rinse the chickpeas and top with 2 qt [1.9 L] fresh water and the other half of the baking soda. The timing doesn't need to be exact, but they must soak for at least a total of 16 hours, ideally 24. They must be hydrated all the way through to their cores.

To make the falafel: Once your chickpeas are done soaking, place a heavy Dutch oven or stockpot on a back burner (make sure it's safely out of the way). Fill it with the neutral oil and set over medium heat. Keep an eye on it to make sure it doesn't go above 380°F [193°C].

Place the garlic, cilantro, green onions, paprika, black pepper, coriander, cumin, cinnamon, sesame seeds, salt, and the ¼ tsp of baking soda in a food processor fitted with the blade attachment. Blend until everything is finely chopped.

Rinse the soaked chickpeas under cold water and add them to the food processor along with the flour and water. Blend until the mixture is the consistency of couscous (finely minced, not quite puréed) and bright green.

Shape the falafel into heaping tablespoons (not too large). Shape by gently squeezing a bit of mix together into a cohesive ball in one hand, and move it back and forth from hand to hand, gently squeezing it just until it holds together. Don't squeeze too tightly, or they will be dense.

Fry in batches of about six or seven. They're done once they're light and fluffy on the inside and dark and crunchy on the outside, 4 to 6 minutes total. Keep the temperature between 350°F and 380°F [177°C and 193°C].

Serve in pita with torshi, lemon tahini sauce, and extra cilantro for garnish.

Note: You can replace the torshi by making a simple Jerusalem salad instead: Combine three parts (by volume) diced tomato, three parts diced cucumber, one part finely diced red onion, and one part chopped fresh parsley and toss together with salt, fresh lemon juice, and extra-virgin olive oil.

Torshi (Middle Eastern Pickled Cauliflower, Carrots, and Hot Peppers)

This recipe is for lacto-fermented torshi, but if you don't feel like bothering with fermentation, make a simple refrigerator pickle instead: Bring to a simmer 1 cup [235 g] water, ½ cup [120 g]

vinegar, 1 Tbsp plus 1 tsp fine sea salt, and 2 tsp yellow curry powder. Place the veggies from the recipe in a clean jar, pour over the hot pickling liquid, and let cool to room temperature. Seal the jar after they've cooled, store in the refrigerator, and wait a day or two to enjoy (they will last for a week or two).

Different sea salts have different volumes, so if you choose to substitute a coarse or flaky sea salt, use an equal weight [20 g], not an equal volume. The salt allows the torshi to ferment safely, so don't cut back on it, and try to be as precise as possible. If you're new to fermentation, I highly recommend using the weight measurements for this recipe, although master fermenters can probably get away with playing it fast and loose with volumetric measurements and winging it.

1½ cups [350 g] filtered water
1 Tbsp plus 1 tsp [20 g] fine sea salt
2 tsp [4 g] yellow curry powder
½ small head cauliflower (6¼ oz [180g])
2 carrots, peeled (3½ oz [100 g])
1 jalapeño (¾ oz [20 g])

Combine the water, sea salt, and curry powder in a clean measuring cup. Stir together until the salt completely dissolves.

Make sure your vegetables are rinsed well. Cut the cauliflower into small, bite-size florets. Grate the carrots coarsely on a box grater. Very thinly slice the jalapeño.

Find a very clean 24 oz [710 ml] jar and sprinkle a thin layer of carrots on the bottom. Next, add a layer of cauliflower, followed by more carrots and a few slices of jalapeño. Shake the jar to help the carrots and jalapeños settle into the gaps (add more carrots to fill in the gaps completely). Repeat with another layer of cauliflower, carrots, and jalapeño, finishing with some carrots and jalapeños on top.

Top the produce with the brine so that everything is completely covered. If any veggies are floating up to the top, weight them down with a tiny ramekin or another food-safe ceramic or plastic object.

Cover the top with a clean towel or paper towel, secured tightly with a rubber band. Set aside at room temperature (between 70°F and 75°F [21°C and 24°C]) for 4 to 8 days (it will ferment more slowly in a cool kitchen). Do not screw on the lid, or it will explode.

During the first day or two at room temperature, you should start to notice some bubbles under the surface of the water. Gently jiggle the jar a couple of times a day to help the bubbles rise to the surface and dissipate, and check on it to make sure everything is fully submerged.

Once the bubbles have died down, transfer the jar to the refrigerator. After 48 hours bubble-free in the fridge, remove the towel and seal it with a lid. They should taste tangy and smell pleasantly funky and fermented but should not smell funky like rotting food. If the pickles smell off to you, discard them or check with a friend who is very experienced with fermenting if you're unsure. If they develop any visible mold or slime, discard them (mold has roots—do not take the risk). Fermented pickles will last in the refrigerator for a couple of months.

Winter Sandwiches

Meatball Sub with Caramelized Fennel

Makes 3 very large or 6 smaller servings

This recipe uses fresh cilantro instead of basil, which is much more reasonably priced (and usually much better quality) in the winter. Cilantro tends to bolt in the summertime, so it's a relatively cool weather–friendly crop. And while cilantro is still very easy to find in the summer, you can swap it out for basil if you've got a lot that you want to take advantage of, and you can use any of your favorite sautéed vegetables in place of the caramelized fennel. Lightly sautéed broccolini, asparagus, or zucchini all work great at various times of the year.

One 20 in [51 cm] baguette
1 batch Turkey Meatballs (page 219), made
    into 15 larger meatballs (2 heaping Tbsp
    [40 g] each) with ¾ cup [30 g] chopped fresh
    cilantro instead of basil
Caramelized Fennel (recipe follows)
½ batch Unseasonably Good Tomato Sauce
    (page 223)
1 cup [100 g] shredded mozzarella
Handful fresh cilantro leaves or fennel fronds,
    for serving

Preheat your broiler for just a few minutes.

Slice your baguette open so that it stays connected on one side. Cut into three separate pieces and open each like a book. Place them open-side up under the broiler just until they toast (depending on your broiler, this can take between 1 and 5 minutes—don't wander away, and keep a very close eye on them).

Remove from the broiler and add the meatballs, followed by half the caramelized fennel,

1 cup [240 g] of the tomato sauce, the rest of the fennel, and the mozzarella.

Place back under the broiler for another few minutes, just until the cheese bubbles and browns in spots.

Garnish with cilantro at the table and serve with extra tomato sauce on the side.

Caramelized Fennel

4 Tbsp [55 g] unsalted butter
2 fennel bulbs, very thinly sliced (560 g)
½ tsp salt

Place the butter in a large nonstick sauté pan or skillet set over medium-high heat. Once it melts, add the sliced fennel and salt. Stir together and cook for about 30 minutes, stirring occasionally. Lower the heat gradually throughout the cooking until medium-low and keep an eye on the fennel so it does not burn. The fennel will soften, then fall apart a bit and turn very dark brown. It's done once it's caramelized, sweet, and very soft.

Spring Sandwiches

Bánh Mì

Makes 4 servings

Bánh mì are great year-round, but my favorite version incorporates pickled cool-weather vegetables. Later in the summer, I throw in some long, thin slices of cucumbers and jalapeños, traditional additions in Saigon-style bánh mì. You'll find endless variations out there, with lots of delicious Vietnamese sausages and head cheeses, but when I'm making it at home, I usually go with panfried tofu.

In the United States, tofu is often marketed to vegetarians, but in much of the world it's just another delicious ingredient that everyone eats, and it's not surprising to see it paired with meat for some extra-savory flavor. So here you'll find it along with chicken liver pâté, but if you're a vegetarian, you can always make a vegetarian pâté instead. Use store-bought, or try Andrea Nguyen's pâté from her book *Into the Vietnamese Kitchen* (you'll also find an edamame pâté in her book, *The Banh Mi Handbook*).

10½ oz [300 g] firm tofu, cut into ½ in [13 mm] thick rectangles
1 Tbsp fresh lime juice
1 Tbsp Maggi sauce or sweet soy sauce, plus more for serving
1 tsp fish sauce
1 tsp garlic powder
One 24 in [60 cm] baguette (soft on the inside, a little crusty on the outside)
¼ cup [60 g] mayonnaise
1 Tbsp sriracha
Neutral oil, such as avocado or canola, for frying
3 Tbsp [30 g] cornstarch

3 oz [85 g] chicken liver pâté

6 to 8 green onions, green parts only (35 g)

1 bunch cilantro, leaves and tender stems only
(30 g)

1 cup [150 g] packed and wrung-out Pickled
Carrots and Daikon Radishes (recipe follows)

Place the tofu pieces on a clean kitchen towel
and cover with the other side of the towel. Press
down gently until much of the moisture has
been absorbed.

Combine the lime juice, Maggi sauce, fish
sauce, and garlic powder on a plate. Flip the
tofu around in the sauce so it's covered. Let
sit for about 15 minutes, giving it another flip
whenever you think to.

Slice the baguette open lengthwise, leaving
one side attached. Scoop out about half of
the interior.

Stir together the mayonnaise and sriracha in a
small mixing bowl.

Preheat a sauté pan or skillet with about ¼ in
[6 mm] of neutral oil over medium heat. Line a
plate with paper towels.

Place the cornstarch on a plate. Roll one piece
of tofu around in the cornstarch until evenly
coated, then brush away the excess. Repeat
with the other pieces. Once the oil is hot, add
the tofu to the pan in a single layer. Cook for
about 4 minutes on one side, then flip to cook
for about 4 minutes on the second side. Once
they're golden brown, remove to the paper
towel–lined plate.

Slather one side of the bread with the pâté and
the other side with the sriracha mayo. Add the
tofu to the pâté side and add the green onions,
cilantro, and pickled carrots and radishes to the
sriracha mayo side. Close it and drizzle a little
Maggi sauce through the opening (serve with
more sauce at the table).

Pickled Carrots and Daikon Radishes

½ peeled daikon or white radish, julienned
(260 g)

1 carrot, peeled and julienned (90 g)

1 cup [235 g] water

1½ Tbsp granulated sugar

2 tsp salt

⅓ cup [80 g] rice wine vinegar

Tightly nest the radish and carrots in two small
heatproof jars or a large container.

Combine the water, sugar, and salt in a small
saucepan. Place over high heat and bring just
to a simmer. Remove from the heat, add the
vinegar, and let cool for a few minutes until it's
just warm and the sugar has dissolved. Pour the
cooled liquid over the vegetables. Make sure
they're fully submerged, let the jar cool, then
cover and store in the refrigerator. They're
ready to eat after 2 hours, but they'll be better
the next day (and they keep for weeks).

Whole Chicken

While you can roast or grill a chicken just about any time of the year, there are so many techniques that involve seasonal cues and produce. The seasonal variations in this section feature four different chicken-cooking techniques that easily incorporate seasonal produce pretty much year-round. While you might be more predisposed to grill in the summer or roast in the winter, I've included lots of ideas for making each of these recipes work beautifully for other seasons.

Whatever technique you're using to cook your chicken, there are a few essential things to keep in mind:

1. ALWAYS BRINE YOUR CHICKEN.

There's no way around it—deeply infusing your chicken with salt helps it stay super juicy as it cooks (even if you overcook it by several degrees). You can achieve this with either a wet or dry brine, and I almost always prefer dry-brining.

While dry-brining is arguably the tastiest, it's also the easiest to throw together and the hardest to mess up. Instead of creating a salt solution, you simply sprinkle your chicken all over with salt and let it rest in the fridge for a while. Since you sprinkle salt directly on the chicken, it's easy to gauge how much you're using, and it's difficult to oversalt it. Pretty much all the salt you sprinkle will end up in the chicken (no more, no less), even if you let it keep brining for days.

On the other hand, with a wet brine, it's harder to intuit how much salt will transfer from the solution to the chicken, so it can't always be used flexibly, and if your brine is very concentrated, you have to remove the chicken from the solution at a certain point to make sure it doesn't become too salty. Wet-brining is not only high maintenance but also messy, so I just stay away from it altogether.

While you can absolutely estimate with a dry brine, aim for a little over ½ tsp table salt per 1 lb of bone-in meat if using the US system, or 1 g table salt per 130 g bone-in meat if using the metric system. To calculate the amount of salt with the metric system, just divide the weight of the chicken in grams by 130 (or divide the weight in kilograms by 0.13)—the number you end up with is how many grams of table salt you should use. To calculate the amount of salt with US measurements, just divide the number of pounds by 2—the number you end up with is the number of teaspoons of table salt (just round up slightly).

While kosher salt is a popular choice among chefs and serious home cooks, I like to develop recipes using table salt because it tends to be more consistent across different brands, and nearly every single kitchen has it on hand. If you prefer using kosher salt (or fine sea salt, or whatever salt you've got), feel free to use it here (or in just about any recipe in this book). If you make the swap, use your salt of choice entirely to taste (different salts have different volumes and different sodium contents).

While it's hard to over-salt a whole chicken, be more cautious if you're working with thinly sliced pieces (as on page 205). If you tend to like things on the less-seasoned side, feel free to cut back the recommended salt amount so that it suits your own taste. But don't be too stingy—it is the key to the right flavor and texture.

2. KEEP DIFFERENT COOK TIMES IN MIND WHEN COMBINING CHICKEN AND PRODUCE.

Whether you're grilling, roasting, or sautéing, make sure you add vegetables in stages if they take different amounts of time to cook. My winter roasted chicken with potatoes recipe has you cook everything together in one pot, because the potatoes will become crispy and fluffy by the time the chicken is done. If you were to try roasting a chicken along with cherry tomatoes, on the other hand, you might wish to add them in later in the roasting if you'd like them to remain mostly whole (or add them earlier if you don't mind them disintegrating).

Similarly, when you're grilling vegetables alongside chicken, make sure you skewer them separately so you can control their doneness. Just about anything in the roasted vegetable section that you can skewer (see page 110) can be grilled. I like to grill most vegetables over high heat, lowering it to medium after a few minutes for certain things that take a little longer to cook through (such as tough things like squash and root vegetables). Vegetables and fruits that only need to char and don't need to cook through (such as tomatoes, figs, peaches, or anything else you'd eat raw) should be cooked for only a few minutes over the highest possible heat.

3. ROAST IT AT 425°F [220°C], AND CHECK FOR DONENESS ONCE IT'S NICELY BROWNED.

Dry-brining your chicken means you can get away with fudging the doneness temperature a bit more than usual. Even if you go a few degrees over, your chicken will remain juicy. But do keep an eye on the internal temperature, and make sure you wait for it to reach 165°F [74°C] without going too far over. If you don't have a thermometer, stop roasting once the juices run clear and are no longer pinkish. Always let your chicken rest for about 10 minutes before slicing and serving.

Summer Grilled Chicken

Dry-Rubbed Grilled Chicken Parts with
Skewered Summer Veggies

Makes 4 servings

Grilling is the perfect opportunity to spend some time outside and not worry about heating up your home. Separate your chicken into parts or butterfly it to give yourself more control—grills don't heat very evenly, but when you're working with separate pieces, you can remove them from the grill one by one as they finish cooking.

For the best grilled vegetables, be sure to skewer them separately, again to control their doneness. You can mix things up in the summer-time, subbing in some skewered eggplant or cherry tomatoes or even a few ears of corn. Or if you're the year-round grilling type, use whatever grillable seasonal produce you've got around. Anything that can be roasted at a high tempera-ture and can be skewered can be grilled over high heat (see page 110 for ideas).

3 to 4 lb [1.4 to 1.8 kg] whole chicken
Salt
1 batch Spice Rub for Chicken (recipe follows)
¼ cup [75 g] mirin
¼ cup [60 g] soy sauce
2 Tbsp rice wine vinegar
1 Tbsp brown sugar
1 green onion, quartered lengthwise (30 g)
1 small onion, cut into 1 in [2.5 cm] dice and
  broken into layers (100 g)
1 zucchini, cut into 1 in [2.5 cm] dice (200 g)
1 or 2 bell peppers, cut into 1 in [2.5 cm] dice
  (265 g)
Olive oil

Separate your chicken pieces (or buy a butch-ered whole chicken), ideally four half-breast pieces (two with wing attached), two thighs, and two drumsticks.

Salt the chicken pieces all over with 1¾ to 2¼ tsp of salt (a little over ½ tsp table salt per 1 lb of bone-in meat, or 1 g salt per 130 g bone-in meat).

Sprinkle the chicken all over with the spice rub and pat it on top of and under the skin. Be sure the rub is evenly coating the chicken all over, even in the nooks and crannies, and do not skimp on it. Place the seasoned chicken in a resealable container or plastic bag and refriger-ate for at least 3 hours, up to overnight.

Combine the mirin, soy sauce, vinegar, brown sugar, and green onion in a small sauce-pan. Bring to a boil over medium-high heat, lower the heat to medium-low, and simmer at a low boil for about 5 minutes, until it becomes a syrupy glaze. Remove the green onions (enjoy them!) and set the sauce aside to cool.

Skewer the onions, zucchini, and bell peppers separately.

When you're ready to cook the chicken, preheat your grill over medium-low heat with the top closed and coat the chicken in a light layer of oil.

Once the grill reaches 340°F [170°C], place your chicken pieces on the grill, close the grill lid, and keep an eye on the temperature after the first couple of minutes. Adjust to make sure it's maintaining around 340°F [170°C], no higher than 350°F [180°C]. Cook for 20 to 35 minutes, flipping the chicken pieces once or twice so they sear evenly, and brushing them with the sauce once or twice during the second half of cooking.

Place the onions on the grill while the chicken cooks. The onions should cook for at least 25 minutes, until they've softened and charred. About halfway through cooking, brush the onions with a light layer of sauce.

Once the chicken registers an internal temperature of 165°F [74°C], transfer it to a plate to rest.

Increase the temperature to high. Place the vegetable skewers on the hot grill, brush all the vegetables with a light layer of sauce, and let cook with the lid up for about 12 minutes for zucchini and 15 minutes for bell peppers. Frequently rotate and brush with more light layers of sauce as they cook. Discard any leftover sauce, place everything together on a platter, and enjoy.

Spice Rub for Chicken

1 Tbsp brown sugar
1 Tbsp sweet paprika
1 Tbsp ground cumin
1 tsp garlic powder
1 tsp dried thyme
½ tsp cinnamon
½ tsp celery seed (optional)

Add the brown sugar, paprika, cumin, garlic powder, dried thyme, cinnamon, and celery seed to a small mixing bowl or jar and stir to combine.

Fall Roasted Chicken

Butterflied Chicken and Stuffing with Brussels Sprouts, Celery, Apples, and Herbs

Makes 4 servings

Growing up, we always made box-mix stuffing for Thanksgiving. I usually opt for homemade these days, but there's something about the box mix's crumbly texture that my stuffing has always missed. Then one day it occurred to me to add a handful of bread crumbs to the bread cubes; the combination results in lots of little crumbles and a bunch of big chewy pieces. You can use store-bought crumbs or make your own with stale leftover bread.

3 to 4 lb [1.4 to 1.8 kg] whole chicken
Salt
1 small boule crusty bread, cut into 1 in [2.5 cm] cubes (300 g)
½ cup [55 g] bread crumbs
1 Tbsp packed fresh thyme leaves, plus more for garnish
1 Tbsp packed chopped fresh sage leaves, plus more for garnish
2 celery stalks, thinly sliced (110 g)
1 Granny Smith apple, thinly sliced (100 g)
8 Brussels sprouts, quartered (150 g)
1 Tbsp minced or pressed garlic
½ tsp freshly ground black pepper
1⅓ cups [315 g] chicken or vegetable stock, plus more for basting
1 large egg
Extra-virgin olive oil, for coating the chicken

Butterfly your chicken, then salt the chicken back and front with 1¾ to 2¼ tsp of salt (a little over ½ tsp of table salt per 1 lb of bone-in meat, or 1 g of salt per 130 g of bone-in meat). Place the seasoned chicken in a sealable container or plastic bag and refrigerate for at least 3 hours, up to overnight.

Preheat the oven to 350°F [180°C] once your chicken is done dry-brining.

Place the bread cubes on a rimmed baking sheet in an even layer, spaced out as much as possible. Bake for about 20 minutes, so that they dry out and turn light golden brown. Transfer to a large mixing bowl, but don't bother washing the pan.

Raise the oven temperature to 425°F [220°C].

Add the bread crumbs, thyme, sage, celery, apple, Brussels sprouts, garlic, and black pepper to the bowl with the bread (don't add salt, unless your chicken broth is low sodium—the chicken drippings will add a decent amount of salt as well).

In a separate bowl, whisk together the stock and egg. Add the chicken stock mixture to the bread mixture and slowly and gently fold everything together until the liquid is absorbed (about 2 minutes).

Place the chicken in the center of the baking sheet and lightly coat its surface with olive oil. Surround with an even layer of stuffing. Place in the oven.

About 30 minutes into roasting, use tongs to gently flip sections of the stuffing so that the browned top bits face down and the pieces soaked in drippings face up. If there are no drippings and the stuffing is not soaked underneath, drizzle with 2 to 3 Tbsp [30 to 45 g] of stock or water first (taste a bite—if it needs salt, use stock, otherwise use water. You may not need to use any extra liquid at all, depending on how many drippings your bird gives off and how quickly they evaporate in your oven). Repeat this about every 20 minutes or any time you think the stuffing is getting too crispy on top, but be careful not to overdo it with any added liquid.

Roast for 50 to 70 minutes total, until the chicken registers an internal temperature of 165°F [74°C] and the stuffing is golden brown, chewy throughout, and crispy on top. Let the chicken rest for about 10 minutes before carving. If you like your stuffing extra soft, make sure you drizzle it with any remaining drippings and let it sit for 10 minutes, covered in a serving dish, before serving. Top with a little more fresh sage and thyme before serving.

Winter Roasted Chicken

Citrus-Stuffed, Oven-Roasted Chicken with Lemon-Pepper Greek Potatoes

Makes 4 servings

This is my favorite way to cook chicken on a cold winter day. As the potatoes soak up all the lemon and chicken juices, they become incredibly tender on the bottom and crispy on top. The David Leite–inspired garlic butter and lemon slices under the skin baste the chicken without any babysitting. It's wonderful served with a side of garlicky winter greens. Feel free to experiment with all your favorite root vegetables with this one—anything that holds up to moderately long roasting works great (carrots, celeriac, and parsnips are perfect, and sweet potatoes work well as long as you don't mind them softening), so it's great for cold-weather produce.

3 to 4 lb [1.4 to 1.8 kg] whole chicken
Salt
3 Tbsp [45 g] unsalted butter, at room temperature
2 Tbsp minced or pressed garlic
2 tsp freshly ground black pepper
2 tsp dried thyme
1 lemon, very thinly sliced and seeded (100 g)
3 russet potatoes, cut into ½ in [13 mm] wedges (615 g)
1 Tbsp fresh lemon juice, plus more for basting
1 tsp lemon zest
1 tsp olive oil

Salt the chicken inside and out with 1¾ to 2¼ tsp of salt (a little over ½ tsp of table salt per 1 lb of bone-in meat, or 1 g of salt per 130 g of bone-in meat). It may look like too much, but remember that a whole chicken has very little surface area. Place the seasoned chicken in a sealable container or plastic bag and refrigerate for at least 3 hours, up to overnight.

Once your chicken is ready to roast, preheat the oven to 425°F [220°C].

Mix together the butter with half of the garlic, half of the black pepper, and half of the thyme.

Transfer the chicken to an ovenproof casserole dish or large Dutch oven (the chicken should fit in it with a 1 to 3 in [2.5 to 7.5 cm] gap around it). Loosen the skin on the breast and thighs by using your fingers or the back of a spoon (careful not to tear it, or it will split more as it roasts). Spread the garlic butter under the skin (if your chicken is cold, use a little at a time, otherwise it will harden and become difficult to work with). Once you've used all the butter, place slightly overlapping lemon slices under the breast and thigh skin. Tuck the wings behind its back. Before washing your hands, rub whatever garlic butter is left on the outside of the chicken.

Put the potatoes in a mixing bowl, top with the lemon juice, lemon zest, olive oil, remaining garlic, remaining black pepper, and remaining thyme, and season with about ½ tsp of salt. Toss together until evenly coated. Place the potatoes in the gap between the chicken and the sides of the pan and sprinkle with any bits that didn't cling.

Transfer the chicken to the oven. About 45 minutes into roasting, baste the potatoes with a little more lemon juice (about 1 Tbsp) and tilt the chicken so that any juices in its cavity spill out over the potatoes. Roast for 60 to 90 minutes total, until the chicken registers an internal temperature of 165°F [74°C] and the potatoes are meltingly tender on the bottom and crispy on top. Let the chicken rest for about 10 minutes before carving and serve with the potatoes and a little spoonful of pan juices.

Note: If you want to end up with a delicious pot of chicken stock in addition to a whole roast chicken, be sure to start by roasting everything in a big Dutch oven. After you're done carving and serving right from the pot, transfer any leftover potatoes and chicken meat to a storage container, but leave the chicken bones, lemon bits, and any juices behind in the pot. Top off the chicken bones with 2 in [5 cm] of water and set on the stove to simmer for 1 hour or longer, then strain away the spent solids. It'll become the most intensely flavorful chicken stock you've ever made, and you won't have had to dirty a single extra dish or prep any additional vegetables. Just don't forget to season it with salt.

Spring Chicken Cutlets

Chicken Piccata with Asparagus

Makes 4 servings

Chicken piccata goes so wonderfully with anything green and zesty, so it's ideal for spring produce. Here, I've included asparagus, but you can absolutely substitute fiddlehead ferns (see page 21), green beans later on in the summer, or Tuscan kale in the fall and winter. Anything that can be sautéed and served with lemon will work great.

3 to 4 lb [1.4 to 1.8 kg] whole chicken, or deboned whole chicken, or 3 or 4 chicken breasts
Salt
½ tsp freshly ground black pepper
⅓ cup plus 1 Tbsp [55 g] all-purpose flour
3 Tbsp [45 g] unsalted butter
Extra-virgin olive oil

3 garlic cloves, crushed through a press
1 cup [235 g] chicken stock
¼ cup [60 g] fresh lemon juice
¼ cup [40 g] rinsed capers
1 large bunch asparagus, trimmed (200 g)
¼ cup [10 g] chopped fresh parsley
Thin lemon wedges, for serving

Separate your chicken into pieces, then debone them (if using whole, bone-in).

Butterfly the chicken breast pieces: First remove the tenderloin with a little bit of breast meat attached to it to make one cutlet. Then carefully slice down the middle of the remaining breast like a hamburger bun, pressing it flat on the cutting board while keeping your fingers completely out of the way. Repeat with the other breast. You should end up with three flat pieces from each breast. The leg and thigh meat should be similarly flat already. (See Note.)

Sprinkle the chicken cutlets very evenly with 1 to 1½ tsp [5.5 to 8 g] of salt and the black pepper and refrigerate for at least 1 hour, up to overnight. If you didn't do a great job clearing the meat from the bones, use a touch less salt, and if your chicken is gigantic, use a touch more. Don't salt it as liberally as you would a bone-in chicken.

Once the chicken has dry-brined for an hour or so, place ⅓ cup [45 g] of the flour on a large plate. Place a large sauté pan or skillet over medium-high heat and add the butter and ¼ cup [55 g] of olive oil. Once the butter melts and sizzles loudly, dredge a piece of chicken in the flour, shake off the excess, and gently lower into the oil. Repeat with two to three more chicken pieces (don't crowd the pan, and lower the heat if they brown too quickly or the oil gets too hot) and let cook for 3 to 4 minutes before flipping, then cook for about 3 minutes on the second side. They should be golden brown all over and completely cooked through. Transfer them to a plate and repeat in batches.

Once the chicken is all fried, pour off all but about 2 Tbsp of oil from the pan. Add the garlic and the remaining 1 Tbsp of flour to the pan. Stir together for just 30 seconds, then add the chicken stock and lemon juice. Add most of the capers (reserve some for garnish), stir together, taste, and add a little more salt if needed. Bring up to a simmer and let it bubble for about 2 minutes, just until it thickens very slightly. Set aside briefly off the heat while you sauté the asparagus.

Set another pan over medium-high heat. Once hot, add about 1 tsp of olive oil, swirl to coat, and then add the asparagus. Season with a pinch of salt and gently toss around for about 3 minutes, just until they turn brighter green and are slightly softened. Remove from the heat.

Bring the sauce back to a simmer and return the chicken to the pan. Toss the pieces around to make sure they're coated, then toss in the asparagus to coat it. Garnish with the parsley, lemon wedges, and any reserved capers and serve with a little bit of the sauce.

Note: Save the wings, skin, and/or the carcass for another use, such as stock (add to the Vegetable Stock on page 139 to make it chicken stock).

Ravioli

While many of my favorite dishes are magnets for leftover ingredients, ravioli is the best for using up small amounts of truly random bits and pieces, and it's the least likely dish to *seem* as if it were made from odds and ends. Flavor concentration is the key to getting a lot of goodness out of such a small amount of filling.

To concentrate your vegetables' flavors, you'll need to sauté them until they shrink down and caramelize. The following recipe has you covered, but keep this concept in mind as you go, and remember to never pile a bunch of watery raw or boiled veggies into your filling, and never skip the additional straining when applicable. Your filling should be thick and creamy and should pack a punch.

Once you've filled your ravioli, you can boil them right away or freeze them in their raw state for later. To freeze, simply place filled ravioli in a single layer on a parchment-lined baking sheet, freeze solid, and transfer them to a freezer bag to store for several months. Boil them right from frozen, and add an extra minute to their cook time.

Make Your Own Ravioli Grid

Ingredients to swap in for the base recipe on the facing page

HERBS

+ **Leafy**

  Cilantro, dill, parsley, chives, basil

+ **Woody**

  Thyme, rosemary, sage, oregano

PASTA SAUCES

+ Syrupy roasted tomato sauce (see page 221)
+ Pesto, in many forms (page 226)
+ Unseasonably Good Tomato Sauce (page 223)
+ Garlic herb brown butter (see page 224)
+ Barely Cooked Fresh Tomato Sauce (page 212)

TO ESTIMATE

If you're starting with something that takes up a lot more space (spinach, kale, etc.), keep in mind that you'll need to start with a lot more than 4 cups. Likewise, if you start with something that has a lot of water (e.g., zucchini, spinach, etc.), keep in mind you may need to use a larger amount [500 g] to end up with a decent quantity. Just make sure you end up with 2 to 3 cups [300 g] of produce after cooking it.

SEASONAL PRODUCE

Summer

Corn kernels, coarsely chopped green beans, thinly sliced zucchini or summer squash, chopped figs (use raw, and include another vegetable or meat), chopped bell peppers, chopped Swiss chard leaves

Fall

Chopped figs (use raw, and include another vegetable or meat), thinly sliced fennel, large-diced sweet potatoes/squash/pumpkin, chopped blanched broccoli rabe, chopped broccoli or broccolini, roasted chestnuts (do not sauté; see page 62), chanterelles, chopped spinach or kale

Winter

Thinly sliced fennel, large-diced sweet potatoes/squash/pumpkin, chopped blanched broccoli rabe, chopped broccoli or broccolini, spinach, kale

Spring

Chopped broccoli or broccolini, chopped blanched broccoli rabe, coarsely chopped asparagus or prepped fiddlehead ferns (see page 21), peas, thinly sliced morels, chopped spinach or kale

Anytime

Thinly sliced mushrooms, frozen spinach (wring out well instead of sautéeing)

Ravioli

Makes 60 ravioli

For the pasta dough
3 cups [390 g] all-purpose flour
4 large eggs
1 large egg yolk
1 Tbsp extra-virgin olive oil
½ tsp salt

Can substitute small wonton
wrappers instead of pasta dough

For the filling
1 Tbsp olive oil
**2½ to 5 cups [400 to 500 g] produce (see grid
     on facing page)**
One 8 oz [225 g] container ricotta
**½ cup [25 g] finely grated Parmesan cheese
     (optional)**
1 large egg yolk
**¼ cup [10 g] chopped fresh leafy herbs (1 Tbsp
     dried) or 1 to 2 Tbsp chopped fresh woody
     herbs (1½ tsp dried)**
3 garlic cloves, crushed through a press
2 tsp citrus zest (optional)
¼ cup [35 g] toasted pine nuts (optional)
¼ to ½ tsp salt
¼ tsp freshly ground black pepper
Sauce of choice, for serving

To make the pasta dough: Reserve ¼ cup [30 g]
of the flour and set aside. Combine the majority
of the flour along with the eggs, yolk, olive oil,
and salt in the bowl of a stand mixer (or knead
by hand). Bring it all together at medium speed
with the dough hook. Once it comes together

into a firm dough, continue kneading while you
slowly sprinkle in some of the remaining flour,
until it becomes very firm yet still pliable (about
3 minutes total). You will likely only need half
of the remaining flour. You may need to pause
to scrape the dough down or to knead by hand
for a minute if your mixer has trouble bringing
it together.

Once you've kneaded it, smooth the dough
into a ball, wrap tightly in plastic wrap, and let
rest for about 30 minutes to 1 hour. Make the
filling while you wait.

To make the filling: Place a nonstick or cast-
iron skillet over medium-high heat and let it
preheat for a few minutes. Once hot, add the
olive oil, followed by the produce (work in
batches with one vegetable at a time, so everything finishes cooking at the same time). Stir
occasionally, and remove from the heat once
they're reduced in size and have caramelized
in spots. If you're using anything like squash
or sweet potato, mash it after sautéing. If your
produce gives off a lot of moisture (such as
fresh spinach or mushrooms), be sure to let it all
cook off, and strain very wet things like spinach
using the method on page 213. You should end
up with 1½ to 2½ cups [300 g] after sautéing. If
it seems you have too much, set some aside for
another project.

Move your produce to a medium mixing
bowl. Add the ricotta, Parmesan (if using), egg
yolk, herbs, garlic, citrus zest (if using), pine
nuts (if using), salt, and pepper. Mix well.

Bring a large stockpot of water to a boil.

To assemble: Lightly flour a clean countertop and set up a pasta roller. Divide the dough into eight pieces and pat each piece into a flat oval. Roll two of them out to about number 3, into 13 by 5 in [33 by 12 cm] rectangles. Start with the widest setting and then gradually scale it down. Flour them well once they're rolled out.

Fill the ravioli by using a mold or doing it freehand on the counter. If using a mold, create indentations. Evenly distribute 12 heaping tsp [10 g each] of filling (do not overstuff).

Dab lightly around the filling with water, and place the other rectangle on top. Lift one half up and slowly lower it back down, patting as you go to make sure all the air bubbles are out. Repeat with the other side. Trim them into separate pieces using your mold or a knife.

Repeat with the remaining dough and filling. Collect the scraps as you go, form into a ball, divide in half, and let rest for at least 10 minutes so you can roll out one last batch.

Simmer the ravioli about 12 at a time for about 3 minutes. Serve with your sauce of choice.

Note: If you want to incorporate some meat, use the following quantities:

- 1½ to 2½ cups [230 g] produce with 1¼ cups [225 g] seared and chopped Italian sausage (from about 3 links). After sautéing, you should end up with about 1 cup [120 g] produce. (See Summer Ravioli for a sausage ravioli example.)
- 2 cups [235 g] sautéed or 1 cup [235 g] puréed produce with 10 pieces [250 g] bacon, chopped, pan-seared until crisp-chewy, and fat discarded. (See page 65 to learn how to cook pieces of bacon this way.)

Summer Ravioli

Zucchini, Italian Sausage, Black Pepper, Barely Cooked Fresh Tomato Sauce

In the middle of summer, when tomatoes are at their best, I want to preserve as much of their fresh flavor as possible, so they taste nothing like those that come from a can. For the sauce that accompanies these sunny ravioli, you simply fry the tomatoes until they start to fall apart, and stop as soon as some of their juices evaporate and they meld into a barely cooked sauce. You can make the sauce ahead of time, or you can allow the tomatoes to dissolve those delicious bits stuck on the pan after you make the filling.

Extra-virgin olive oil
1 medium zucchini, sliced into thin half-moons (230 g)
½ tsp salt
3 Italian sausages, removed from their casing (255 g)
Barely Cooked Fresh Tomato Sauce (recipe follows)
¼ cup [10 g] packed fresh basil leaves
3 garlic cloves, crushed through a press
One 8 oz [225 g] container ricotta
¼ tsp freshly ground black pepper
1 large egg yolk
1 batch fresh, rested pasta dough (see page 209) or 60 small wonton wrappers

Place a large sauté pan or skillet over medium-high heat and let it preheat for a few minutes. Once hot, add about 1 Tbsp of olive oil, followed by the zucchini and ¼ tsp of the salt. Let the zucchini cook for about 8 minutes, giving them a gentle stir every few minutes. They should shrink down significantly, caramelize, and be very soft by the time they're done.

Transfer the zucchini to a medium mixing bowl, and leave the pan on the heat.

Add about 1 tsp of oil to the pan, followed by the sausage. Break it up with a spoon into very small pieces. Cook for about 5 minutes, stirring occasionally. The sausage should brown and caramelize. Once it's browned all over, transfer to the bowl. If you haven't made the tomato sauce, start making it at this point in the dirty pan.

Bring a large stockpot of water to a boil.

Coarsely chop the basil leaves and add to the mixing bowl with the filling. Add the garlic, ricotta, pepper, and egg yolk and season with the remaining ¼ tsp of salt. Mix together until well combined.

Roll out the pasta dough and fill the ravioli with the zucchini-sausage mixture according to the instructions on page 211.

Simmer the ravioli about 12 at a time for about 3 minutes. Transfer the cooked ravioli to the tomato sauce, stir to coat, and serve.

Barely Cooked Fresh Tomato Sauce

1 to 2 Tbsp olive oil
3 garlic cloves, crushed through a press
5 tomatoes, cut into large dice (690 g)
¼ tsp black pepper
¼ tsp salt
¼ cup [10 g] packed basil leaves

If you're starting with a dirty pan from making the filling, lower the pan's heat to medium. Otherwise, set a pan over medium heat and let it preheat for a few minutes.

Once the pan is hot, add the olive oil followed immediately by the garlic, and cook for about 30 seconds. Immediately add the tomatoes, pepper, and salt and cook, stirring occasionally, for 5 to 8 minutes, just until the tomatoes break down into a chunky sauce. Add the basil leaves, stir together, and remove from the heat. Use immediately or store, refrigerated, for up to 1 week.

Fall Ravioli

Pumpkin, Fried Sage, Browned Butter

Every fall I impulse-buy a Cinderella pumpkin from the farmers' market, and the literal weight of my decision slowly dawns on me with every step home, as I simultaneously daydream and panic about all the pumpkin recipes the future has in store. It's quite a feat to use up an entire pumpkin, but you'll find lots of ideas throughout this book, and this ravioli recipe is my favorite way to kick things off. But if you're not up for the challenge, don't feel like you have to stick to pumpkin here—you can use just about any firm-fleshed winter squash. Try half of a small butternut squash or one medium acorn squash instead.

If you do go the giant pumpkin route and end up with a lot left over, browse around this book for more ideas. Once cut open, pumpkin and winter squash will last in the refrigerator for 3 to 5 days, so purée and freeze whatever you don't plan to use in the near future. Try substituting pumpkin in the roasted butternut squash recipe on page 115, and stash away some purée to make a Loaf Cake at a later date (page 257).

1 Tbsp extra-virgin olive oil
4 cups [400 g] cubed pumpkin or firm-fleshed squash
½ tsp salt
One 8 oz [225 g] container ricotta
½ cup [25 g] finely grated Parmesan cheese
1 large egg yolk

3 garlic cloves, crushed through a press

2 Tbsp chopped fresh sage, plus more whole
    leaves for frying

¼ tsp freshly ground black pepper

4 Tbsp [55 g] butter

1 batch fresh rested pasta dough (see
    page 209) or 60 small wonton wrappers

Sea salt (optional)

Place a large skillet over medium-high heat and let it preheat for a few minutes. Once hot, add the olive oil, followed by the pumpkin and ¼ tsp of the salt. Let cook for about 8 minutes, stirring every few minutes. The pumpkin is done once it's caramelized and softened. Transfer to a medium mixing bowl and smash with the back of a fork.

Add the ricotta, Parmesan, egg yolk, garlic, sage, pepper, and remaining ¼ tsp salt. Mix well.

Bring a large stockpot of water to a boil.

Roll out the pasta dough and fill the ravioli with the pumpkin filling according to the instructions on page 211.

Simmer the ravioli about 12 at a time for about 3 minutes. Transfer to a serving bowl as they finish cooking.

While the ravioli are simmering, place the butter in a sauté pan or skillet over medium heat. Swirl the butter around as it melts. Once it melts completely, let it continue to sizzle until it starts to lightly brown and quiets down (1 to 2 minutes after melting). Add a small handful of sage leaves. Let them sizzle and crisp up for about 1 minute (stop before they turn too brown). As soon as the leaves crisp up, pour the brown butter and fried sage over the ravioli and gently toss together. Sprinkle lightly with sea salt (or table salt).

Winter Ravioli

Spinach, Pine Nuts, Lemon,
Dried Basil, Tomato Sauce

While you can absolutely make this recipe with fresh spinach as written, it also works great with frozen. Both fresh and frozen spinach will lose about half their weight after straining, so you'll want to use two 8 oz [225 g] containers of frozen spinach for this recipe. Instead of sautéing frozen spinach, simply thaw it and wring it out before adding it to the filling. If you're buying bagged spinach, three 6 oz [170 g] bags or two 8 oz [225 g] bags will work great. If you're buying bunches, go with one giant or two medium bunches.

Extra-virgin olive oil

17½ oz [500 g] packed coarsely chopped
    spinach

Salt

One 8 oz [225 g] container ricotta

½ cup [25 g] finely grated Parmesan cheese

1 large egg yolk

3 garlic cloves, crushed through a press

1 Tbsp dried basil

2 tsp lemon zest

¼ cup [35 g] toasted pine nuts

¼ tsp freshly ground black pepper

1 batch fresh rested pasta dough (see
    page 209) or 60 small wonton wrappers

1 batch Unseasonably Good Tomato Sauce
    (page 223)

Place a large stockpot or Dutch oven over medium-high heat and let it preheat for a few minutes. Once hot, add about 1 tsp of olive oil, followed by about half of the spinach and a pinch of salt. Let the spinach cook for about 4 minutes, tossing it constantly and squeezing it against the side of the pot. It's done once it's wilted down completely and any excess moisture has cooked off. Transfer to a medium mixing bowl, and repeat with the remaining spinach and another 1 tsp of olive oil. If the cooked spinach is still noticeably leaking liquid, wring it out by pressing it against the side of the bowl and letting the juices run into the sink. You should end up with about 1 cup [250 g] of wilted spinach.

Add the ricotta, Parmesan, egg yolk, garlic, dried basil, lemon zest, pine nuts, pepper, and about ¼ tsp salt to the mixing bowl with the spinach. Mix well.

Bring a large stockpot of water to a boil.

Roll out the pasta dough and fill the ravioli according to the instructions on page 211.

Simmer the ravioli about 12 at a time for about 3 minutes. Transfer to a serving bowl as they finish cooking, and toss with the tomato sauce.

Spring Ravioli

Mushrooms, Peas, Chives, Leeks, Lemon, Olive Oil, Parmesan

Mushrooms are one of my favorite vegetables to pair with spring produce—their earthiness nicely complements sharper flavors. Most mushrooms are cultivated indoors, so they're readily available year-round, although certain wild varieties are available only for short seasonal windows. If you happen to find some spring morels at the farmers' market or on a wild mushroom hunt, they would work wonderfully here as well, but regular old brown or button mushrooms are always a good call. If you do go wild mushroom hunting, always be sure to do so under the guidance of an expert forager if you're not one yourself.

Extra-virgin olive oil
8 oz [225 g] brown mushrooms, thinly sliced
Salt
2½ cups [225 g] chopped leek (white and light green parts only)
One 8 oz [225 g] container ricotta
1 large egg yolk
⅓ cup [50 g] blanched shelled peas, plus more for garnish
3 garlic cloves, crushed through a press
¼ cup [15 g] chopped fresh chives
¼ tsp freshly ground black pepper
1 batch fresh rested pasta dough (see page 209) or 60 small wonton wrappers
Parmesan cheese, for serving
Lemon wedges, for serving

Place a large stockpot or Dutch oven over medium-high heat and let it preheat for a few minutes. Once hot, add about 2 tsp of olive oil, followed by the mushrooms and a big pinch of salt. Let the mushrooms cook for about

10 minutes, stirring them every few minutes. They should shrink down significantly and caramelize by the time they're done. Transfer to a medium mixing bowl.

Leave the pan on the heat and add the leeks, another 1 tsp of olive oil, and a pinch of salt. Let the leeks cook for about 3 minutes, just until they soften and shrink down significantly. Transfer to the bowl with the mushrooms.

Add the ricotta, egg yolk, peas, garlic, chives, pepper, and about ¼ tsp of salt to the mushroom-leek mixture. Mix well.

Bring a large stockpot of water to a boil.

Roll out the pasta dough and fill the ravioli according to the instructions on page 211.

Simmer the ravioli about 12 at a time for about 3 minutes. Transfer to a serving bowl as they finish cooking, and toss together with a drizzle of olive oil and any extra peas. Use a vegetable peeler to top with big shavings of Parmesan. Serve with lemon wedges.

Pasta with Meatballs

While this dish's al dente pasta, turkey meatballs, and gooey mozzarella pearls stay constant, the sauce, herbs, and vegetables change dramatically from season to season. I've got an unseasonably good tomato sauce for the longest of winters, all kinds of seasonal pestos, a few excellent ways of turning fresh tomatoes into tomato sauce, plus lots of ideas for incorporating seasonal produce.

This recipe works great as a weeknight dinner—make a simple sauce (or use your favorite store-bought one), and blanch your favorite vegetables in the stockpot right alongside the pasta during its last few minutes. Or if you feel like going all out, you can even make your own fresh pasta. Simply make one batch of the ravioli dough on page 209 but omit the olive oil. Roll it out to a number 1 or 2 and dust liberally with flour. Fold a piece in half crosswise several times, slice into long ribbons, and then unfurl them. Boil for just 1 to 2 minutes.

While you can roast or sauté many ingredients and then throw them into the final dish with your cooked pasta, blanching is your friend here. Any of the vegetables on page 218 can be just thrown in the pasta water in the last minute or two of cooking. Just make sure you prep them as specified so that everything finishes cooking at the same time (if you don't go quite as thin as ⅛ in [3 mm] when called for, add them a minute or two earlier).

Make Your Own Pasta with Meatballs Grid

Ingredients to swap in for the base recipe on the facing page

PASTA SAUCE

+ Syrupy roasted tomato sauce (see page 221)
+ Pesto, in many forms (see page 226)
+ Unseasonably Good Tomato Sauce (page 223)
+ Garlic herb brown butter (see page 224)
+ 1½ batches of Barely Cooked Fresh Tomato Sauce (page 212)

TO ESTIMATE

Be careful not to use too much pasta and vegetables for the amount of sauce you have. It's better to have too much sauce and then hold some back.

NOTE

If you're throwing fresh baby spinach or arugula in with your pasta (or any other tender greens), use a couple of handfuls and don't bother blanching them—they can be thrown right in with the drained pasta, and they'll wilt from the residual heat.

SEASONAL PRODUCE

Summer

Corn kernels, green bean segments, ¼ in [6 mm] sliced zucchini or summer squash, ⅛ in [3 mm] sliced bell peppers, Swiss chard leaves

Fall

⅛ in [3 mm] sliced pumpkin, squash, parsnips, or carrots, bite-size cauliflower or broccoli florets, chopped broccoli rabe

Winter

⅛ in [3 mm] sliced pumpkin, squash, parsnips, or carrots, bite-size cauliflower or broccoli florets, chopped broccoli rabe

Spring

Peas, snow peas, snap peas, ⅛ in [3 mm] sliced parsnips or carrots, bite-size broccoli or cauliflower florets, chopped broccoli rabe, favas (see page 98 for special instructions), prepped fiddlehead ferns (see page 21), asparagus segments

Pasta with Meatballs

Makes 6 servings

1 batch Turkey Meatballs (recipe follows)
Pasta sauce of your choice
Salt
12 oz [340 g] pasta
2 to 3 cups [300 g] produce (see grid on facing
    page)
1 bunch basil, stemmed (40 g leaves), or 1 Tbsp
    dried basil
8 oz [225 g] mozzarella pearls or large-diced
    buffalo mozzarella
Finely grated Parmesan or pecorino romano
    cheese, for serving (optional)

Prepare your turkey meatballs and sauce.

Bring a large stockpot of water to a boil and salt somewhat liberally. Once boiling, add the pasta and cook until al dente, according to the package instructions. Once there are about 2 minutes left, add the produce so that your produce and pasta are al dente at the same time.

Drain the pasta and return to the stockpot. Add the cooked turkey meatballs to the pot, along with the sauce and basil. Fold together until evenly distributed. Add the mozzarella pearls, fold together a couple of times just to distribute, and immediately transfer to a serving bowl so the mozzarella doesn't melt onto the pot. Serve with Parmesan or pecorino romano at the table, if using.

Turkey Meatballs

½ cup [55 g] bread crumbs
½ cup [120 g] whole milk
1 lb [455 g] ground turkey
¾ cup [30 g] chopped fresh basil leaves, or
    1 Tbsp dried basil
3 garlic cloves, crushed through a press, or
    1½ tsp garlic powder
1 tsp freshly ground black pepper
½ to ¾ tsp salt
1 Tbsp neutral oil, such as avocado or canola

Put the bread crumbs and milk in a medium mixing bowl and let soak for about 2 minutes. Add the turkey, basil, garlic, and pepper to the softened bread crumbs and mix everything together until evenly distributed. Shape into 25 to 30 meatballs (about 1 heaping Tbsp [20 to 25 g] each) and then season their surfaces evenly with the salt. Do not put salt *in* the mixture, or they will be tough.

Heat a large nonstick or cast-iron sauté pan or skillet over medium heat for a few minutes. Once hot, add the oil to the pan and swirl to coat. Add the meatballs and allow them to brown on one side before turning. Carefully turn each meatball three or four times, until browned all over (10 to 12 minutes total).

Once browned more or less evenly, add about ¼ cup [60 g] of water to the pan and immediately cover. Let steam to cook all the way through, about 3 minutes more (cut one open to check).

Once they're done, continue cooking, uncovered, shaking the pan to toss them around gently while the liquid reduces. They should

end up coated in a thin brown sauce, with no more liquid left at the bottom of the pot (about 3 minutes more).

Summer Pasta

Spaghetti, Syrupy Roasted Tomato Sauce, Baby Arugula, Fresh Basil

This recipe is perfect for that late summer/ early fall moment when your garden has a crazy amount of tomatoes and the weather is getting cool enough that you don't mind leaving the oven on for a while. Even if you don't have a tomato garden, you'll probably find some stunners at a very fair price at the farmers' market as the season crescendos. Get them while the getting's good, slow-roast as many as you can, and pack them away in the freezer for the months ahead.

8 vine-ripened tomatoes, halved across their equators
Neutral oil, such as avocado or canola
Salt
Freshly ground black pepper
1 batch Turkey Meatballs (page 219), made with fresh basil
12 oz [340 g] spaghetti
2 big handfuls baby arugula (100 g)
1 bunch basil, stemmed and torn (40 g leaves)
8 oz [225 g] mozzarella pearls or large-diced buffalo mozzarella

Preheat the oven to 350°F [180°C].

Coat the tomato halves in a light layer of oil, place on a rimmed baking sheet cut-side up, and sprinkle with about ¼ tsp of salt and ¼ tsp pepper.

Roast for 75 minutes, opening the door once or twice to allow the steam to escape, until

they've shrunk down and become syrupy but are still quite soft.

While the tomatoes are roasting, cook your Turkey Meatballs (page 219).

Place the roasted tomatoes in a medium mixing bowl. Use scissors to cut each tomato into three or four pieces and then smash them with the back of a fork, just until they start to form a chunky sauce (don't try to blend them completely—you want lots of big pieces). Taste and adjust the seasoning. Set aside.

Bring a large stockpot of water to a boil and salt it somewhat liberally. Once boiling, add the spaghetti and cook until al dente.

Drain the pasta and return it to the pot. Add the cooked turkey meatballs to the pot, along with the tomato sauce, arugula, and basil leaves. Fold together until the arugula and basil are wilted. Fold in the mozzarella pearls, immediately transfer to a serving bowl, and serve.

Fall Pasta

Penne, Pesto, Sweet Potatoes, Crushed Red Pepper

I like to make a big batch of homemade pesto at the end of summer, during the days when you'll find oversize bouquets of basil selling for reasonable prices at farmers' markets. I freeze it in ice cube trays, pop them out into a freezer-safe container, and enjoy all year long. For this fall recipe, if you don't have a treasure trove of fresh summer pesto, you can always buy a premade container at the supermarket. Look for one that's creamy and bright green (or thereabouts) and try to stay away from drab ones that have lots of oil pooling on the top.

1 batch Turkey Meatballs (page 219), made with dried basil

Salt

1 Tbsp neutral oil, such as avocado or canola

1 very large sweet potato cut into ½ in [13 mm] wedges (300 g)

Freshly ground black pepper

12 oz [340 g] penne

1 cup [235 g] basil Pesto (page 227)

¼ tsp red pepper flakes, plus more as needed

8 oz [225 g] mozzarella pearls or large-diced buffalo mozzarella

Set the cooked turkey meatballs aside in a bowl.

Bring a large stockpot of water to a boil and salt it somewhat liberally.

Place a large nonstick or cast-iron sauté pan or skillet over medium heat and let it preheat for a few minutes. Once hot, add the oil and swirl to coat. Add the sweet potato wedges, season with salt and pepper, and let cook for about 7 minutes on each side. After about 14 minutes total, they should be soft on the inside and nicely browned on the outside. Set aside with the meatballs.

Meanwhile, once the pot of water is boiling, add the penne and cook until al dente.

Drain the pasta and return it to the stockpot. Add the cooked turkey meatballs and sweet potatoes to the pot, along with the pesto and red pepper. Fold together until evenly distributed. Fold in the mozzarella pearls, immediately transfer to a serving bowl, and serve.

Winter Pasta

Fusilli, Tomato Sauce, Kale, Dried Herbs

Most of this book's tomato sauce recipes feature fresh tomatoes, but this canned one is so good, I sometimes find myself making it in the middle of summer. The secret is to cook the tomatoes and aromatics down and then to use an immersion blender (or regular blender) to emulsify them until they become almost like a creamy vodka sauce. It's unseasonably good, and unreasonably good.

1 batch Unseasonably Good Tomato Sauce
(recipe follows)
1 batch Turkey Meatballs (page 219), made with
dried basil
Salt
12 oz [340 g] fusilli (a.k.a. rotini)
Leaves from 1 medium bunch kale
8 oz [225 g] mozzarella pearls or large-diced
buffalo mozzarella

Start by making the tomato sauce, and work on the rest while it simmers away.

Prepare your turkey meatballs.

Bring a large stockpot of water to a boil and salt it somewhat liberally.

Once the water is boiling, add the fusilli and cook until al dente. When there are 2 minutes left on the timer, add the kale and let it blanch while the pasta finishes cooking.

Drain the pasta and kale and return them to the stockpot. Add the cooked turkey meatballs to the pot, along with the tomato sauce. Fold together until evenly distributed. Fold in the mozzarella pearls, immediately transfer to a serving bowl, and serve.

Unseasonably Good Tomato Sauce

⅓ cup [70 g] extra-virgin olive oil
½ medium onion, diced (90 g)
Salt
1 Tbsp minced or pressed garlic
One 28 oz [794 g] can diced tomatoes
1 Tbsp dried basil
1 tsp dried oregano
½ tsp ground fennel seed (optional)
¼ tsp freshly ground black pepper

Set a small Dutch oven or large stockpot on the stove. Add the olive oil, onion, and a pinch of salt and set over medium heat. Once the onion starts sizzling, cook for 8 to 10 minutes, just until softened. Add the garlic, stir together for just a few seconds, and immediately add the diced tomatoes, basil, oregano, fennel seed, and black pepper.

Increase the heat to medium-high, bring up to a simmer, and lower the heat back down to medium so it stays at a simmer. Let the sauce simmer for about 20 minutes while stirring occasionally (don't let it scorch) and remove from the heat once it has reduced by about one-quarter (three-quarters its original volume). Taste and adjust the seasoning (depending on how much sodium was in your diced tomatoes).

Use an immersion blender to purée and emulsify the sauce: Use oven mitts to tilt the pot so that it pools in one corner. Move the immersion blender around, being careful of splattering and pausing to lift it up occasionally. Stop once all the oil droplets have disappeared and the sauce has lightened significantly in color. (You can skip the blending, but the sauce will have a very different texture.)

Spring Pasta

Orecchiette, Garlic Herb Brown Butter, Carrots, Snap Peas, Asparagus

Pasta primavera is one of those things that folks went wild for in the 1970s and then pretty much stopped making afterward. But when done well, it's not just a totally delightful nostalgia trip—it's a truly delicious way to serve spring produce. Here, I've included snow peas, asparagus, and carrots, but you can use whatever spring produce you'd like (e.g., fiddlehead ferns [see page 21], sugar snap peas, shelling peas, favas [see page 98], or thinly sliced parsnips).

1 batch Turkey Meatballs (page 219), made with
    dried basil
Salt
12 oz [340 g] orecchiette or shells
2 cups [150 g] snow peas
1 bunch asparagus, trimmed and broken into
    1 in [2.5 cm] pieces (100 g)
1 carrot, thinly sliced into ⅛ in [3 mm] half-
    moons (70 g)
4 Tbsp [55 g] unsalted butter
1 Tbsp minced or pressed garlic
½ cup [20 g] chopped fresh parsley
¼ cup [10 g] chopped fresh dill
½ tsp black pepper
8 oz [225 g] mozzarella pearls or large-diced
    buffalo mozzarella
Finely grated Parmesan cheese, for serving

Prepare your turkey meatballs first and set aside.

Once your meatballs are done, bring a large stockpot of water to a boil and salt it somewhat liberally. Once boiling, add the orecchiette and cook until al dente. When there are 2 minutes left on the timer, add the snow peas, asparagus, and carrots and let them blanch while the pasta finishes cooking.

Meanwhile, place the butter in a small saucepan and melt it over medium-low heat. Let it continue to sizzle until it starts to turn brown. As soon as it browns, remove from the heat and add the garlic. Cook with the residual heat for about 1 minute, then transfer to a bowl (use a spatula to scrape the pan out so you don't leave any behind). Once it cools down a bit, stir in the parsley, dill, and black pepper. Season with about ¼ tsp of salt.

Drain the pasta and vegetables and return them to the stockpot. Add the cooked turkey meatballs to the pot, along with the herb butter sauce. Fold together until evenly distributed. Fold in the mozzarella pearls and immediately transfer to a serving bowl. Serve with finely grated Parmesan at the table.

Make Your Own Pesto Grid

Ingredients to swap in for the base recipe on the following page

Ingredients to swap in for the base recipe on the following page

NOTE

The perfect amount of herbs or greens to add to this recipe is a scant 3 oz [80 g], but since that looks different for every vegetable, use the following chart if you feel like eyeballing it.

SEASONAL

Summer

Basil leaves from 2 medium bunches, parsley leaves from 2 small bunches, mint leaves from 2 medium bunches, 1 large or 2 medium bunches of chives

Fall

Kale leaves from 1 very small bunch, 2 big handfuls of arugula

Winter

Kale leaves from 1 very small bunch

Spring

1 large or 2 medium bunches of chives, 2 big handfuls of arugula, 2 big handfuls of watercress, 4 medium ramps

Anytime

Cilantro leaves and tender stems from 1 large bunch

Pesto

Makes 1 cup [235 g]

Blend up a batch of seasonal pesto and then stash it in the freezer for later. Classic basil pesto will always be my favorite, but lots of other herbs and flavorful greens work wonderfully as well.

Once you have a stash of pesto, use it wisely. While it's tempting to mix it into everything for a dose of savory herbiness, pesto works best in recipes where extra oil is welcome. A good rule of thumb is to use pesto when you might otherwise use mayo, aioli, or butter, but when you also want an herby kick. If you'd like to add some herby savory flavor to something that's already quite rich, simply mix in some finely minced fresh herbs and garlic instead.

To keep your pesto from turning brown, use the freshest herbs possible, get rid of stems, and dry them very well before using them in this recipe. If you want to make absolutely sure your pesto won't turn brown, blanch the herbs or greens in boiling water for exactly 5 seconds and then shock them immediately in an ice bath. You can also add the optional citrus juice for further insurance.

Ways to use pesto: crostini (see page 104), pasta (see page 221), quesadillas (see page 162), roast chicken, burgers, meatballs, sandwiches, salad dressing (add a little vinegar or lemon juice along with a little water to thin it out, and then season with salt), topping baked potatoes or sweet potatoes, lobster rolls and chicken salad (in place of all or some of the mayo; see page 189), coating vegetables before roasting (instead of oil), topping corn on the cob (instead of butter).

1 to 3 garlic cloves
⅓ cup [45 g] pine nuts
Tightly packed herbs/vegetables (see the grid on the facing page for quantity)
1 Tbsp fresh lemon or lime juice (optional; see Note)
⅔ cup [35 g] finely grated pecorino romano or Parmesan cheese
¼ tsp freshly ground black pepper
¼ tsp salt
¼ cup [50 g] extra-virgin olive oil

Place the garlic and pine nuts in the bowl of a food processor fitted with the blade attachment. Process until it turns into a thick, chunky paste. Scrape down the sides and add the herbs/vegetables, citrus juice (if using), pecorino, black pepper, and salt and pulse several times until it's puréed. With the food processor running, very slowly drizzle the olive oil through the feed tube, allowing it to emulsify into a creamy, bright green pesto.

Store in a jar in the refrigerator for up to 3 days or freeze. It will last in the freezer for 3 months in a regular sealed container or bag, and will last more like 1 year in the freezer in a vacuum-sealed bag.

Notes: Lemon juice or lime juice is totally optional. I add lime juice to cilantro pesto, and lemon juice to kale or mint pesto, but I prefer classic basil pesto without any extra acidity.

SWEETS

Fruit Tarts

While pastry crusts aren't quite as intimidating as they may seem, there's nothing easier than a cookie crust, such as the kind that holds together your favorite New York–style cheesecake. For a perfect seasonal sweet, you need nothing more than a cookie crust, a simple custard, and all your favorite produce.

That custard tart is exactly what you'll find as this section's base recipe, but don't be afraid to get creative with your layers by using components from one or more of the seasonal variations (e.g., no-bake cheesecake, baked cheesecake, ganache, or curd). Just make sure that the first layer always sets completely before pouring on the next, and be sure never to place fresh fruit on a piping-hot layer.

While you can technically combine pretty much any layers from this section, certain combinations work better than others, and you want to make sure you don't choose so many layers that you run out of space for them. Here are a few examples of combinations that work well together:

FILLING	TOPPINGS
Custard (page 233)	Fruit
Chocolate Ganache (page 236)	Curd, curd and fruit, or just fruit
Baked cheesecake (see page 238) or No-Bake Cheesecake (page 240)	Curd, curd and fruit, half-recipe ganache and fruit, or just fruit

You can also sub in any of the cookie crusts in this section (cookies and cream on page 235, biscoff on page 238, and Pretzel Crust on page 240).

Make Your Own Fruit Tart Grid

Ingredients to swap in for the base recipe on the facing page

CUSTARD FLAVORINGS

+ 2 tsp vanilla extract
+ 1 tsp orange blossom water
+ ½ to 1 tsp rose water
+ 1 to 1½ tsp almond extract

NOTE

Make sure that your fruit is just-ripe, not overripe.

You can turn any of these into mini fruit tarts if you have mini tart pans. Each recipe will yield six 4¾ in [12 cm] fruit tarts. If you're making the baked cheesecake layer on page 238, it will only need to bake for 8 minutes in mini tart form. The crusts themselves bake for about the same amount of time in mini form (but keep an eye on them in the last 2 minutes of baking, and pull them early if you need to, especially if your tart shells are smaller than 4¾ in [12 cm]).

SEASONAL

Summer

Sliced plums, peaches, nectarines, apricots, Anjou pears, or figs, whole berries or currants, sliced or halved strawberries, pitted cherries

Fall

Sliced Bosc/Bartlett/Anjou pears, plums, or figs, pomegranate arils, small whole black grapes, passion fruit pulp (use in moderation or make the curd on page 236 instead), sliced persimmons in late fall

Winter

Sliced persimmons or Bosc/Bartlett/Anjou pears, citrus supremes (chill the custard tart, pat the supremes dry, then top the custard and serve immediately, or make the curd on page 239 instead)

Spring

Rhubarb Compote (page 241), sliced Anjou pears or loquats, sliced/halved strawberries in late spring

Anytime

Bananas, mangos, kiwi, dragonfruit, frozen passion fruit pulp (use in moderation or make the curd on page 236 instead)

Fruit Tarts

Makes 6 to 8 servings

For the tart shell
21 or 22 honey graham crackers or digestive biscuits (10½ oz [300 g])
½ cup [115 g] unsalted butter, melted
2 Tbsp honey
2 Tbsp granulated sugar
¼ tsp salt

For the custard
2 cups [480 g] milk
½ cup [100 g] granulated sugar
Flavorings
¼ tsp salt
2 large eggs
3 Tbsp [30 g] cornstarch

For the topping
About 4 cups [500 g] prepared produce (choose two or three different fruits, see grid on facing page)
3 Tbsp [60 g] apricot jam

Preheat the oven to 350°F [180°C].

To make the tart shell: Place the graham crackers or digestive biscuits in a food processor and process until they're the texture of dry sand. Add the butter, honey, sugar, and salt and blend until it's the texture of wet sand. Dump the mixture into a 10 in [25 cm] tart pan. Use your fingers and the back of a measuring cup to tightly pack the mixture into an even layer across the bottom and sides. Start by packing the bottom with the cup, and then use your fingers to pack the sides tightly (one hand on top and one hand on the side to create even pressure).

Bake the shell for about 12 minutes. It's done once it begins to brown a bit more and smells nutty.

To make the custard: Combine the milk, sugar, flavorings, and salt in a small saucepan. Place over medium heat and let it come almost up to a simmer. While the milk heats, whisk together the eggs and cornstarch in a medium mixing bowl until completely lump-free. Once the milk mixture is barely simmering, slowly dribble about half of it into the egg mixture while whisking constantly. Add the egg mixture to the remaining milk mixture in the saucepan and immediately whisk together. Bring to a simmer, whisking constantly. Once bubbles break the surface, continue cooking for another 60 seconds or so while whisking constantly.

To fill the fruit tart: Immediately pour the filling into the tart shell and smooth out the surface. Wait about 2 minutes for the surface to cool slightly, and then top with produce (push down slightly so they sink in a little). Microwave the apricot jam for 30 to 60 seconds (just until runny) and brush over the surface of the fruit. Chill the tart for at least 1 hour. If your pan has a removable bottom, remove the collar just before serving (if not, simply serve out of the pan). Leftovers will keep in the refrigerator for a day or two, but the tart is best served a few hours after it is assembled.

Summer Tart

Graham Cracker Crust, Almond Custard, Mixed Berries, Apricot Glaze, Sliced Almonds

This is my favorite straightforward variation on the base recipe in this section. Simply take a stirred custard, flavor it with almond extract, pour it into a graham cracker or digestive biscuit crust, and top with all the summer berries you can find. If you've got mulberries growing in your backyard, feel free to sub them in, but even just a strawberry-blueberry-raspberry trio you find at the supermarket will be lovely.

1 tart shell (see page 233)
1 batch custard (see page 233), made with 1 tsp
    almond extract
2 cups [240 g] sliced strawberries
1 cup [130 g] blueberries
1 cup [110 g] raspberries
3 Tbsp [60 g] apricot jam
¼ tsp almond extract
1 heaping Tbsp sliced almonds

Make the graham cracker crust and custard (see page 233).

Immediately pour the custard into the baked tart shell and smooth out the surface. Wait about 2 minutes for its surface to cool slightly and then top with the berries (push them down slightly so they sink in a little). Microwave the apricot jam stirred together with the almond extract for 30 to 60 seconds (just until runny) and brush over the surface of the berries. Top immediately with the sliced almonds. Chill the tart for at least 1 hour, and serve the day it is assmbled.

Fall Tart

Cookies and Cream, Chocolate Ganache, Passion Fruit Curd

Over the last four years, I've been lucky enough to live in Hong Kong and Melbourne, two cities where you can always find heaps of passion fruit for a reasonable price. This tropical fruit is most at home in a warm climate where it can grow and ripen year-round. In climates like Melbourne (temperate with mild winters), vines tend to flower and fruit through the spring and summer, to harvest annually in the early fall.

Even if you don't live in a climate that can grow passion fruits, you can find frozen packets year-round in Caribbean, Latin American, and Asian markets. Whether you're using frozen or fresh pulp, just make sure you zip it through the food processor to loosen the membranes before turning it into a curd—I learned this technique from Erin Clarkson (of the blog *Cloudy Kitchen*).

The dark chocolate ganache goes with any sweet/tart produce, so sliced mango, whole summer raspberries, a small amount of candied fall hibiscus calyxes, and fall/winter pomegranate arils all work wonderfully in place of the passion fruit curd.

35 Oreos (340 g)
4 Tbsp [55 g] unsalted butter, melted
¼ tsp salt
1 batch Chocolate Ganache (recipe follows)
1 batch Passion Fruit Curd (recipe follows)

Preheat your oven to 350°F [180°C].

To make the tart shell: Place the Oreos in a food processor and process until they're the texture of dry sand. Add the butter and salt and blend until it's the texture of wet sand. (Don't wash the food processor.) Dump the mixture into a 10 in [25 cm] tart pan. Use your fingers and the back of a measuring cup to tightly pack the mixture into an even layer across the bottom and sides. See page 233 for more details.

Bake the shell for about 14 minutes. It's done once it smells nutty and firms up a bit.

When the shell is almost done baking, make the ganache. Pour it into the tart shell and smooth out with an offset spatula or the back of a spoon. Wait until the pan is no longer hot, and then place in the refrigerator for about 30 minutes to set.

While you wait for the ganache to chill, make the curd. Pour the curd over the chocolate ganache. The ganache will start to melt underneath, so pour it on evenly and do not try to smooth it out or disturb it. Return the tart pan to the refrigerator for at least 2 hours.

The tart will keep in the refrigerator for about 3 days but is best served within a day or two after assembling. Leftover slices keep in the freezer, and it tastes phenomenal frozen.

Chocolate Ganache

¾ cup [175 g] heavy cream
6 oz [170 g] dark chocolate (at least 69% cacao)
Pinch of salt

Bring the cream to a bare simmer over medium heat in a small saucepan. Once the cream is barely simmering, remove from the heat and add the chocolate and salt. Swirl to make sure the chocolate is completely submerged. Let sit for about 1 minute and then whisk it together until it's thickened and completely homogenous. Do not reheat and pour within 5 to 10 minutes of making (or if you accidentally let it firm up, simply spread it instead of pouring).

Passion Fruit Curd

¾ cup plus 2 Tbsp [205 g] passion fruit pulp, from about 5 very large or 10 small passion fruits
¾ cup [150 g] granulated sugar
Pinch of salt
3 large eggs
4 Tbsp [55 g] unsalted butter, cut into 4 pieces

Wipe out the food processor so there are no big cookie crumbs. Place the passion fruit pulp, sugar, salt, and eggs in the food processor (make sure it's below the liquid line). Pulse several times just to mix. It's ready once it's completely homogenous and no longer gloopy.

Place the curd over medium-low heat in a small saucepan. Whisk constantly until it thickens significantly, being careful not to let it overheat and lowering the heat gradually as it progresses. It will thicken at about 167°F to 170°F [75°C to 77°C], which takes about 10 minutes to reach. Do not let it exceed 180°F [82°C].

Once the curd thickens, remove from the heat and immediately add the butter and whisk constantly until the butter melts and disappears completely.

Winter Tart

Biscoff, Cheesecake, Fennel Grapefruit
Curd, Candied Grapefruit Peel

In the words of comedian Gary Gulman, grapefruit is "so bad it should be a vegetable." If you
tend to agree, feel free to use a different citrus
fruit for the curd and candied peels. If you're
going with another citrus, also replace the fennel
with another flavoring. Try lime curd with a little
fresh mint leaf, orange with vanilla, or lemon with
rose water.

But if you absolutely love grapefruit, or even
if you enjoy the occasional pamplemousse
sparkling water, you've got to try this recipe as
written. Fennel, grapefruit, and cheese classi-
cally go together in salads, but they also work
nicely together in sweets. Try baking an olive
oil apple fennel seed grapefruit loaf cake with
cream cheese icing sometime (see page 256).
But first: this tart.

For the biscoff crust
38 biscoff cookies (300 g)
7 Tbsp [100 g] unsalted butter, melted
¼ tsp salt

For the cheesecake
**One 8 oz [225 g] package cream cheese, at
    room temperature**
1 large egg
⅓ cup [65 g] granulated sugar
⅛ tsp salt

For the topping
**1 batch Citrus Curd, made with grapefruit zest
    and juice (recipe follows)**
½ tsp ground fennel seed
**1 batch Candied Citrus Peels, made with
    grapefruit (recipe follows; optional)**

Preheat your oven to 350°F [180°C].

To make the crust: Place the cookies in a
food processor and process until they're the
texture of dry sand. Add the butter and salt and
blend until it's the texture of wet sand. Dump
the mixture into a 10 in [25 cm] tart pan. Use
your fingers and the back of a measuring cup
to tightly pack the mixture into an even nearly
½ in [13 mm] layer across the bottom and sides.
See page 233 for more details.

Bake the shell for about 10 minutes for this
recipe (or bake for 12 minutes if you do not plan
to use it with the baked cheesecake layer). It's
done once it begins to brown a bit more and
smells nutty. Leave the oven on.

To make the cheesecake: Combine the
cream cheese, egg, sugar, and salt in a medium
mixing bowl. Pour into the tart shell and
smooth out with an offset spatula or spoon.
Bake for 12 to 14 minutes, just until set. Store in
the refrigerator or proceed right to topping with
the curd.

To make the topping: While the cheesecake
is baking, make the curd (don't forget to zest/
peel the grapefruits for the curd and the candied
peels *before* juicing them). Once the curd is
done, stir in the ground fennel seed and immediately pour the finished grapefruit curd over
the cheesecake layer (either cooled down or
right from the oven). Place it in the refrigerator
for at least 2 hours.

While the curd is setting, make the candied
grapefruit peels, and then decorate the curd
with them.

Serve within a day or two of assembling and
make sure the curd is set before slicing. It's delicious frozen, and keeps well in the freezer.

Citrus Curd

This citrus curd can be made with anything you can zest and juice (lime, lemon, Meyer lemon, orange, blood orange, grapefruit, etc.). If you feel like adding a little extra acidity to an orange curd, go ahead and replace 1 Tbsp of orange juice with lemon or lime juice. If you'd like your lemon or lime curd to be a little less acidic, replace 1 or 2 Tbsp of their juice with water.

Curds are traditionally made with egg yolks, but I prefer using whole eggs. If you're after a more deeply golden curd (and don't mind making a trillion meringues later on), feel free to use about 6 egg yolks in place of 2 large eggs. Above all, make sure your eggs are super fresh. If you're using this curd for another recipe (or on its own), it will keep for 5 to 10 days in the refrigerator, but it will last for months in the freezer.

1 small beet, for coloring (optional)
2 large eggs
¾ cup [150 g] granulated sugar
⅓ cup [80 g] citrus juice
1 Tbsp citrus zest
4 Tbsp [55 g] unsalted butter, cut into 4 pieces

If you're making grapefruit or orange curd and want to make sure it's richly hued (100 percent optional), start with the beet. Peel it, cut it into wedges, and place it in a small saucepan with 1 cup [235 g] of water. Bring to a boil, cover, lower the heat to low, and let it simmer for about 15 minutes. Save the beets for a salad and reserve the liquid as a food coloring.

Add the eggs, sugar, citrus juice, citrus zest, and 1 tsp of the beet liquid to color grapefruit curd or ½ tsp to color orange curd (if using) to a blender or large food processor. Pulse several times to mix thoroughly.

Once the eggs have blended in completely, transfer to a small saucepan over medium-low

heat. Whisk constantly until it thickens significantly, being careful not to let it overheat and lowering the heat gradually as it progresses. It thickens at about 167°F to 170°F [75°C to 77°C], which takes about 10 minutes to reach. Do not let it exceed 180°F [82°C].

Once the curd thickens, remove from the heat and immediately add the butter and whisk constantly until the butter melts completely.

Candied Citrus Peels

You can candy any citrus peels using this technique. Feel free to double the recipe by adding twice as many citrus peels to the same amount of syrup—doubling the peels takes just about 2 minutes longer. For a tripled or quadrupled batch, also double the syrup; a much larger batch takes a few minutes longer to cook.

1 small grapefruit or other citrus
    (see Note)
1½ cups [350 g] water
1 cup [200 g] granulated sugar, plus more for
    dusting

Use a vegetable peeler to peel thick strips of colorful skin from your citrus, avoiding the majority of the white pith underneath. Slice the strips into ⅛ in [3 mm] wide pieces (you should have ⅓ cup [30 g]). Cover and save the peeled citrus in the refrigerator for another project.

Bring the water and the sugar to a boil in a small saucepan over high heat (do not use a wide pan). Once the sugar dissolves, add the citrus peels, lower the heat to medium, and maintain a low boil for about 15 minutes uncovered. They are done once they become translucent and the liquid has reduced by about half. Keep an eye on them and don't let them cook past this point.

Drain the peels. Save the simple syrup in the refrigerator for up to 2 months and use it for cocktails (lemon syrup and juice to make lemonade or whiskey sours, lime syrup and juice for limeade or gimlets, and grapefruit or orange syrup for old-fashioneds).

Line a baking sheet with parchment paper.

Move the drained peels to the prepared baking sheet and spread out as much as possible. Let cool for a couple minutes, then sprinkle liberally with about 1 Tbsp [15 g] of sugar. Toss together. At this point, you can use the candied citrus peels on baked goods or preserve them by spreading them out again and letting them dry uncovered for 2 hours in a climate-controlled room. Seal once they're dehydrated and store at room temperature for up to a month. They'll be chewy for the first day or two, and will gradually become crunchy.

Note: About 1 large orange, 3 large limes, or 2 medium lemons

Spring Tart

Pretzel Crust, No-Bake Cheesecake, Rhubarb Compote

I grew up in the Midwest, so I'm used to the idea of "salad" denoting a big bowl of ingredients like cookies, pretzels, and/or marshmallows suspended in Jell-O. I have no idea how these neon spectacles got their name, but as a big fan of sweet and savory, I do love taking inspiration from Midwestern salads for dessert. For this fruit tart, we've got a pretzel crust, a no-bake cheesecake layer, and a rhubarb topping, but you can adapt it to suit any time of the year by topping it simply with whatever fresh fruit you've got on hand in place of the rhubarb compote. And if you're not so into things inspired by Midwestern "salads," feel free to substitute a biscoff or graham cracker crust (see page 238 or 235, respectively) in place of the pretzel one.

1 batch Pretzel Crust (recipe follows)
1 batch No-Bake Cheesecake (recipe follows)
1 batch Rhubarb Compote (recipe follows)

Let the pretzel crust cool down completely, then top with the no-bake cheesecake, smooth it out, and chill for at least 2 hours until set. Spoon the cooled compote on top of the set cheesecake and spread to the edges.

Pretzel Crust

8 oz [225 g] salted pretzels
6 Tbsp [85 g] unsalted butter, melted
3 Tbsp [60 g] honey
2 Tbsp sugar

Preheat the oven to 350°F [180°C].

Place the pretzels in a food processor and blend until they're the texture of dry sand. Add the butter, honey, and sugar and blend until the mixture is the texture of wet sand. Dump the mixture into a 10 in [25 cm] tart pan. Use your fingers and the back of a measuring cup to tightly pack the mixture into an even nearly ½ in [13 mm] layer across the bottom and sides. (See page 233 for more details.)

Bake the shell for about 12 minutes. It's done once it begins to brown a bit more and smells nutty.

No-Bake Cheesecake

8 oz [225 g] cream cheese, at room temperature
¼ cup [50 g] granulated sugar
⅛ tsp salt
3 Tbsp [45 g] heavy whipping cream

Place the cream cheese, sugar, and salt in the bowl of your stand mixer fitted with the whisk attachment. Beat at medium-high speed until smooth and fluffy (about 2 minutes). Lower the speed to medium and gradually stream in the whipping cream with the mixer running. Once it's all been incorporated, increase the speed to high. Beat for about 1 minute, just until it becomes thicker and fluffier.

Rhubarb Compote

About 6 medium stalks rhubarb, cut into ½ in [13 mm] slices (210 g)
¼ cup [50 g] granulated sugar
Pinch of salt
1 Tbsp water

Place the rhubarb, sugar, salt, and water in a small sauté pan or skillet. Cover and set over medium heat for 2 minutes. Remove the lid, give it a stir, and turn the heat down to low or medium-low. Maintain a gentle simmer until the rhubarb breaks down, about 10 minutes. Stir occasionally while it simmers uncovered. You can tell it's done once it's thickened, slow to move, and no longer runny. Purée the mixture with an immersion blender for a smoother appearance, if desired.

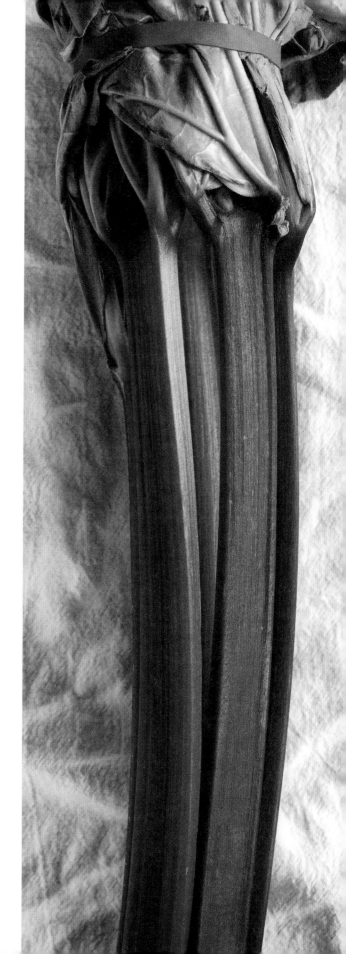

Fruit Galettes

There's nothing quite as cheerful as a galette made with your favorite seasonal fruit, sweetened with a touch of sugar, and baked to perfection in a rustic, flaky pie crust. This base recipe doesn't have many bells and whistles, but it's usually exactly what I'm looking for when I've got some delicious seasonal produce I want to show off.

This crust is inspired by Rose Levy Beranbaum's cream cheese pie dough. Cream cheese makes the pastry a dream to work with, especially when compared to all-butter crusts. It's much less likely to crack and split as you roll it out, which means your galette is much less likely to spring a leak, and yet it still bakes up super flaky and flavorful, a bit like a rugelach dough. If you don't have cream cheese on hand, you can use another not-too-crumbly pie dough recipe (e.g., one that includes yogurt, ricotta, or shortening).

You can easily turn these into mini galettes (great for picnics and bake sales). Simply divide the dough into six small disks, cover and chill as in the following recipe, then roll each one out to about 6 or 7 in [15 to 18 cm]. Fill and proceed with the recipe as usual. These smaller versions will take less time to bake, about 35 minutes.

Also feel free to smarten up your galette with a chocolate crust (see page 249), cinnamon sugar dusting over the egg wash (see page 248), streusel topping (see page 260), or frangipane layer (see page 250). As long as you follow the chart on page 244 to make sure you use the right amount of cornstarch and sugar, it'll go off without a hitch.

Make Your Own Fruit Galette Grid

Ingredients to swap in for the base recipe on the facing page

CORNSTARCH

Cornstarch acts as a thickener, and because this recipe has you add liquid to the filling, it's extremely adaptable and failproof. You can absolutely use a different thickener here (although you may need to experiment with adding more or less), but I love cornstarch because it works great and it's a staple in most kitchens.

You can always add a little more or less. If your produce is particularly juicy, use a touch more cornstarch. If you like a runny filling, use a little less. Use the following chart to get an idea of how much to use for different fruits.

SUGAR

Most things need ¼ cup [50 g] of granulated sugar. If your produce is extremely sweet, cut back on the added sugar slightly. If your produce is tart, add more sugar. Rhubarb, for instance, needs at least ⅓ cup [65 g] of sugar.

LEMON JUICE

Use water for tart produce, and use lemon juice for sweet produce. For example, rhubarb does not need lemon juice, so replace the lemon juice with water. Do not just omit the liquid altogether, or it will throw off the ratio of ingredients. Use half lemon juice/half water if your fruit is somewhere in the middle in tartness (e.g., Granny Smith apples or raspberries). Note that reducing the acidity will help it set more firmly.

SEASONAL PRODUCE

Use 3⅓ to 4 cups [400 g] of produce. It should be ripe enough to enjoy out of hand but not overly so.

Add 2 Tbsp cornstarch	Add 1 Tbsp cornstarch or less
Summer	
Whole mulberries, blackberries, or raspberries; whole pitted cherries (for sour cherries, use more sugar and use water in place of lemon juice); ½ in [13 mm] sliced strawberries, Anjou pears, peaches, plums, nectarines, or apricots	½ in [13 mm] sliced figs, blueberries
Fall	
½ in [13 mm] sliced Bosc/Bartlett/Anjou pears, persimmons, or plums	Peeled ½ in [13 mm] sliced apples
Winter	
½ in [13 mm] sliced persimmon (see Note on page 107 to select a ripe one) or Bosc/Bartlett/Anjou pears	
Spring	
½ in [13 mm] sliced strawberries, halved loquats, ½ in [13 mm] sliced sour plums (pair with something sweeter), ½ in [13 mm] sliced rhubarb (for sour plums and rhubarb: use more sugar and use water in place of lemon juice)	

SPICES AND FLAVORINGS

Use a total of ½ to 2 tsp spices (for cardamom, anise, and other very strong flavors, do not add more than ¼ tsp of each), 1 tsp citrus zest, 2 tsp fresh grated ginger, 1½ tsp vanilla extract, 2 tsp orange blossom water, or 1 tsp rose water.

Fruit Galettes

Makes 6 to 8 servings

For the cream cheese butter pie dough

1⅓ cups [175 g] all-purpose flour,
  plus more for dusting

½ cup [115 g] cold unsalted butter, cut into
  chunks

¼ tsp salt

4 oz [115 g] cold cream cheese, cut into chunks

2 Tbsp very cold water

For the filling

2 Tbsp cornstarch, or as needed
  (see the grid on the facing page)

¼ cup [50 g] granulated sugar, or as needed

3⅓ to 4 cups [400 g] berries or sliced fruit (see
  grid on facing page)

2 Tbsp fresh lemon juice or water

¼ tsp salt

Spices and flavorings

Egg wash (1 egg yolk beaten with 1 tsp water)
Ice cream, for serving (optional)

To make the pie dough: Place the flour, butter, and salt in a food processor fitted with the blade attachment (see Note). Pulse about ten times and stop once the butter has blended into the flour with lots of pea-size lumps left. Add the cream cheese and pulse a few more times, just until the cream cheese has blended in but the mixture is still quite lumpy. Sprinkle the water over the surface and pulse a few more times, just until the mixture can be squeezed together into a ball.

Shape the dough into a ball by squeezing it together, flatten the ball into a disk, and cover tightly with plastic wrap. Gently tap and roll the sides of the disk on the counter to help them become less jagged. Once they're smooth and no longer have big cracks, place the disk flat on the counter and gently press and pat the top to make sure it's nice and flat. As you gently press down on the top, the plastic wrap compresses the sides and ensures that any jagged edges are smoothed out. Refrigerate for 30 minutes. If you chill it completely, let it sit at room temperature for 30 to 50 minutes, just until it's pliable but still chilled.

Preheat the oven to 400°F [205°C]. Line a rimmed baking sheet with parchment paper.

Meanwhile, to make the filling: Decide how much cornstarch and sugar you'll use, using the guide on the facing page (2 Tbsp cornstarch and ¼ cup [50 g] sugar works for most things). In a medium mixing bowl, fold together the fruit, sugar, cornstarch, lemon juice / water, salt, and spices. If you're using particularly acidic fruit, use water (see guide, facing page), otherwise use lemon juice or a combination of the two. Set aside.

On a lightly floured surface, roll out the chilled dough to just under ¼ in [6 mm] thick and about 12 in [30.5 cm] across. Rotate occasionally as you work but try not to handle the dough too much and try to keep the edges from cracking too deeply.

Once it's rolled out, gently wrap the dough around your rolling pin to transfer it to the prepared baking sheet. Place the filling in the very center of the rolled-out dough and be sure to scrape the bowl with a spatula so you don't

miss anything. Arrange in an even layer, leaving a 2 in [5 cm] border around the edges. Fold the edges over in a rustic overlapping pattern so that the middle stays open and brush the crust's surface all over with the egg wash.

Bake for 40 to 50 minutes, until the whole thing is bubbly and the crust is golden brown (a frangipane-filled galette needs 50 minutes). Remove from the oven and let cool before slicing (at least 15 minutes, ideally 1 hour to allow it to set completely). Slice and serve plain or with ice cream, if desired.

Note: You can do this by hand with a pastry cutter or just the tips of your fingers. Squeeze the bits of butter in the flour so that they break down into smaller bits and mix together with the flour. Use a fork to mash in the cream cheese, then sprinkle the water and bring it all together with your hands.

Summer Galette

Blackberry Sumac

This galette should remind you a bit of strawberry rhubarb pie, with a sweet-tart flavor profile, but it's got a lot of extra depth from those more complex and moody blackberries—think European currant-flavored hard candies, or maybe even blue-raspberry Jolly Ranchers.

1 batch Cream Cheese Butter Pie Dough
   (page 245)
3⅔ cups [400 g] whole blackberries
¼ cup [50 g] granulated sugar
2 Tbsp cornstarch
1 Tbsp sumac, plus more for serving
¼ tsp salt
2 Tbsp water
Flour, for dusting

Egg wash (1 egg yolk beaten with 1 tsp water)
Vanilla ice cream, for serving (optional)

Chill the prepared dough for 30 minutes (see page 245).

Meanwhile, preheat the oven to 400°F [205°C] and line a rimmed baking sheet with parchment paper.

In a medium mixing bowl, fold together the blackberries, sugar, cornstarch, sumac, salt, and water.

On a lightly floured surface, roll out the chilled dough to just under ¼ in [6 mm] thick and about 12 in [30.5 cm] across. Rotate occasionally as you work but try not to handle the dough too much and try to keep the edges from cracking too deeply.

Once it's rolled out, gently wrap the dough around your rolling pin to transfer it to the prepared baking sheet. Place the filling in the very center of the rolled-out dough and be sure to scrape the bowl with a spatula so you don't miss anything. Arrange in an even layer, leaving a 2 in [5 cm] border around the edges. Fold the edges over in a rustic overlapping pattern so that the middle stays open and brush the crust's surface all over with egg wash.

Bake for about 40 minutes, until the whole thing is bubbly and the crust is golden brown.

Let cool before slicing (at least 15 minutes, ideally 1 hour). Serve plain or with vanilla ice cream, if desired, and a little pinch of sumac.

Fall Galette

Pear, Saffron, Cinnamon

There's nothing quite so autumnal as cinnamon and seasonal fruit, but if you're in search of an update on the classic, try incorporating a pinch of saffron. Always bloom your saffron in some liquid first, and never add more than a little taste. If you don't have saffron, add a pinch of cardamom in its place or stick with cinnamon.

1 batch Cream Cheese Butter Pie Dough (page 245)

About 40 saffron threads (1 medium pinch)

2 Tbsp fresh lemon juice

3½ cups [400 g] ½ in [13 mm] Bosc pear slices (from about 3 or 4 peeled pears; see Note)

¼ cup [50 g] granulated sugar

2 Tbsp cornstarch

2½ tsp cinnamon

¼ tsp salt

Flour, for dusting

Egg wash (1 egg yolk beaten with 1 tsp water)

Cinnamon sugar, for dusting the crust

Salted caramel ice cream, for serving (optional)

Chill the prepared dough for 30 minutes (see page 245).

Meanwhile, preheat the oven to 400°F [205°C] and line a rimmed baking sheet with parchment paper.

In a small bowl, combine the saffron and lemon juice and let steep for at least 5 minutes.

In a medium mixing bowl, fold together the pears, sugar, cornstarch, cinnamon, salt, and saffron-steeped lemon juice.

On a lightly floured surface, roll out the chilled dough to just under ¼ in [6 mm] thick and about 12 in [30.5 cm] across. Rotate occasionally as you work but try not to handle the dough too much and try to keep the edges from cracking too deeply.

Once it's rolled out, gently wrap the dough around your rolling pin to transfer it to the prepared baking sheet. Place the filling in the very center of the rolled-out dough and be sure to scrape the bowl with a spatula so you don't miss anything. Arrange in an even layer, leaving a 2 in [5 cm] border around the edges. Fold the edges over in a rustic overlapping pattern so

that the middle stays open and brush the crust's surface all over with the egg wash. Sprinkle the crust with cinnamon sugar right before baking.

Bake for about 40 minutes, until the whole thing is bubbly and the crust is golden brown.

Let cool before slicing (at least 15 minutes, ideally 1 hour). Serve plain or with salted caramel ice cream, if desired.

Note: Use ripe pears, but try not to use ones that are extremely ripe.

Winter Galette

(Frozen) Peach, Anise, Chocolate Crust

When I was little, my favorite *I Spy* book featured a mesmerizing photo of black and pastel-striped licorice allsorts. When I was a few years older, I finally came across these candies in an old-fashioned confectioner's, where I funneled way too many scoopfuls into my little cellophane bag. On the drive home, I tried a nonpareil button, only to experience an intense and unfamiliar rush of a flavor nothing like the one I had imagined. At that point I'd had enough anise for a lifetime.

Many years later, I've finally made peace with licorice and anise flavors and started to even love them. This change of heart started when I realized that it's lovely in moderation, almost like a sharp vanilla. But if you're not quite there, that's totally fine—feel free to substitute ½ tsp of vanilla extract.

This galette uses frozen peaches, so it's perfect for winter, but persimmons work here as well. I find that persimmons tend to be a tad expensive, so I usually savor them on their own, but if you've got a persimmon orchard or find them on sale somewhere, give them a try in this galette (see Note on page 107 to learn how to tell when they're ripe). And if you're making this in the middle of summer, go with fresh peaches instead of frozen.

For the chocolate pie dough
1¼ cups [165 g] all-purpose flour
½ cup [115 g] cold unsalted butter, cut into chunks
¼ cup [25 g] cocoa powder, plus more for dusting
2 Tbsp granulated sugar
¼ tsp salt
4 oz [115 g] cold cream cheese, cut into chunks
2 Tbsp very cold water

For the filling
4 cups [400 g] frozen sliced peaches (see Note)
¼ cup [50 g] granulated sugar
2 Tbsp cornstarch
¼ tsp salt
Up to ¼ tsp ground anise seed
2 Tbsp fresh lemon juice
Egg wash (1 egg yolk beaten with 1 tsp water)
Chocolate ice cream, for serving (optional)

To make the pie dough: Place the flour, butter, cocoa powder, sugar, and salt in a food processor fitted with the blade attachment (see Note). Pulse about ten times and stop once the butter has blended into the flour with lots of pea-size lumps left. Add the cream cheese and pulse a few more times, just until the cream cheese has blended in but the mixture is still quite lumpy. Sprinkle the water over the surface and pulse a few more times, just until the mixture can be squeezed together into a ball.

Shape the dough into a ball by squeezing it together, flatten the ball into a disk, and cover tightly with plastic wrap. Gently tap and roll the sides of the disk on the counter to help them become less jagged. Once they're smooth and

no longer have big cracks, place the disk flat on the counter and gently press and pat the top to make sure it's nice and flat. As you gently press down on the top, the plastic wrap compresses the sides and ensures that any jagged edges are smoothed out. Refrigerate for 30 minutes.

Meanwhile, preheat the oven to 400°F [205°C] and line a rimmed baking sheet with parchment paper.

To make the filling: In a medium mixing bowl, fold together the frozen peaches, sugar, cornstarch, salt, anise (use just a pinch if you're not an anise lover), and lemon juice. Let sit for about 15 minutes to slightly thaw.

On a surface lightly dusted with cocoa powder, roll out the chilled dough to just under ¼ in [6 mm] thick and about 12 in [30.5 cm] across. Rotate occasionally as you work but try not to handle the dough too much and try to keep the edges from cracking too deeply.

Once it's rolled out, gently wrap the dough around your rolling pin to transfer it to the prepared baking sheet. Place the filling in the very center of the rolled-out dough and be sure to scrape the bowl with a spatula so you don't miss anything. Arrange in an even layer, leaving a 2 in [5 cm] border around the edges. Fold the edges over in a rustic overlapping pattern so that the middle stays open and brush the crust's surface all over with the egg wash.

Bake for about 40 minutes, until the whole thing is bubbly.

Let cool before slicing (at least 15 minutes, ideally 1 hour). Serve plain or with chocolate ice cream, if desired.

Notes: You can make the dough by hand using the Note on page 247.

If you're making this in the middle of summer, feel free to use 3¼ cups [400 g] fresh peach slices instead.

Spring Galette

Rhubarb, Pistachio Frangipane

Rhubarb, the tangy darling of springtime pies, is surprisingly earthy underneath it all. If you find quality rhubarb, don't combine it with any other fruit, add a little less sugar than you'd normally be tempted to overcompensate with, and you'll taste that funky combination of punchy and earthy. And if you're like me, you'll love it. Here, I've even added a delicious pistachio frangipane layer to highlight that depth. But if you're not so sure you're ready to experience rhubarb in all its glory, replace half with strawberries; while doing so, just be sure to add a bit less sugar than this recipe calls for.

1 batch Cream Cheese Butter Pie Dough (page 245)

For the pistachio frangipane
½ cup [60 g] finely ground pistachios, plus extra for sprinkling
1 large egg white
2 Tbsp granulated sugar
1 Tbsp unsalted butter, at room temperature
1 heaping Tbsp all-purpose flour, plus more for dusting

For the filling
4 cups [400 g] ½ in [13 mm] sliced rhubarb
⅓ cup [65 g] granulated sugar
2 Tbsp cornstarch
2 Tbsp water
¼ tsp salt
Egg wash (1 egg yolk beaten with 1 tsp water)
Almond ice cream, for serving (optional)

Chill the prepared dough for 30 minutes (see page 245).

To make the frangipane: Combine the pistachios, egg white, sugar, and butter in a stand mixer and beat at high speed with the paddle attachment until light and fluffy, about 2 minutes. Stir in the flour once it's fluffy. Set aside at cool room temperature.

Meanwhile, preheat the oven to 400°F [205°C] and line a rimmed baking sheet with parchment paper.

To make the filling: In a medium mixing bowl, fold together the rhubarb, sugar, cornstarch, water, and salt.

On a lightly floured surface, roll out the chilled dough to just under ¼ in [6 mm] thick and about 12 in [30.5 cm] across. Rotate occasionally as you work but try not to handle the dough too much and try to keep the edges from cracking too deeply.

Once it's rolled out, gently wrap the dough around your rolling pin to transfer it to the prepared baking sheet. Spread the frangipane in the center of the rolled-out dough, leaving a 2 in [5 cm] border around the edges.

Place the rhubarb filling on the frangipane layer and be sure to scrape the bowl with a spatula so you don't miss anything. Arrange in an even layer, leaving a 2 in [5 cm] border around the edges. Fold the edges over in a rustic overlapping pattern so that the middle stays open and brush the crust's surface all over with the egg wash.

Bake for about 50 minutes, until the whole thing is bubbly and the crust is golden brown.

Let cool before slicing (at least 15 minutes, ideally 1 hour). Serve plain or with almond ice cream and extra pistachios, if desired.

Turnovers

Makes 12 turnovers

1.1 lb [490 g] puff pastry, thawed
1 batch galette filling made with 1 Tbsp less
    water/lemon juice (see page 245), or ¾ cup
    [240 g] jam plus 7 oz [200 g] soft cheese
1 large egg yolk, beaten
⅔ cup [75 g] confectioners' sugar (optional)
1 Tbsp lemon juice (optional)

Preheat the oven to 400°F [205°C]. Line two rimmed baking sheets with parchment paper.

Roll out the puff pastry a little thinner than ⅛ in [2 mm]. Cut into twelve 5 in [13 cm] squares and place them on the prepared baking sheets.

Distribute the galette filling evenly or use 1 Tbsp chilled jam and 1 Tbsp cheese per pastry square. Leave as much of a border as possible around the filling, and then brush the border with an extremely light layer of water using your finger.

Fold one side of the pastry over to form a triangle. Press down around the edges to seal it shut with your fingers. Further seal it shut by crimping it: Fold up the bottom edge and pinch, going down the edge in overlapping pleats, pinching with each one (alternatively, use the back of a fork to crimp it shut). Use scissors or a paring knife to make a tiny slit in the top, but don't pierce through to the bottom. Brush with the beaten egg yolk.

Bake for 20 minutes, until golden brown with one or two badly sealed ones oozing juices. Let cool for 20 minutes.

Mix together the confectioners' sugar and lemon juice (if desired), drizzle over the turnovers, and enjoy.

Summer Turnovers

Make the galette filling (see page 245) with nectarines, 1 Tbsp lemon juice, and 1½ Tbsp chopped fresh basil, and decorate with icing and a few little basil leaves.

Fall Turnovers

Make the galette filling (see page 245) with Granny Smith apples. Instead of 1 Tbsp liquid, use 1 tsp rose water plus 2 tsp lemon juice. Decorate with icing and edible dried rose petals (make the icing with 2 tsp lemon juice plus 1 tsp rose water instead of 1 Tbsp fresh lemon juice).

Winter Turnovers

Make a quince jam (see page 51) in late fall or early to mid-winter (or find some store-bought). Fill the turnovers with quince jam and Camembert, and glaze them with more jam that's been briefly warmed in the microwave.

Spring Turnovers

Find some fresh local spring goat cheese (or just pick some up from the supermarket) and fill the turnovers with raspberry preserves and goat cheese.

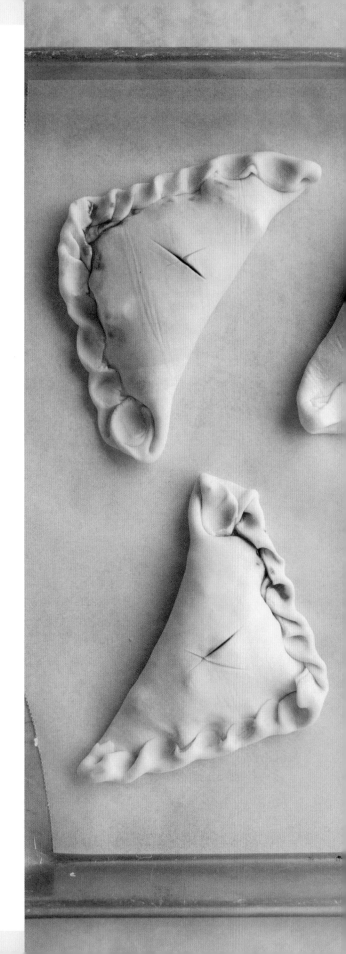

Loaf Cakes

If you've ever baked a carrot cake or made a loaf of banana or zucchini bread, you've already got the general idea of this recipe: Produce adds flavor, moisture, and texture to a simple loaf cake. The trick is knowing exactly how to prep everything. To infuse the batter itself with moisture and flavor, choose one item to grate or purée. Then optionally choose one or two fruits or vegetables to mix in for some added bursts of flavor, texture, and color.

The grated/puréed produce in the following chart's first column is essential to the base recipe, but if you don't feel like adding any fresh produce mix-ins from the second column, that's absolutely fine, and it won't negatively affect the structure of the batter. You can also add some dry mix-ins (such as chocolate chips and nuts), either in addition to the produce mix-ins or in place of them. The produce mix-ins and dry mix-ins are both totally optional, but it's best to include at least one of the two to give the cake a little excitement.

Make Your Own Loaf Cake Grid

Ingredients to swap in for the base recipe on the facing page

SWEET DRY MIX-INS

+ Chocolate chips
+ **Dried fruits**
  Raisins
  Craisins
  Chopped dried apricots
  Chopped dried figs
  Chopped dates

SAVORY DRY MIX-INS

+ Toasted coconut flakes
+ **Nuts**
  Chopped pistachios
  Chopped walnuts
  Whole pine nuts
  Sliced almonds

FLAVORINGS

+ 1 to 3 tsp spices (go even easier on cardamom, anise, fennel, and other strong flavors)
+ 2 tsp citrus zest
+ 1 Tbsp fresh grated ginger
+ 1 to 2 tsp vanilla extract
+ 1 Tbsp orange blossom water
+ 2 tsp rose water
+ 1 tsp almond extract

SEASONAL PRODUCE

Grated/Puréed Produce	Produce Mix-ins
Summer	
Grated and wrung-out zucchini (measured after wringing, liquid discarded)	Whole blueberries, blackberries, or raspberries, very tiny strawberries, corn kernels
Fall	
Grated and wrung-out apples or pears (measured after wringing, liquid discarded), poached and puréed quince (see page 259), steamed and puréed pumpkin or other squash (see page 262)	Whole cranberries, pomegranate arils, sliced figs, thinly sliced apples
Winter	
Steamed and puréed pumpkin or other squash (see page 262)	Thinly sliced apples
Spring	
Grated carrots or parsnips	Thinly sliced rhubarb (if you use rhubarb as a mix-in, choose something sweeter for the puréed produce, such as applesauce or bananas)
Anytime	
Unsweetened applesauce, mashed overripe bananas	Small frozen berries (do not thaw before adding to the batter, and avoid anything large or sliced), frozen corn kernels, a whole ripe banana split in half and placed on top before baking

Loaf Cakes

Makes one 8 by 4 in [20 by 10 cm] cake

1 cup [230 g] puréed or 1½ to 2 cups [230 g] grated produce (see grid on facing page)

½ cup [105 g] oil (see Note)

2 large eggs

⅔ cup [130 g] sugar (see Note)

Flavorings (optional)

1½ cups [195 g] all-purpose flour

¾ tsp salt

½ tsp baking powder

¼ tsp baking soda

½ cup [60 g] savory dry mix-ins (optional)

½ cup [90 g] sweet dry mix-ins (optional)

1 to 1½ cups [150 g] fresh produce mix-ins from the grid on facing page (optional)

1 batch cream cheese frosting (see page 262) or citrus icing (see page 262), both optional

Butter an 8 by 4 in [20 by 10 cm] loaf pan, line it with a parchment sling (see Note), and preheat the oven to 350°F [180°C].

In a medium mixing bowl, whisk together the puréed or grated produce, oil, eggs, sugar, and any wet flavorings (e.g., extracts) until completely incorporated. Set aside.

In another medium mixing bowl, sift together the flour, salt, baking powder, baking soda, and any dry flavorings (e.g., spices).

Pour the wet ingredients over the dry ingredients and fold together until there are only a couple of remaining dry flour streaks. Add the savory, sweet, and produce mix-ins, if using, and gently fold to combine. Do not overmix.

Scoop the batter into the loaf pan, and bake for 50 to 65 minutes (cakes with lots of fresh fruit mix-ins will take longer to bake), until a toothpick inserted into the center comes out clean. Remove from the pan and cool on a rack for at least 45 minutes before icing or serving. The cake keeps at room temperature for a couple of days, and you can freeze whatever you do not plan to eat in the near future. Cake with cream cheese frosting should be kept in the refrigerator for a day, and frozen for any longer (to make it ahead, leave the unfrosted cake at room temperature and frost it before serving).

Notes: You can use extra-virgin olive oil or melted coconut oil if you want one of their flavors. Otherwise, use a neutral oil, such as avocado or canola.

You can use granulated sugar or brown sugar interchangeably here, or a combination of the two.

To make a parchment sling, cut a piece of parchment paper to about 7½ by 10 in [19 by 25 cm]. Place the parchment sheet over the pan; the sheet's length should go in the opposite direction of the pan's length. Press the parchment paper into the pan so that it *just* covers the pan's bottom and long sides. Fold the flaps so that they drape over the sides (optionally secure them with metal binder clips if they're unwieldy). Press it into the buttered pan so it sticks really well.

Summer Loaf Cake

Blueberry Corn Zucchini

This take on zucchini bread is the closest thing to eating an actual slice of summer. The sweet corn and blueberries work wonderfully together, a bit like a berry-studded cakey cornbread. Eating a slice of this loaf cake almost re-creates the experience of sitting in a veggie garden in July and enjoying a snack, with the smell of fresh tomatoes and zucchini wafting over. Double the batch and freeze half for winter to bring back good memories of lazy summer days.

1½ cups [230 g] packed grated and wrung-out zucchini, from about 1 large zucchini

½ cup [105 g] neutral oil, such as canola or avocado

2 large eggs

⅔ cup [130 g] granulated sugar

1 cup [130 g] all-purpose flour

⅔ cup [105 g] polenta or cornmeal

¾ tsp salt

½ tsp baking powder

¼ tsp baking soda

¾ cup [115 g] blueberries (fresh or frozen), plus more for topping

½ cup [80 g] corn kernels, plus more for topping

Butter an 8 by 4 in [20 by 10 cm] loaf pan, line it with a parchment sling (see Note on page 257), and preheat the oven to 350°F [180°C].

In a medium mixing bowl, whisk together the zucchini, oil, eggs, and sugar until completely incorporated. Set aside.

In another medium mixing bowl, sift together the flour, cornmeal, salt, baking powder, and baking soda.

Pour the wet ingredients over the dry ingredients and fold together until there are only a couple of remaining dry flour streaks. Add the blueberries and corn and gently fold to combine. Do not overmix.

Scoop the batter into the loaf pan, sprinkle a small handful of blueberries and corn over the batter to decorate the top, and bake for 55 to 60 minutes, until a toothpick inserted into the center comes out clean. Remove from the pan and cool on a rack for at least 45 minutes before serving.

Fall Loaf Cake

Spiced Apple Streusel

So many of my favorite pome fruits are ready for harvest in the fall—there's quince, pear, and of course everyone's go-to: the tried-and-true apple. If you'd like to change things up, you can turn this into a pear cake or quince cake. To substitute quince, poach them for about 45 minutes, drain them, and then purée them. One large or two small quince will yield about 1 cup [235 g] of purée, which you can sub in for the grated apples (and omit the sliced apples altogether). To substitute pear, simply grate them and wring the gratings out so you end up with 2 cups [230 g], from three or four pears.

Stick with warm fall spices for any pome fruit—lots of cinnamon, a little cardamom, and a touch of allspice—or change things up and replace the spices with 2 tsp rose water, and add a rose water glaze in place of the apple glaze (see page 253).

For the cake

1 tart-crisp apple, thinly sliced (150 g)

1 Tbsp granulated sugar

1 Tbsp fresh lemon juice

2 cups [230 g] grated and wrung out tart-crisp apples, from about 4 apples

½ cup [105 g] neutral oil, such as canola or
  avocado
2 large eggs
⅔ cup [130 g] brown sugar
1½ cups [195 g] all-purpose flour
¾ tsp salt
½ tsp baking powder
¼ tsp baking soda
2 tsp cinnamon
½ tsp cardamom
¼ tsp allspice

For the streusel
2 Tbsp brown sugar
2 Tbsp flour
2 Tbsp salted butter

For the glaze
3 Tbsp confectioners' sugar

Butter an 8 by 4 in [20 by 10 cm] loaf pan, line it
with a parchment sling (see Note on page 257),
and preheat the oven to 350°F [180°C].

To make the cake: In a small mixing bowl,
toss the sliced apples with the granulated sugar
and lemon juice and set aside.

In a medium mixing bowl, whisk together the
grated apples, oil, eggs, and brown sugar until
completely incorporated. Set aside.

In another medium mixing bowl, sift together
the flour, salt, baking powder, baking soda,
cinnamon, cardamom, and allspice.

Pour the wet ingredients over the dry ingredients and fold together until there are only a
couple of remaining dry flour streaks. Lift most
of the sliced apples out of their bowl (reserving
their liquid and about five slices for decoration),
snap them in half, and place in the bowl with the
batter. Gently fold to incorporate and do not
overmix.

Scoop the batter into the loaf pan and fan out
the reserved apple slices across the batter.

To make the streusel: In a small bowl,
combine the brown sugar, flour, and butter and
work together with your fingers until crumbly.
Sprinkle the streusel over the apples in large
chunks.

Bake for about 55 minutes, until a toothpick inserted into the center comes out clean.
Remove from the pan and cool on a rack for at
least 45 minutes before icing or serving.

While the cake cools, make the glaze: Combine 1 Tbsp of the reserved apple juices with the
confectioners' sugar and stir to combine into a
runny glaze. Carefully brush over the cooled
cake.

Winter Loaf Cake

Lime Coconut Pumpkin

While pumpkin loaf cake is a perfect opportunity to go pumpkin spice crazy, there are a
ton of other possibilities out there. Here, lime
and coconut give pumpkin a weirdly wonderful
tropical-wintry vibe. But if fall is not fall until you
have your season's first PSL, feel free to substitute 1 Tbsp of your favorite pumpkin spice blend
in place of the lime zest and other spices, skip
the coconut, skip the lime zest in the icing, and
replace the lime juice with lemon juice.

For the cake
1 cup [230 g] puréed cooked pumpkin (see
  Note)
½ cup [105 g] melted extra-virgin coconut oil
2 large eggs
⅔ cup [130 g] granulated sugar
2 tsp lime zest
1½ cups [195 g] all-purpose flour
¾ tsp salt
½ tsp baking powder
¼ tsp baking soda

2 tsp ground cinnamon

1 tsp ground ginger

½ cup [30 g] unsweetened coconut flakes, plus
more for sprinkling

⅓ cup [45 g] chopped dates

For the icing

¾ cup [85 g] confectioners' sugar

1 Tbsp fresh lime juice (see Note)

1 tsp lime zest, plus more for sprinkling

Butter an 8 by 4 in [20 by 10 cm] loaf pan, line it
with a parchment sling (see Note on page 257),
and preheat the oven to 350°F [180°C].

To make the cake: In a medium mixing bowl,
whisk together the pumpkin purée, coconut
oil, eggs, sugar, and lime zest until completely
incorporated. Set aside.

In another medium mixing bowl, sift together
the flour, salt, baking powder, baking soda,
cinnamon, and ginger.

Pour the wet ingredients over the dry ingredients and fold together until there are only a
couple of remaining dry flour streaks. Add the
coconut flakes and chopped dates and gently
fold to combine. Do not overmix.

Scoop the batter into the loaf pan and bake
for about 50 minutes, until a toothpick inserted
into the center comes out clean. Remove from
the pan and cool on a rack for at least 45 minutes before icing.

To make the icing: While the cake cools,
combine the confectioners' sugar with the lime
juice and the lime zest and stir together to form
an opaque icing.

Drizzle the icing over the cooled cake and
decorate with extra coconut flakes and lime zest.

Notes: To purée the pumpkin: Cover and
microwave pumpkin chunks for about 5 minutes, until completely tender, then mash.

To adapt this icing for other recipes, you can
use whatever citrus zest and juice you want

to incorporate (grapefruit, lemon, lime, and
orange all work great).

Spring Loaf Cake

Cardamom Caraway Carrot

Ruby Tandoh and Samin Nosrat have two of my
favorite carrot cake recipes of all time—respectively, caraway poppy cake and saffron cardamom carrot cake. It turns out, cardamom and
caraway are also a lovely match, and this cake is
very much inspired by these two. If you want to
make a more classic carrot cake, simply skip the
caraway, cardamom, and pistachios and add an
extra ½ tsp cinnamon.

For the cake

2 cups [230 g] grated carrots, plus more for
topping

½ cup [105 g] neutral oil, such as canola or
avocado

2 large eggs

⅓ cup [65 g] granulated sugar

⅓ cup [65 g] brown sugar

1½ cups [195 g] all-purpose flour

1 tsp ground cinnamon

¾ tsp ground caraway, plus more for topping

¾ tsp salt

½ tsp ground cardamom, plus more for topping

½ tsp baking powder

¼ tsp baking soda

½ cup [60 g] chopped pistachios, plus more for
topping

¼ cup [40 g] raisins (optional)

For the cream cheese frosting

8 oz [225 g] cream cheese, at room temperature

¼ cup [85 g] honey

Butter an 8 by 4 in [20 by 10 cm] loaf pan, line it with a parchment sling (see Note on page 257), and preheat the oven to 350°F [180°C].

To make the cake: In a medium mixing bowl, whisk together the carrots, oil, eggs, granulated sugar, and brown sugar until completely incorporated. Set aside.

In another medium mixing bowl, sift together the flour, cinnamon, caraway, salt, cardamom, baking powder, and baking soda.

Pour the wet ingredients over the dry ingredients and fold together until there are only a couple of remaining dry flour streaks. Add the pistachios and raisins (if using) and gently fold to combine. Do not overmix.

Scoop the batter into the loaf pan and bake for about 50 minutes, until a toothpick inserted into the center comes out clean. Remove from the pan and cool on a rack for at least 45 minutes before icing or serving.

To make the frosting: While the cake cools, place the cream cheese in the bowl of a stand mixer and beat for about 1 minute. Drizzle in the honey with the mixer running and continue to beat for 1 minute more, until light and fluffy.

Once the loaf has cooled, dollop the frosting on top and make swooshes with an offset spatula or knife. Decorate with pistachios, shredded carrots, caraway, and cardamom.

Upside-Down Cakes

This is my favorite simplified upside-down cake—it's perfect for all baking levels yet always impressive. The cake batter in this base recipe is a classic plain butter cake. It goes with just about anything and can be spiced up with a few extra flavorings. But you can also borrow the almond (page 269), semolina (page 270), gingerbread (page 272), or chocolate (page 273) cake batters from the seasonal variations.

All the batters in this section are designed to be just a touch too sturdy and dry to be baked on their own without any fruit—that way, as they cool, they soak up all that delicious syrup, yet they have the structure to keep from turning to goo in the process. The final product is dewy on top with a moist texture throughout.

As with any recipe where you're baking with fruit, if you're using the kind of fruit that you usually set on the counter to allow to ripen for a couple of days, make sure it isn't *overly* ripe—you want it to be ripe enough to enjoy but not so much that its juices run everywhere.

Make Your Own Upside-Down Cake Grid

Ingredients to swap in for the base recipe on the facing page

SPICES

+ ½ tsp cinnamon
+ ¼ tsp cardamom
+ ¼ tsp cloves
+ ¼ tsp fennel seed
+ 1 pinch anise

Add to the dry batter ingredients and/or the fruit bottom.

LIQUID FLAVORINGS

+ 1 tsp vanilla extract
+ 2 tsp rose water
+ 1 Tbsp orange blossom water
+ 1 to 2 tsp spices
+ 1 tsp citrus zest

Add to the wet batter ingredients and/or the fruit bottom.

TO ESTIMATE

While baking is all about precision, you can easily get away with not weighing your fruit for this recipe. Just be sure to line the bottom of the cake pan with ½ in [13 mm] thick pieces of fruit, with a little bit of breathing room between each piece (see photos). Don't overload it or try to cram a lot of extra fruit in, or else the cake will go from syrupy and soft to waterlogged and mushy.

NOTE

Replace some of your fruit with a small handful of pomegranate arils or cranberries (fall), or jarred maraschino cherries (anytime), but use these in moderation.

SEASONAL PRODUCE

Summer

Halved small or quartered or sliced large apricots, figs, or strawberries, ½ in [13 mm] sliced peaches, plums, or nectarines, whole pitted cherries, blackberries, blueberries, or raspberries

Fall

Halved small or quartered large figs, ½ in [13 mm] sliced apples, pears, persimmons, or quince

Winter

Halved kumquats, ½ in [13 mm] sliced just-ripe Fuyu persimmon

Spring

Sliced strawberries, sour plums, rhubarb, loquats

Anytime

Frozen berries (do not thaw), sliced bananas (anywhere from just-ripe to overripe), sliced mangos, canned pineapple rings (drained and patted dry)

Upside-Down Cakes

Makes 8 servings

For the fruit
4 Tbsp [55 g] unsalted butter, melted
½ cup [100 g] dark brown sugar
Spices or flavorings (optional)
2 to 3 cups [300 g] fresh prepared fruit (see grid on facing page)

For the cake batter
1½ cups [195 g] all-purpose flour
1¼ tsp baking powder
¼ tsp baking soda
½ tsp salt
Spices or flavorings (optional)
2 large eggs, at room temperature
4 Tbsp [55 g] unsalted butter, melted
¾ cup [150 g] granulated sugar
½ cup [120 g] buttermilk (see Note)

Preheat the oven to 350°F [180°C]. Butter a 9 in [23 cm] round cake pan. Cover the bottom with a parchment round.

To prep the fruit: Combine the melted butter, brown sugar, and spices or flavorings (if using) in a small mixing bowl. Whisk together until completely combined. Pour into the prepared cake pan. Use an offset spatula to spread everything out evenly until the bottom is covered.

Slice the fruit so it is ½ in [13 mm] thick. (If you're working with something small, such as kumquats or small apricots, slice them in half. Tiny things, like blueberries or raspberries, should be left whole.)

Arrange the fruit in a single layer over the buttery brown sugar (cut-side down, if they're sliced in half).

To make the cake batter: In a medium mixing bowl, sift together the flour, baking powder, baking soda, salt, and dry spices (if using).

In a large mixing bowl, beat the eggs and melted butter together until they are very well incorporated. Then add the granulated sugar, buttermilk, and any liquid flavorings (if using) and beat to combine well.

Pour the wet mixture over the dry mixture and stir together just until everything is combined. It won't be completely smooth, and there might be some tiny lumps; this is completely fine. Don't overmix!

Carefully pour the batter over the fruit, smooth out the top a little bit with a spatula, and bake for 30 to 45 minutes, until a toothpick inserted into the center comes out clean.

Let cool for 5 to 10 minutes in the cake pan. Then trace around the edge with a butter knife to make sure it's loosened from the pan. Invert onto a serving plate, let cool for at least 30 minutes more, and serve.

Note: See page 44 for a buttermilk substitute.

Summer Cake

Apricots, Raspberries, Chocolate, Almond Cake

It's a familiar scene for fans of Agatha Christie murder mysteries: The titular detective suspiciously wafts a snifter of brandy and exclaims "Ah, bitter almonds—this man has been poisoned!" Indeed, you can find that bitter almond scent (and actual traces of cyanide) safely stored away in the pits of many stone fruits. It's always struck me as eerie, then, that almond extract and stone fruits are so often paired with each other in classic desserts, but perhaps it's best not to ask too many questions and just enjoy their delicious pairing.

Feel free to substitute any of your favorite other stone fruits, which all go with raspberries, chocolate, and of course almonds (cut larger fruit pieces into ½ in [13 mm] wedges instead of halving them).

For the fruit
4 Tbsp [55 g] unsalted butter, melted
½ cup [100 g] dark brown sugar
5 to 7 pitted apricots (175 g)
1 heaping cup [125 g] raspberries
2 Tbsp dark chocolate chips

For the almond cake batter
¾ cup [100 g] all-purpose flour
1 cup [100 g] almond flour
1¼ tsp baking powder
¼ tsp baking soda
½ tsp salt
2 large eggs, at room temperature
4 Tbsp [55 g] unsalted butter, melted
¾ cup [150 g] granulated sugar
½ cup [120 g] buttermilk (see Note)
½ tsp almond extract

½ cup [90 g] dark chocolate chips
Melted chocolate, for decorating (optional)

Preheat the oven to 350°F [180°C]. Butter a 9 in [23 cm] round cake pan. Cover the bottom with a parchment round.

To prep the fruit: Combine the melted butter and brown sugar in a small mixing bowl. Whisk together until completely combined. Pour into the prepared cake pan. Use an offset spatula to cover the bottom evenly.

Arrange the apricot halves cut-side down in a single layer over the buttery brown sugar in the pan, then sprinkle the raspberries and chocolate chips evenly around them (if they're the right size, place 1 raspberry in the center of each apricot, underneath).

To make the cake batter: Sift the flour, almond flour, baking powder, baking soda, and salt into a large mixing bowl.

In another large mixing bowl, beat the eggs and melted butter together until they are very well incorporated. Then add the sugar, buttermilk, and almond extract and beat to combine well.

Pour the wet mixture over the dry mixture, add the chocolate chips, and stir together just until everything is combined. Don't overmix!

Carefully pour the batter over the fruit, smooth out the top a little bit with a spatula, and bake for about 40 minutes, until a toothpick inserted into the center comes out clean.

Let cool for 5 to 10 minutes in the cake pan. Then trace around the edge with a butter knife to make sure it's loosened from the pan. Invert onto a serving plate, let cool for at least 30 minutes more, drizzle with a little chocolate, if desired, and serve.

Note: See page 44 for a buttermilk substitute.

Fall Cake

Figs, Orange Blossom, Semolina, Honey

Figs and honey go together beautifully, perhaps in part because of the crucial role pollinating insects play in their production. A particular species of wasp has a symbiotic relationship with fig trees, and you can't have honey without honeybees. With many pollinators facing extinction, one of the most useful things you can do (if you have the space, time, and resources) is to plant a pesticide-free pollinator garden to create a habitat for local butterflies and bees.

Orange blossom honey goes great here, but even plain old clover honey paired with orange blossom water will make you very happy. If you don't have any orange blossom products handy, use 1 tsp of vanilla extract in the batter instead for a very different (but equally lovely) flavor profile.

For the fruit
4 Tbsp [55 g] unsalted butter, melted
¼ cup [50 g] dark brown sugar
2 Tbsp honey
6 to 10 fresh figs (300 g)

For the semolina cake batter
1 cup [130 g] all-purpose flour
¼ cup [50 g] coarse semolina
1¼ tsp baking powder
¼ tsp baking soda
½ tsp salt
2 large eggs, at room temperature
4 Tbsp [55 g] unsalted butter, melted
½ cup [100 g] granulated sugar
¼ cup [85 g] honey
½ cup [120 g] buttermilk (see Note)
1 Tbsp orange blossom water (see Note)
Toasted almonds, for decoration

Preheat the oven to 350°F [180°C]. Butter a 9 in [23 cm] round cake pan. Cover the bottom with a parchment round.

To prep the fruit: Combine the melted butter, brown sugar, and honey in a small mixing bowl. Whisk together until completely combined. Pour into the prepared cake pan. Use an offset spatula to cover the bottom evenly.

If the figs are tiny, slice them in half. If they are medium or large, slice them into ½ in [13 mm] rounds. Arrange the them cut-side down in a single layer over the buttery brown sugar in the pan.

To make the semolina cake batter: Sift the flour, semolina, baking powder, baking soda, and salt in a large mixing bowl.

In another large mixing bowl, beat the eggs and melted butter together until they are very well incorporated. Then add the sugar, honey, buttermilk, and orange blossom water and beat to combine well.

Pour the wet mixture over the dry mixture and stir together just until everything is combined. Don't overmix!

Carefully pour the batter over the figs, smooth out the top a little bit with a spatula, and bake for about 35 minutes, until a toothpick inserted into the center comes out clean.

Let cool for 5 to 10 minutes in the cake pan. Then trace around the edge with a butter knife to make sure it's loosened from the pan. Invert onto a serving plate, let cool for at least 30 minutes more, sprinkle with toasted almonds, and serve.

Notes: See page 44 for a buttermilk substitute.

You can find orange blossom water in most Middle Eastern markets, as well as supermarkets with a large international section.

Winter Cake

Pineapple, Orange, Cardamom, Gingerbread Cake

This recipe is inspired by the original pineapple maraschino cherry upside-down cake, made entirely with shelf-stable pantry ingredients. Here, I've added an orange cardamom gingerbread batter for an extra-warm wintry vibe. You can substitute ½ in [13 mm] thick persimmon slices if you've got some on hand (or bake as written and save your persimmons for eating with a spoon). On the other hand, if you're baking this recipe in the middle of summer, use a classic buttermilk batter (see page 267) and fresh cherries if you've got an extra handful in the fridge. If you want to add a little extra something to a more classic pineapple cake, take a note from Quin Liburd (of the blog *Butter Be Ready*): Brown your butter, let it cool to room temperature, then add it to both the batter and the pan's bottom.

For the fruit

4 Tbsp [55 g] unsalted butter, melted
½ cup [100 g] dark brown sugar
One 15 oz [425 g] can pineapple rings
About 15 jarred drained morello or maraschino
    cherries (40 g)

For the gingerbread cake batter

1½ cups [195 g] all-purpose flour
2 Tbsp cocoa powder
1 Tbsp ground ginger
1 tsp cinnamon
½ tsp cardamom
½ tsp salt
1¼ tsp baking powder
¼ tsp baking soda
2 large eggs, at room temperature
4 Tbsp [55 g] unsalted butter, melted
½ cup [100 g] dark brown sugar

¼ cup [85 g] molasses
½ cup [120 g] buttermilk (see Note)
1 Tbsp freshly grated ginger
1 tsp orange zest (from about ½ orange), plus
    more for decoration
Confectioners' sugar, for decoration

Preheat the oven to 350°F [180°C]. Butter a 9 in [23 cm] round cake pan. Cover the bottom with a parchment round.

To prep the fruit: Combine the melted butter and brown sugar in a small mixing bowl. Whisk together until completely combined. Pour into the prepared cake pan. Use an offset spatula to cover the bottom evenly.

Drain the pineapple rings and pat them dry (reserve the juice for another project or make some rum punch), so you end up with six to eight rings [9 oz/260 g]. Arrange the rings in a single layer over the buttery brown sugar in the pan (break one up and place in the gaps around the edges if it doesn't fit). Place a cherry in the center of each, as well as in between the pineapple rings.

To make the gingerbread cake batter: Sift the flour, cocoa powder, ginger, cinnamon, cardamom, salt, baking powder, and baking soda in a large mixing bowl.

In another large mixing bowl, beat the eggs and melted butter together until they are very well incorporated. Then add the brown sugar, molasses, buttermilk, ginger, and orange zest and beat to combine well.

Pour the wet mixture over the dry mixture and stir together just until everything is combined. Don't overmix!

Carefully pour the batter over the fruit, smooth out the top a little bit with a spatula, and bake for about 35 minutes, until a toothpick inserted into the center comes out clean.

Let it cool for 5 to 10 minutes in the cake pan. Then trace around the edge with a butter knife to make sure it's loosened from the pan. Invert onto a serving plate and let it cool for at least

30 minutes more, and serve. Right before serving, sprinkle a little more orange zest over the top and dust lightly with confectioners' sugar.

Note: See page 44 for a buttermilk substitute.

Spring Cake

Strawberries, Rhubarb, Chocolate Cake

You don't see chocolate paired with rhubarb as much as you see it paired with mellower flavors such as vanilla cake and all-butter crust. But I'm a big fan of chocolate and tanginess, which work in perfect harmony here. Once rhubarb becomes harder to track down later in the spring, simply use extra strawberries.

It was hard not to make every single spring recipe in this book's dessert section a celebration of rhubarb. But this is your friendly reminder that every single spring sweet in this book can *become* a celebration of rhubarb, if you want it to be. Just check out the base recipes throughout the dessert section to learn how you can incorporate it into everything from turnovers to loaf cakes.

For the fruit
4 Tbsp [55 g] unsalted butter, melted
½ cup [100 g] dark brown sugar
4 stalks rhubarb, cut into ½ in [13 mm] slices (150 g)
10 to 12 hulled strawberries, cut into ½ in [13 mm] slices (150 g)

For the chocolate cake batter
1 cup [130 g] all-purpose flour
½ cup [50 g] cocoa powder
1¼ tsp baking powder
¼ tsp baking soda

½ tsp salt
2 large eggs, at room temperature
4 Tbsp [55 g] unsalted butter, melted
¾ cup [150 g] granulated sugar
½ cup [120 g] buttermilk (see Note)
1 tsp vanilla extract

Preheat the oven to 350°F [180°C]. Butter a 9 in [23 cm] round cake pan. Cover the bottom with a parchment round.

To prep the fruit: Combine the melted butter and brown sugar in a small mixing bowl. Whisk together until completely combined. Pour into the prepared cake pan. Use an offset spatula to cover the bottom evenly.

Arrange the rhubarb and strawberry slices cut-side down in a single layer over the buttery brown sugar in the pan.

To make the chocolate cake batter: Sift the flour, cocoa powder, baking powder, baking soda, and salt into a large mixing bowl.

In another large mixing bowl, beat the eggs and melted butter together until they are very well incorporated. Then add the sugar, buttermilk, and vanilla and beat to combine well.

Pour the wet mixture over the dry mixture and stir together just until everything is combined. Don't overmix!

Carefully pour the batter over the fruit, smooth out the top a little bit with a spatula, and bake for about 35 minutes, until a toothpick inserted into the center comes out clean.

Let cool for 5 to 10 minutes in the cake pan. Then trace around the edge with a butter knife to make sure it's loosened from the pan. Invert onto a serving plate, let it cool for at least 30 minutes more, and serve.

Note: See page 44 for a buttermilk substitute.

ABOUT
THE AUTHOR

Kathryn Pauline is the creator of the blog
Cardamom and Tea. She is a recipe developer
and food photographer and has been
nominated for two *Saveur* Blog Awards,
winning one in 2017. She grew up in Chicago
and lives in Melbourne, Australia.

ACKNOWLEDGMENTS

This book belongs to many people.

Every reader who has trusted my recipes.

Folks in the food world who have supported me, guided me, and given me opportunities at pivotal moments, especially Dianne Jacob, Grace Bonney, Kristina Gil, Julia Turshen, Maureen Abood, the *Saveur* editorial team, Mai Kakish, Mica McCook, Sherrod Faulks, Maryam Jillani, Lisa Kiorkis, Renate (*Renate Bakes*), and so many more.

My agent, Andrianna Yeatts, for taking a chance on me, believing in my work, and opening door after door (along with the occasional window).

Cristina Garces, Lizzie Vaughan, Deanne Katz, Sarah Billingsley, and the whole team at Chronicle for making this book real.

Abderazzaq Noor for allowing me to beautify this book with photos of his Melbourne garden.

Friends who've tested a recipe, cooked for me, written with me, and just generally cheered me on over these last few years.

Abeer Najjar for always understanding and for making this work joyful. If nothing else, I'm so thankful that this all brought about our friendship.

Tim for being my first paying client before I knew the value of my work, and Rebecca for believing I was a fellow writer before I knew myself.

Simon's family, who've accepted me like a daughter/sister/cousin/granddaughter ever since we were two kids in love.

My parents for cheering me on, my big fat crazy family for being crazily supportive, and especially my mom and nana for teaching me to love food, starting with my very first meal and surely until my last.

Meghan for being my best friend since the summer of 1990.

Simon for being a true partner through all of life's seasons.

INDEX